Brief C++

Late Objects

3/e

Cay Horstmann

San Jose State University

WILEY

PUBLISHER	Laurie Rosatone
EDITORIAL DIRECTOR	Don Fowley
DEVELOPMENTAL EDITOR	Cindy Johnson
ASSISTANT DEVELOPMENT EDITOR	Ryann Dannelly
EXECUTIVE MARKETING MANAGER	Dan Sayre
SENIOR PRODUCTION EDITOR	Laura Abrams
SENIOR CONTENT MANAGER	Valerie Zaborski
EDITORIAL ASSISTANT	Anna Pham
SENIOR DESIGNER	Tom Nery
SENIOR PHOTO EDITOR	Billy Ray
PRODUCTION MANAGEMENT	Cindy Johnson
COVER IMAGE	© Monty Rakusen/Getty Images

This book was set in Stempel Garamond LT Std by Publishing Services, and printed and bound by Quad/Graphics, Versailles. The cover was printed by Quad/Graphics, Versailles.

This book is printed on acid-free paper. ∞

Founded in 1807, John Wiley & Sons, Inc. has been a valued source of knowledge and understanding for more than 200 years, helping people around the world meet their needs and fulfill their aspirations. Our company is built on a foundation of principles that include responsibility to the communities we serve and where we live and work. In 2008, we launched a Corporate Citizenship Initiative, a global effort to address the environmental, social, economic, and ethical challenges we face in our business. Among the issues we are addressing are carbon impact, paper specifications and procurement, ethical conduct within our business and among our vendors, and community and charitable support. For more information, please visit our website: *www.wiley.com/go/citizenship*.

Evaluation copies are provided to qualified academics and professionals for review purposes only, for use in their courses during the next academic year. These copies are licensed and may not be sold or transferred to a third party. Upon completion of the review period, please return the evaluation copy to Wiley. Return instructions and a free of charge return shipping label are available at *www.wiley.com/go/returnlabel*. If you have chosen to adopt this textbook for use in your course, please accept this book as your complimentary desk copy. Outside of the United States, please contact your local representative.

ISBN 13: 978-1-119-40042-4

The inside back cover will contain printing identification and country of origin if omitted from this page. In addition, if the ISBN on the back cover differs from the ISBN on this page, the one on the back cover is correct.

Printed in the United States of America.

10 9 8 7 6 5 4 3 2 1

PREFACE

This book is an introduction to C++ and computer programming that focuses on the essentials—and on effective learning. The book is designed to serve a wide range of student interests and abilities and is suitable for a first course in programming for computer scientists, engineers, and students in other disciplines. No prior programming experience is required, and only a modest amount of high school algebra is needed.

Here are the key features of this book:

Present fundamentals first.

This book uses the C++ programming language as a vehicle for introducing computer science concepts. A substantial subset of the C++ language is covered, focusing on the modern features of standard C++ that make students productive. The book takes a traditional route, first stressing control structures, procedural decomposition, and array algorithms. Objects are used when appropriate in the early chapters. Students start designing and implementing their own classes in Chapter 9.

Guidance and worked examples help students succeed.

Beginning programmers often ask "How do I start? Now what do I do?" Of course, an activity as complex as programming cannot be reduced to cookbook-style instructions. However, step-by-step guidance is immensely helpful for building confidence and providing an outline for the task at hand. "Problem Solving" sections stress the importance of design and planning. "How To" guides help students with common programming tasks. Additional Worked Examples are available in the E-Text or online.

Tip: Source files for all of the program examples in the book, including the Worked Examples, are provided with the source code for this book. Download the files to your computer for easy access as you work through the chapters.

Practice makes perfect.

Of course, programming students need to be able to implement nontrivial programs, but they first need to have the confidence that they can succeed. The Enhanced E-Text immerses students in activities designed to foster in-depth learning. Students don't just watch animations and code traces, they work on generating them. The activities provide instant feedback to show students what they did right and where they need to study more. A wealth of practice opportunities, including code completion questions and skill-oriented multiple-choice questions, appear at the end of each section, and each chapter ends with well-crafted review exercises and programming projects.

Problem solving strategies are made explicit.

Practical, step-by-step illustrations of techniques help students devise and evaluate solutions to programming problems. Introduced where they are most relevant, these strategies address barriers to success for many students. Strategies included are:

- Algorithm Design (with pseudocode)
- First Do It By Hand (doing sample calculations by hand)
- Flowcharts

- Selecting Test Cases
- Hand-Tracing
- Storyboards
- Solve a Simpler Problem First
- Reusable Functions
- Stepwise Refinement
- Adapting Algorithms
- Discovering Algorithms by Manipulating Physical Objects
- Draw a Picture (pointer diagrams)
- Tracing Objects (identifying state and behavior)
- Discovering Classes

A visual approach motivates the reader and eases navigation.

Photographs present visual analogies that explain the nature and behavior of computer concepts. Step-by-step figures illustrate complex program operations. Syntax boxes and example tables present a variety of typical and special cases in a compact format. It is easy to get the "lay of the land" by browsing the visuals, before focusing on the textual material.

© Terraxplorer/iStockphoto.

Visual features help the reader with navigation.

Focus on the essentials while being technically accurate.

An encyclopedic coverage is not helpful for a beginning programmer, but neither is the opposite—reducing the material to a list of simplistic bullet points. In this book, the essentials are presented in digestible chunks, with separate notes that go deeper into good practices or language features when the reader is ready for the additional information. You will not find artificial over-simplifications that give an illusion of knowledge.

Reinforce sound engineering practices.

A multitude of useful tips on software quality and common errors encourage the development of good programming habits. The focus is on test-driven development, encouraging students to test their programs systematically.

Engage with optional engineering and business exercises.

End-of-chapter exercises are enhanced with problems from scientific and business domains. Designed to engage students, the exercises illustrate the value of programming in applied fields.

New to This Edition

Updated for Modern Versions of C++

A number of features of the C++ 2011 and C++ 2014 standards are described either as recommended "best practice" or as Special Topics.

New and Reorganized Topics

The book now supports two pathways into object-oriented programming and inheritance. Pointers and structures can be covered before introducing classes. Alternatively, pointers can be deferred until after the implementation of classes.

A sequence of Worked Examples and exercises introduces "media computation"—generating and modifying images, sounds, and animations.

Lower-Cost, Interactive Format

This third edition is published as a lower-cost Enhanced E-Text that supports active learning through a wealth of interactive activities. These activities engage and prepare students for independent programming and the Review Exercises, Practice Exercises, and Programming Projects at the end of each E-Text chapter. The Enhanced E-Text may also be bundled with an Abridged Print Companion, which is a bound book that contains the entire text for reference, but without exercises or practice material.

Interactive learning solutions are expanding every day, so to learn more about these options or to explore other options to suit your needs, please contact your Wiley account manager (www.wiley.com/go/whosmyrep) or visit the product information page for this text on wiley.com (http://wiley.com/college/sc/horstmann).

The Enhanced E-Text is designed to enable student practice without the instructor assigning the interactivities or recording their scores. If you are interested in assigning and grading students' work on them, ask your Wiley Account Manager about the online course option implemented in the Engage Learning Management System. The Engage course supports the assignment and automatic grading of the interactivities. Engage access includes access to the Enhanced E-Text.

Features in the Enhanced E-Text

The interactive Enhanced E-Text guides students from the basics to writing complex programs. After they read a bit, they can try all of the interactive exercises for that section. Active reading is an engaging way for students to ensure that students are prepared before going to class.

There five types of interactivities:

Code Walkthrough Code Walkthrough activities ask students to trace through a segment of code, choosing which line will be executed next and entering the new values of variables changed by the code's execution. This activity simulates the hand-tracing problem solving technique taught in Chapters 3 and 4—but with immediate feedback.

Example Table Example table activities make the student the active participant in building up tables of code examples similar to those found in the book. The tables come in many different forms. Some tables ask the student to determine the output of a line of code, or the value of an expression, or to provide code for certain tasks. This activity helps students assess their understanding of the reading—while it is easy to go back and review.

Algorithm Animation An algorithm animation shows the essential steps of an algorithm. However, instead of passively watching, students get to predict each step. When finished, students can start over with a different set of inputs. This is a surprisingly effective way of learning and remembering algorithms.

Rearrange Code Rearrange code activities ask the student to arrange lines of code by dragging them from the list on the right to the area at left so that the resulting code fulfills the task described in the problem. This activity builds facility with coding structure and implementing common algorithms.

Object Diagram Object diagram activities ask the student to create a memory diagram to illustrate how variables and objects are initialized and updated as sample code executes. The activity depicts variables, objects, and references in the same way as the figures in the book. After an activity is completed, pressing "Play" replays the animation. This activity goes beyond hand-tracing to illuminate what is happening in memory as code executes.

Code Completion Code completion activities ask the student to finish a partially-completed program, then paste the solution into CodeCheck (a Wiley-based online code evaluator) to learn whether it produces the desired result. Tester classes on the CodeCheck site run and report whether the code passed the tests. This activity serves as a skill-building lab to better prepare the student for writing programs from scratch.

A Tour of the Book

This book is intended for a two-semester introduction to programming that may also include algorithms and data structures. The organization of chapters offers the same flexibility as the previous edition; dependencies among the chapters are also shown in Figure 1.

Part A: Fundamentals (Chapters 1–8)

The first six chapters follow a traditional approach to basic programming concepts. Students learn about control structures, stepwise refinement, and arrays. Objects are used only for input/output and string processing. Input/output is first covered in Chapter 2, which may be followed by an introduction to reading and writing text files in Section 8.1.

In a course for engineers with a need for systems and embedded programming, you will want to cover Chapter 7 on pointers. Sections 7.1 and 7.4 are sufficient for using pointers with polymorphism in Chapter 10.

File processing is the subject of Chapter 8. Section 8.1 can be covered sooner for an introduction to reading and writing text files. The remainder of the chapter gives additional material for practical applications.

Part B: Object-Oriented Design (Chapters 9–10)

After students have gained a solid foundation, they are ready to tackle the implementation of classes. Chapters 9 and 10 introduce the object-oriented features of C++. Chapter 9 introduces class design and implementation. Chapter 10 covers inheritance and polymorphism. By the end of these chapters, students will be able to implement programs with multiple interacting classes.

Any subset of these chapters can be incorporated into a custom print version of this text; ask your Wiley sales representative for details, or visit customselect.wiley.com to create your custom order.

Appendices

Appendices A and B summarize C++ reserved words and operators. Appendix C lists character escape sequences and ASCII character code values. Appendix D documents all of the library functions and classes used in this book.

Appendix E contains a programming style guide. Using a style guide for programming assignments benefits students by directing them toward good habits and reducing gratuitous choice. The style guide is available in electronic form on the book's companion web site so that instructors can modify it to reflect their preferred style.

Appendix F, available in the E-Text, introduces common number systems used in computing.

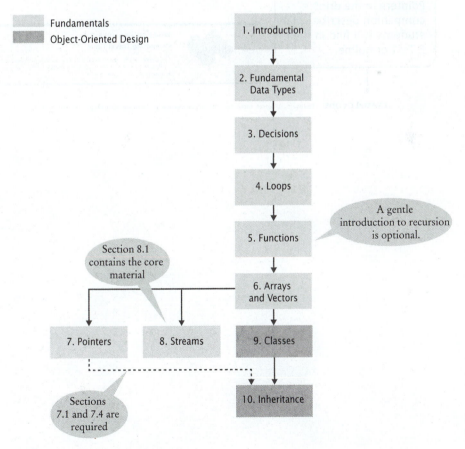

Figure 1   Chapter Dependencies

Web Resources

This book is complemented by a complete suite of online resources. Go to www.wiley.com/go/bclo3 to visit the online companion sites, which include

- Source code for all example programs in the book and its Worked Examples, plus additional example programs.
- Worked Examples that apply the problem-solving steps in the book to other realistic examples.
- Lecture presentation slides (for instructors only).
- Solutions to all review and programming exercises (for instructors only).
- A test bank that focuses on skills, not just terminology (for instructors only). This extensive set of multiple-choice questions can be used with a word processor or imported into a course management system.
- "CodeCheck" assignments that allow students to work on programming problems presented in an innovative online service and receive immediate feedback. Instructors can assign exercises that have already been prepared, or easily add their own. Visit http://codecheck.it to learn more.

Pointers in the print companion describe what students will find in their E-Text or online.

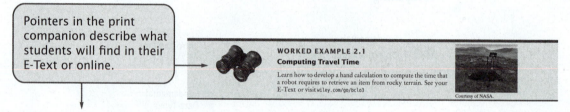

WORKED EXAMPLE 2.1
Computing Travel Time

Learn how to develop a hand calculation to compute the time that a robot requires to retrieve an item from rocky terrain. See your E-Text or visit wiley.com/go/bclo3

Courtesy of NASA.

EXAMPLE CODE   See how_to_1/scores_vector in your companion code for a solution using vectors instead of arrays.

A Walkthrough of the Learning Aids

The pedagogical elements in this book work together to focus on and reinforce key concepts and fundamental principles of programming, with additional tips and detail organized to support and deepen these fundamentals. In addition to traditional features, such as chapter objectives and a wealth of exercises, each chapter contains elements geared to today's visual learner.

> Throughout each chapter, **margin notes** show where new concepts are introduced and provide an outline of key ideas.

> Annotated **syntax boxes** provide a quick, visual overview of new language constructs.

> **Annotations** explain required components and point to more information on common errors or best practices associated with the syntax.

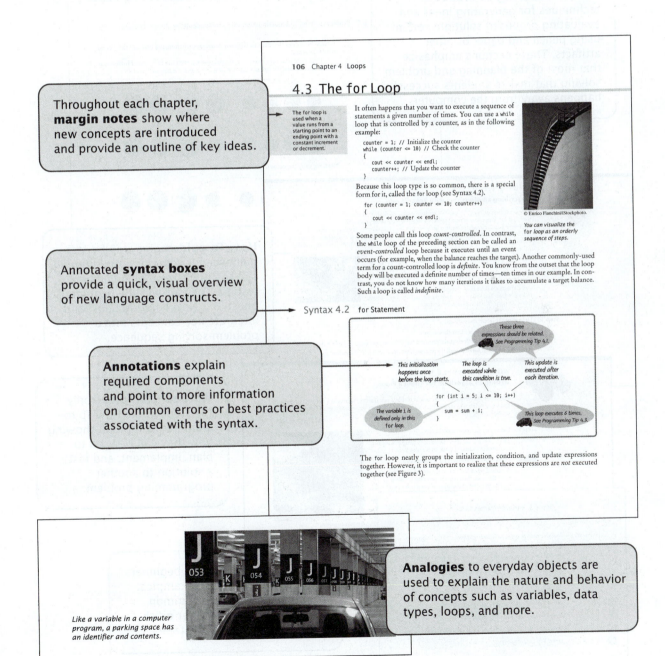

106 Chapter 4 Loops

4.3 The for Loop

The for loop is used when a value runs from a starting point to an ending point with a constant increment or decrement.

It often happens that you want to execute a sequence of statements a given number of times. You can use a while loop that is controlled by a counter, as in the following example:

```
counter = 1; // Initialize the counter
while (counter <= 10) // Check the counter
{
    cout << counter << endl;
    counter++; // Update the counter
}
```

Because this loop type is so common, there is a special form for it, called the for loop (see Syntax 4.2).

```
for (counter = 1; counter <= 10; counter++)
{
    cout << counter << endl;
}
```

© Enrico Fianchini/iStockphoto.

You can visualize the for loop as an orderly sequence of steps.

Some people call this loop *count-controlled*. In contrast, the while loop of the preceding section can be called an *event-controlled* loop because it executes until an event occurs (for example, when the balance reaches the target). Another commonly-used term for a count-controlled loop is *definite*. You know from the outset that the loop body will be executed a definite number of times—ten times in our example. In contrast, you do not know how many iterations it takes to accumulate a target balance. Such a loop is called *indefinite*.

Syntax 4.2   for Statement

These three expressions should be related. See Programming Tip 4.1.

This initialization happens once before the loop starts.

The loop is executed while this condition is true.

This update is executed after each iteration.

```
for (int i = 5; i <= 10; i++)
{
    sum = sum + i;
}
```

The variable i is defined only in this for loop.

This loop executes 6 times. See Programming Tip 4.3.

The for loop neatly groups the initialization, condition, and update expressions together. However, it is important to realize that these expressions are *not* executed together (see Figure 3).

Like a variable in a computer program, a parking space has an identifier and contents.

> **Analogies** to everyday objects are used to explain the nature and behavior of concepts such as variables, data types, loops, and more.

Memorable photos reinforce analogies and help students remember the concepts.

A recipe for a fruit pie may say to use any kind of fruit.
Here, "fruit" is an example of a parameter variable.
Apples and cherries are examples of arguments.

Problem Solving sections teach techniques for generating ideas and evaluating proposed solutions, often using pencil and paper or other artifacts. These sections emphasize that most of the planning and problem solving that makes students successful happens away from the computer.

6.5   Problem Solving: Discovering Algorithms by Manipulating Physical Objects   **277**

Now how does that help us with our problem, switching the first and the second half of the array?

Let's put the first coin into place, by swapping it with the fifth coin. However, as C++ programmers, we will say that we swap the coins in positions 0 and 4:

Next, we swap the coins in positions 1 and 5:

HOW TO 1.1

Describing an Algorithm with Pseudocode

This is the first of many "How To" sections in this book that give you step-by-step procedures for carrying out important tasks in developing computer programs.

Before you are ready to write a program in C++, you need to develop an algorithm—a method for arriving at a solution for a particular problem. Describe the algorithm in pseudocode—a sequence of precise steps formulated in English. To illustrate, we'll devise an algorithm for this problem:

Problem Statement   You have the choice of buying one of two cars. One is more fuel efficient than the other, but also more expensive. You know the price and fuel efficiency (in miles per gallon, mpg) of both cars. You plan to keep the car for ten years. Assume a price of $4 per gallon of gas and usage of 15,000 miles per year. You will pay cash for the car and not worry about financing costs. Which car is the better deal?

© dlewis33/Getty Images.

Step 1   Determine the inputs and outputs.

In our sample problem, we have these inputs:
- *purchase price1* and *fuel efficiency1*, the price and fuel efficiency (in mpg) of the first car
- *purchase price2* and *fuel efficiency2*, the price and fuel efficiency of the second car

How To guides give step-by-step guidance for common programming tasks, emphasizing planning and testing. They answer the beginner's question, "Now what do I do?" and integrate key concepts into a problem-solving sequence.

WORKED EXAMPLE 1.1

Writing an Algorithm for Tiling a Floor

Problem Statement   Your task is to tile a rectangular bathroom floor with alternating black and white tiles measuring 4 × 4 inches. The floor dimensions, measured in inches, are multiples of 4.

Step 1   Determine the inputs and outputs.

The inputs are the floor dimensions (length × width), measured in inches. The output is a tiled floor.

Step 2   Break down the problem into smaller tasks.

A natural subtask is to lay one row of tiles. If you can solve that task, then you can solve the problem by laying one row next to the other, starting from a wall, until

© rban/iStockphoto.

Worked Examples apply the steps in the How To to a different example, showing how they can be used to plan, implement, and test a solution to another programming problem.

Table 3 Variable Names in C++	
Variable Name	Comment
can_volume1	Variable names consist of letters, numbers, and the underscore character.
x	In mathematics, you use short variable names such as *x* or *y*. This is legal in C++, but not very common, because it can make programs harder to understand (see Programming Tip 2.1).
⚠ Can_volume	**Caution:** Variable names are case sensitive. This variable name is different from can_volume.
🚫 6pack	**Error:** Variable names cannot start with a number.
🚫 can volume	**Error:** Variable names cannot contain spaces.
🚫 double	**Error:** You cannot use a reserved word as a variable name.
🚫 ltr/fl.oz	**Error:** You cannot use symbols such as . or /

Example tables support beginners with multiple, concrete examples. These tables point out common errors and present another quick reference to the section's topic.

Consider the function call illustrated in Figure 3:

```
double result1 = cube_volume(2);
```

- The parameter variable side_length of the cube_volume function is created. ❶
- The parameter variable is initialized with the value of the argument that was passed in the call. In our case, side_length is set to 2. ❷
- The function computes the expression side_length * side_length * side_length, which has the value 8. That value is stored in the variable volume. ❸
- The function returns. All of its variables are removed. The return value is transferred to the *caller*, that is, the function calling the cube_volume function. ❹

Progressive figures trace code segments to help students visualize the program flow. Color is used consistently to make variables and other elements easily recognizable.

❶ Function call

```
double result1 = cube_volume(2);
```

result1 =

side_length =

❷ Initializing function parameter variable

```
double result1 = cube_volume(2);
```

result1 =

side_length = 2

❸ About to return to the caller

```
double volume = side_length * side_length * side_length;
return volume;
```

result1 =

side_length = 2

volume = 8

❹ After function call

```
double result1 = cube_volume(2);
```

result1 = 8

Figure 3 Parameter Passing

❶ Initialize counter

```
for (counter = 1; counter <= 10; counter++)
{
    cout << counter << endl;
}
```

counter = 1

❷ Check condition

```
for (counter = 1; counter <= 10; counter++)
{
    cout << counter << endl;
}
```

counter = 1

❸ Execute loop body

```
for (counter = 1; counter <= 10; counter++)
{
    cout << counter << endl;
}
```

counter = 1

❹ Update counter

```
for (counter = 1; counter <= 10; counter++)
{
    cout << counter << endl;
}
```

counter = 2

❺ Check condition again

```
for (counter = 1; counter <= 10; counter++)
{
    cout << counter << endl;
}
```

counter = 2

Figure 3 Execution of a for Loop

Optional **engineering exercises** engage students with applications from technical fields.

Engineering P7.12 Write a program that simulates the control software for a "people mover" system, a set of driverless trains that move in two concentric circular tracks. A set of switches allows trains to switch tracks.

In your program, the outer and inner tracks should each be divided into ten segments. Each track segment can contain a train that moves either clockwise or counterclockwise.

train moves to an adjacent segment in its track or, if that segment is occupied, to e adjacent segment in the other track.

efine a Segment structure. Each segment has a pointer to the next and previous gments in its track, a pointer to the next and previous segments in the other track,

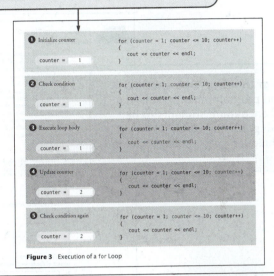

sec02/cube.cpp

```cpp
 1 #include <iostream>
 2
 3 using namespace std;
 4
 5 /**
 6    Computes the volume of a cube.
 7    @param side_length the side length of the cube
 8    @return the volume
 9 */
10 double cube_volume(double side_length)
11 {
12    double volume = side_length * side_length * side_length;
13    return volume;
14 }
15
16 int main()
17 {
18    double result1 = cube_volume(2);
19    double result2 = cube_volume(10);
20    cout << "A cube with side length 2 has volume " << result1 << endl;
21    cout << "A cube with side length 10 has volume " << result2 << endl;
22
23    return 0;
24 }
```

Program listings are carefully designed for easy reading, going well beyond simple color coding. Functions are set off by a subtle outline.

Program Run

```
A cube with side length 2 has volume 8
A cube with side length 10 has volume 1000
```

EXAMPLE CODE See sec04 of your companion code for another implementation of the earthquake program that you saw in Section 3.3. Note that the get_description function has multiple return statements.

Additional example programs are provided with the companion code for students to read, run, and modify.

Common Errors describe the kinds of errors that students often make, with an explanation of why the errors occur, and what to do about them.

Common Error 2.1

Using Undefined Variables

You must define a variable before you use it for the first time. For example, the following sequence of statements would not be legal:

```
double can_volume = 12 * liter_per_ounce;
double liter_per_ounce = 0.0296;
```

In your program, the statements are compiled in order. When the compiler reaches the first statement, it does not know that liter_per_ounce will be defined in the next line, and it reports an error.

Programming Tip 3.6

Hand-Tracing

A very useful technique for understanding whether a program works correctly is called *hand-tracing*. You simulate the program's activity on a sheet of paper. You can use this method with pseudocode or C++ code.

Get an index card, a cocktail napkin, or whatever sheet of paper is within reach. Make a column for each variable. Have the program code ready. Use a marker, such as a paper clip, to mark the current statement. In your mind, execute statements one at a time. Every time the value of a variable changes, cross out the old value and write the new value below the old one.

For example, let's trace the tax program with the data from the program run in Section 3.4. In lines 13 and 14, tax1 and tax2 are initialized to 0.

© thomasd007/iStockphoto.

Hand-tracing helps you understand whether a program works correctly.

```
 6  int main()
 7  {
 8      const double RATE1 = 0.10;
 9      const double RATE2 = 0.25;
10      const double RATE1_SINGLE_LIMIT = 32000;
11      const double RATE1_MARRIED_LIMIT = 64000;
12
13      double tax1 = 0;
14      double tax2 = 0;
15
```

Programming Tips explain good programming practices, and encourage students to be more productive with tips and techniques such as hand-tracing.

tax1	tax2	income	marital status
0	0		

In lines 18 and 22, income and marital_status are initialized by input statements.

```
16      double income;
17      cout << "Please enter your income: ";
18      cin >> income;
19
20      cout << "Please enter s for single, m for married: ";
21      string marital_status;
22      cin >> marital_status;
23
```

tax1	tax2	income	marital status
0	0	80000	m

Because marital_status is not "s", we move to the else branch of the outer if statement (line 36).

```
24
25
26
27
28
29
30
31
32
```

Special Topic 6.5

The Range-Based for Loop

C++11 introduces a convenient syntax for visiting all elements in a "range" or sequence of elements. This loop displays all elements in a vector:

```
vector<int> values = {1, 4, 9, 16, 25, 36};
for (int v : values)
{
    cout << v << " ";
}
```

In each iteration of the loop, v is set to an element of the vector. Note that you do not use an index variable. The value of v is the element, not the index of the element.

If you want to modify elements, declare the loop variable as a reference:

```
for (int& v : values)
{
    v++;
}
```

This loop increments all elements of the vector.

You can use the reserved word auto, which was introduced in Special Topic 2.3, for the type of the element variable:

```
for (auto v : values) { cout << v << " "; }
```

The range-based for loop also works for arrays:

```
int primes[] = { 2, 3, 5, 7, 11, 13 };
for (int p : primes)
{
    cout << p << " ";
```

Special Topics present optional topics and provide additional explanation of others.

range-based for loop is a convenient shortcut for visiting or updating all elements of a or an array. This book doesn't use it because one can achieve the same result by looping index values. But if you like the more concise form, and use C++11 or later, you should nly consider using it.

special_topic_5 of your companion code for a program that demonstrates the range-based op.

Computing & Society 7.1 Embedded Systems

An **embedded system** is a computer system that controls a device. The device contains a processor and other hardware and is controlled by a computer program. Unlike a personal computer, which has been designed to be flexible and run many different computer programs, the hardware and software of an embedded system are tailored to a specific device. Computer controlled devices are becoming increasingly common, ranging from washing machines to medical equipment, cell phones, automobile engines, and spacecraft.

Several challenges are specific to programming embedded systems. Most importantly, a much higher standard of quality control applies. Vendors are often unconcerned about bugs in personal computer software, because they can always make you install a patch or upgrade to the next version. But in an embedded system, that is not an option. Few consumers

would feel comfortable upgrading the software in their washing machines or automobile engines. If you ever handed in a programming assignment that you believed to be correct, only to have the instructor or grader find bugs in it, then you know how hard it is to write software that can reliably do its task for many years without a chance of changing it. Quality standards are especially important in devices whose failure would destroy property or endanger human life. Many personal computer purchasers buy computers that are fast and have a lot of storage, because the investment is paid back over time when many programs are run on the same equipment. But the hardware for an embedded device is not shared—it is dedicated to one device. A separate processor, memory, and so on, are built for every copy of the device. If it is possible to shave a few pennies off the manufacturing cost of every unit, the savings can add up quickly for devices that are pro-

duced in large volumes. Thus, the programmer of an embedded system has a much larger economic incentive to conserve resources than the desktop software programmer. Unfortunately, trying to conserve resources usually makes it harder to write programs that work correctly.

C and C++ are commonly used languages for developing embedded systems.

© Courtesy of Professor Prabal Dutta.

The Controller of an Embedded System

Computing & Society presents social and historical topics on computing—for interest and to fulfill the "historical and social context" requirements of the ACM/IEEE curriculum guidelines.

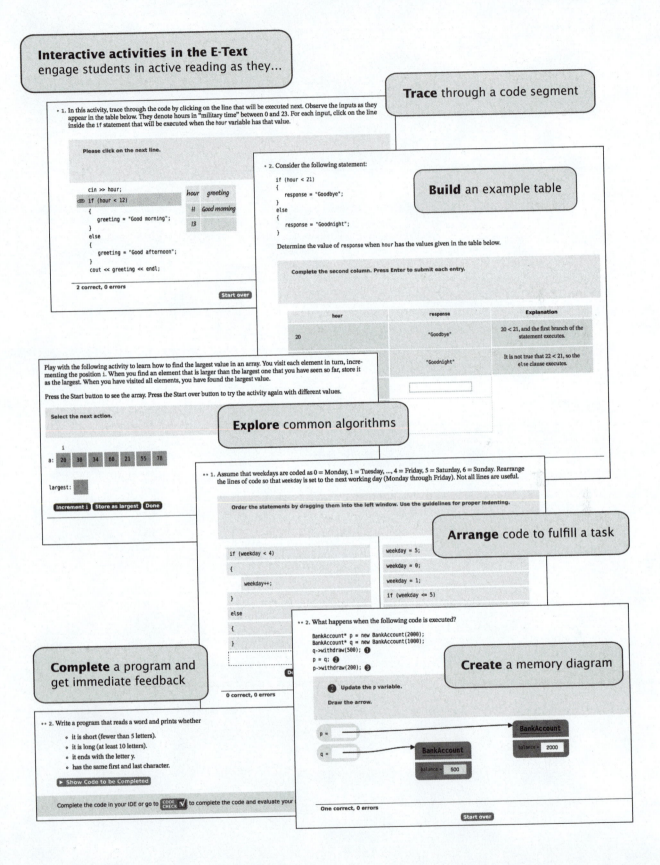

Interactive activities in the E-Text
engage students in active reading as they...

Trace through a code segment

• 1. In this activity, trace through the code by clicking on the line that will be executed next. Observe the inputs as they appear in the table below. They denote hours in "military time" between 0 and 23. For each input, click on the line inside the if statement that will be executed when the hour variable has that value.

Please click on the next line.

```
cin >> hour;
if (hour < 12)
{
    greeting = "Good morning";
}
else
{
    greeting = "Good afternoon";
}
cout << greeting << endl;
```

hour	greeting
11	Good morning
13	

2 correct, 0 errors

Start over

• 2. Consider the following statement:

```
if (hour < 21)
{
    response = "Goodbye";
}
else
{
    response = "Goodnight";
}
```

Build an example table

Determine the value of response when hour has the values given in the table below.

Complete the second column. Press Enter to submit each entry.

hour	response	Explanation
20	"Goodbye"	20 < 21, and the first branch of the statement executes.
	"Goodnight"	It is not true that 22 < 21, so the else clause executes.

Play with the following activity to learn how to find the largest value in an array. You visit each element in turn, incrementing the position i. When you find an element that is larger than the largest one that you have seen so far, store it as the largest. When you have visited all elements, you have found the largest value.

Press the Start button to see the array. Press the Start over button to try the activity again with different values.

Select the next action.

```
        i
a:  20  30  34  60  21  55  78

largest:
```

[Increment i] [Store as largest] [Done]

Explore common algorithms

•• 1. Assume that weekdays are coded as 0 = Monday, 1 = Tuesday, ..., 4 = Friday, 5 = Saturday, 6 = Sunday. Rearrange the lines of code so that weekday is set to the next working day (Monday through Friday). Not all lines are useful.

Order the statements by dragging them into the left window. Use the guidelines for proper indenting.

```
if (weekday < 4)
{
    weekday++;
}
else
{
}
```

```
weekday = 5;
weekday = 0;
weekday = 1;
if (weekday <= 5)
```

Arrange code to fulfill a task

•• 2. What happens when the following code is executed?

```
BankAccount* p = new BankAccount(2000);
BankAccount* q = new BankAccount(1000);
q->withdraw(500); ❶
p = q; ❷
p->withdraw(200); ❸
```

Create a memory diagram

Complete a program and get immediate feedback

❷ Update the p variable.
Draw the arrow.

```
p =
q =
```

BankAccount
balance = 2000

BankAccount
balance = 500

0 correct, 0 errors

•• 2. Write a program that reads a word and prints whether

○ it is short (fewer than 5 letters).
○ it is long (at least 10 letters).
○ it ends with the letter y.
○ has the same first and last character.

▶ Show Code to be Completed

Complete the code in your IDE or go to [CODE CHECK ✓] to complete the code and evaluate your

One correct, 0 errors

Start over

Acknowledgments

Many thanks to Don Fowley, Graig Donini, Dan Sayre, Ryann Dannelly, David Dietz, Laura Abrams, and Billy Ray at John Wiley & Sons for their help with this project. An especially deep acknowledgment and thanks goes to Cindy Johnson for her hard work, sound judgment, and amazing attention to detail.

I am grateful to Mark Atkins, *Ivy Technical College*, Katie Livsie, *Gaston College*, Larry Morell, *Arkansas Tech University*, and Rama Olson, *Gaston College*, for their contributions to the supplemental material. Special thanks to Stephen Gilbert, *Orange Coast Community College*, for his help with the interactive exercises.

Every new edition builds on the suggestions and experiences of new and prior reviewers, contributors, and users. We are very grateful to the individuals who provided feedback, reviewed the manuscript, made valuable suggestions and contributions, and brought errors and omissions to my attention. They include:

Charles D. Allison, *Utah Valley State College*
Fred Annexstein, *University of Cincinnati*
Mark Atkins, *Ivy Technical College*
Stefano Basagni, *Northeastern University*
Noah D. Barnette, *Virginia Tech*
Susan Bickford, *Tallahassee Community College*
Ronald D. Bowman, *University of Alabama, Huntsville*
Robert Burton, *Brigham Young University*
Peter Breznay, *University of Wisconsin, Green Bay*
Richard Cacace, *Pensacola Junior College, Pensacola*
Kuang-Nan Chang, *Eastern Kentucky University*
Joseph DeLibero, *Arizona State University*
Subramaniam Dharmarajan, *Arizona State University*
Mary Dorf, *University of Michigan*
Marty Dulberg, *North Carolina State University*
William E. Duncan, *Louisiana State University*
John Estell, *Ohio Northern University*
Waleed Farag, *Indiana University of Pennsylvania*
Evan Gallagher, *Polytechnic Institute of New York University*
Stephen Gilbert, *Orange Coast Community College*
Kenneth Gitlitz, *New Hampshire Technical Institute*
Daniel Grigoletti, *DeVry Institute of Technology, Tinley Park*
Barbara Guillott, *Louisiana State University*
Charles Halsey, *Richland College*
Jon Hanrath, *Illinois Institute of Technology*
Neil Harrison, *Utah Valley University*
Jurgen Hecht, *University of Ontario*
Steve Hodges, *Cabrillo College*

Jackie Jarboe, *Boise State University*
Debbie Kaneko, *Old Dominion University*
Mir Behrad Khamesee, *University of Waterloo*
Sung-Sik Kwon, *North Carolina Central University*
Lorrie Lehman, *University of North Carolina, Charlotte*
Cynthia Lester, *Tuskegee University*
Yanjun Li, *Fordham University*
W. James MacLean, *University of Toronto*
LindaLee Massoud, *Mott Community College*
Adelaida Medlock, *Drexel University*
Charles W. Mellard, *DeVry Institute of Technology, Irving*
Larry Morell, *Arkansas Tech University*
Ethan V. Munson, *University of Wisconsin, Milwaukee*
Arun Ravindran, *University of North Carolina at Charlotte*
Philip Regalbuto, *Trident Technical College*
Don Retzlaff, *University of North Texas*
Jeff Ringenberg, *University of Michigan, Ann Arbor*
John P. Russo, *Wentworth Institute of Technology*
Kurt Schmidt, *Drexel University*
Brent Seales, *University of Kentucky*
William Shay, *University of Wisconsin, Green Bay*
Michele A. Starkey, *Mount Saint Mary College*
William Stockwell, *University of Central Oklahoma*
Jonathan Tolstedt, *North Dakota State University*
Boyd Trolinger, *Butte College*
Muharrem Uyar, *City College of New York*
Mahendra Velauthapillai, *Georgetown University*
Kerstin Voigt, *California State University, San Bernardino*
David P. Voorhees, *Le Moyne College*
Salih Yurttas, *Texas A&M University*

A special thank you to all of our class testers:

Pani Chakrapani and the students of the University of Redlands
Jim Mackowiak and the students of Long Beach City College, LAC
Suresh Muknahallipatna and the students of the University of Wyoming
Murlidharan Nair and the students of the Indiana University of South Bend
Harriette Roadman and the students of New River Community College
David Topham and the students of Ohlone College
Dennie Van Tassel and the students of Gavilan College

CONTENTS

PREFACE **v**

SPECIAL FEATURES **xxiv**

QUICK REFERENCE **xxviii**

1 INTRODUCTION **1**

1.1 What Is Programming? **2**

1.2 The Anatomy of a Computer **3**
    C&S Computers Are Everywhere 5

1.3 Machine Code and Programming Languages **5**
    C&S Standards Organizations 7

1.4 Becoming Familiar with Your Programming Environment **7**
    PT1 Backup Copies 10

1.5 Analyzing Your First Program **11**
    CE1 Omitting Semicolons 13
    ST1 Escape Sequences 13

1.6 Errors **14**
    CE2 Misspelling Words 15

1.7 PROBLEM SOLVING Algorithm Design **16**
    The Algorithm Concept 16
    An Algorithm for Solving an Investment Problem 17
    Pseudocode 18
    From Algorithms to Programs 19
    HT1 Describing an Algorithm with Pseudocode 19
    WE1 Writing an Algorithm for Tiling a Floor 21

2 FUNDAMENTAL DATA TYPES **25**

2.1 Variables **26**
    Variable Definitions 26
    Number Types 28
    Variable Names 29
    The Assignment Statement 30
    Constants 31
    Comments 31
    CE1 Using Undefined Variables 33

CE2 Using Uninitialized Variables 33
PT1 Choose Descriptive Variable Names 33
PT2 Do Not Use Magic Numbers 34
ST1 Numeric Types in C++ 34
ST2 Numeric Ranges and Precisions 35
ST3 Defining Variables with auto 35

2.2 Arithmetic **36**
    Arithmetic Operators 36
    Increment and Decrement 36
    Integer Division and Remainder 36
    Converting Floating-Point Numbers to Integers 37
    Powers and Roots 38
    CE3 Unintended Integer Division 39
    CE4 Unbalanced Parentheses 40
    CE5 Forgetting Header Files 40
    CE6 Roundoff Errors 41
    PT3 Spaces in Expressions 42
    ST4 Casts 42
    ST5 Combining Assignment and Arithmetic 42
    C&S The Pentium Floating-Point Bug 43

2.3 Input and Output **44**
    Input 44
    Formatted Output 45

2.4 PROBLEM SOLVING First Do It By Hand **47**
    WE1 Computing Travel Time 48
    HT1 Carrying out Computations 48
    WE2 Computing the Cost of Stamps 51

2.5 Strings **51**
    The string Type 51
    Concatenation 52
    String Input 52
    String Functions 52
    C&S International Alphabets and Unicode 55

3 DECISIONS **59**

3.1 The if Statement **60**
    CE1 A Semicolon After the if Condition 63
    PT1 Brace Layout 63
    PT2 Always Use Braces 64
    PT3 Tabs 64

PT4 Avoid Duplication in Branches 65
ST1 The Conditional Operator 65

3.2 Comparing Numbers and Strings   66
CE2 Confusing = and == 68
CE3 Exact Comparison of Floating-Point Numbers 68
PT5 Compile with Zero Warnings 69
ST2 Lexicographic Ordering of Strings 69
HT1 Implementing an if Statement 70
WE1 Extracting the Middle 72
C&S Dysfunctional Computerized Systems 72

3.3 Multiple Alternatives   73
ST3 The switch Statement 75

3.4 Nested Branches   76
CE4 The Dangling else Problem 79
PT6 Hand-Tracing 79

3.5 PROBLEM SOLVING Flowcharts   81

3.6 PROBLEM SOLVING Test Cases   83
PT7 Make a Schedule and Make Time for Unexpected Problems 84

3.7 Boolean Variables and Operators   85
CE5 Combining Multiple Relational Operators 88
CE6 Confusing && and || Conditions 88
ST4 Short-Circuit Evaluation of Boolean Operators 89
ST5 De Morgan's Law 89

3.8 APPLICATION Input Validation   90
C&S Artificial Intelligence 92

4   LOOPS 95

4.1 The while Loop   96
CE1 Infinite Loops 100
CE2 Don't Think "Are We There Yet?" 101
CE3 Off-by-One Errors 101
C&S The First Bug 102

4.2 PROBLEM SOLVING Hand-Tracing   103

4.3 The for Loop   106
PT1 Use for Loops for Their Intended Purpose Only 109
PT2 Choose Loop Bounds That Match Your Task 110
PT3 Count Iterations 110

4.4 The do Loop   111
PT4 Flowcharts for Loops 111

4.5 Processing Input   112
Sentinel Values 112
Reading Until Input Fails 114
ST1 Clearing the Failure State 115
ST2 The Loop-and-a-Half Problem and the break Statement 116
ST3 Redirection of Input and Output 116

4.6 PROBLEM SOLVING Storyboards   117

4.7 Common Loop Algorithms   119
Sum and Average Value 119
Counting Matches 120
Finding the First Match 120
Prompting Until a Match is Found 121
Maximum and Minimum 121
Comparing Adjacent Values 122
HT1 Writing a Loop 123
WE1 Credit Card Processing 126

4.8 Nested Loops   126
WE2 Manipulating the Pixels in an Image 129

4.9 PROBLEM SOLVING Solve a Simpler Problem First   130

4.10 Random Numbers and Simulations   134
Generating Random Numbers 134
Simulating Die Tosses 135
The Monte Carlo Method 136
C&S Digital Piracy 138

5   FUNCTIONS 141

5.1 Functions as Black Boxes   142

5.2 Implementing Functions   143
PT1 Function Comments 146

5.3 Parameter Passing   146
PT2 Do Not Modify Parameter Variables 148

5.4 Return Values   148
CE1 Missing Return Value 149
ST1 Function Declarations 150
HT1 Implementing a Function 151
WE1 Generating Random Passwords 152
WE2 Using a Debugger 152

5.5 Functions Without Return Values   153

5.6 PROBLEM SOLVING Reusable Functions **154**

5.7 PROBLEM SOLVING Stepwise
Refinement **156**
- PT3 Keep Functions Short 161
- PT4 Tracing Functions 161
- PT5 Stubs 162
- WE3 Calculating a Course Grade 163

5.8 Variable Scope and Global Variables **163**
- PT6 Avoid Global Variables 165

5.9 Reference Parameters **165**
- PT7 Prefer Return Values to Reference Parameters 169
- ST2 Constant References 170

5.10 Recursive Functions (Optional) **170**
- HT2 Thinking Recursively 173
- C&S The Explosive Growth of Personal Computers 174

6 ARRAYS AND VECTORS **179**

6.1 Arrays **180**
- Defining Arrays 180
- Accessing Array Elements 182
- Partially Filled Arrays 183
- CE1 Bounds Errors 184
- PT1 Use Arrays for Sequences of Related Values 184
- C&S Computer Viruses 185

6.2 Common Array Algorithms **185**
- Filling 186
- Copying 186
- Sum and Average Value 186
- Maximum and Minimum 187
- Element Separators 187
- Counting Matches 187
- Linear Search 188
- Removing an Element 188
- Inserting an Element 189
- Swapping Elements 190
- Reading Input 191
- ST1 Sorting with the C++ Library 192
- ST2 A Sorting Algorithm 192
- ST3 Binary Search 193

6.3 Arrays and Functions **194**
- ST4 Constant Array Parameters 198

6.4 PROBLEM SOLVING Adapting
Algorithms **198**
- HT1 Working with Arrays 200
- WE1 Rolling the Dice 203

6.5 PROBLEM SOLVING Discovering Algorithms by
Manipulating Physical Objects **203**

6.6 Two-Dimensional Arrays **206**
- Defining Two-Dimensional Arrays 207
- Accessing Elements 207
- Locating Neighboring Elements 208
- Computing Row and Column Totals 208
- Two-Dimensional Array Parameters 210
- CE2 Omitting the Column Size of a Two-Dimensional Array Parameter 212
- WE2 A World Population Table 213

6.7 Vectors **213**
- Defining Vectors 214
- Growing and Shrinking Vectors 215
- Vectors and Functions 216
- Vector Algorithms 216
- Two-Dimensional Vectors 218
- PT2 Prefer Vectors over Arrays 219
- ST5 The Range-Based for Loop 219

7 POINTERS AND
STRUCTURES **223**

7.1 Defining and Using Pointers **224**
- Defining Pointers 224
- Accessing Variables Through Pointers 225
- Initializing Pointers 227
- CE1 Confusing Pointers with the Data to Which They Point 228
- PT1 Use a Separate Definition for Each Pointer Variable 229
- ST1 Pointers and References 229

7.2 Arrays and Pointers **230**
- Arrays as Pointers 230
- Pointer Arithmetic 230
- Array Parameter Variables Are Pointers 232
- ST2 Using a Pointer to Step Through an Array 233
- CE2 Returning a Pointer to a Local Variable 234
- PT2 Program Clearly, Not Cleverly 234
- ST3 Constant Pointers 235

7.3 **C and C++ Strings** **235**
The char Type 235
C Strings 236
Character Arrays 237
Converting Between C and C++ Strings 237
C++ Strings and the [ ] Operator 238
ST4 Working with C Strings 238

7.4 **Dynamic Memory Allocation** **240**
CE3 Dangling Pointers 242
CE4 Memory Leaks 243

7.5 **Arrays and Vectors of Pointers** **243**

7.6 **PROBLEM SOLVING Draw a Picture** **246**
HT1 Working with Pointers 248
WE1 Producing a Mass Mailing 249
C&S Embedded Systems 250

7.7 **Structures** **250**
Structured Types 250
Structure Assignment and Comparison 251
Functions and Structures 252
Arrays of Structures 252
Structures with Array Members 253
Nested Structures 253

7.8 **Pointers and Structures** **254**
Pointers to Structures 254
Structures with Pointer Members 255
ST5 Smart Pointers 256

8 STREAMS **259**

8.1 **Reading and Writing Text Files** **260**
Opening a Stream 260
Reading from a File 261
Writing to a File 262
A File Processing Example 262

8.2 **Reading Text Input** **265**
Reading Words 265
Reading Characters 266
Reading Lines 267
CE1 Mixing >> and getline Input 268
ST1 Stream Failure Checking 269

8.3 **Writing Text Output** **270**
ST2 Unicode, UTF-8, and C++ Strings 272

8.4 **Parsing and Formatting Strings** **273**

8.5 **Command Line Arguments** **274**
C&S Encryption Algorithms 277
HT1 Processing Text Files 278
WE1 Looking for for Duplicates 281

8.6 **Random Access and Binary Files** **281**
Random Access 281
Binary Files 282
Processing Image Files 282
C&S Databases and Privacy 286

9 CLASSES **289**

9.1 **Object-Oriented Programming** **290**

9.2 **Implementing a Simple Class** **292**

9.3 **Specifying the Public Interface of a Class** **294**
CE1 Forgetting a Semicolon 296

9.4 **Designing the Data Representation** **297**

9.5 **Member Functions** **299**
Implementing Member Functions 299
Implicit and Explicit Parameters 299
Calling a Member Function from a Member Function 301
PT1 All Data Members Should Be Private; Most Member Functions Should Be Public 303
PT2 const Correctness 303

9.6 **Constructors** **304**
CE2 Trying to Call a Constructor 306
ST1 Overloading 306
ST2 Initializer Lists 307
ST3 Universal and Uniform Initialization Syntax 308

9.7 **PROBLEM SOLVING Tracing Objects** **308**
HT1 Implementing a Class 310
WE1 Implementing a Bank Account Class 314
C&S Electronic Voting Machines 314

9.8 **PROBLEM SOLVING Discovering Classes** **315**
PT3 Make Parallel Vectors into Vectors of Objects 317

9.9 **Separate Compilation** **318**

9.10 **Pointers to Objects** **322**
Dynamically Allocating Objects 322
The -> Operator 323
The this Pointer 324

9.11 PROBLEM SOLVING Patterns for
Object Data **324**
Keeping a Total 324
Counting Events 325
Collecting Values 326
Managing Properties of an Object 326
Modeling Objects with Distinct States 327
Describing the Position of an Object 328
C&S Open Source and Free Software 329

10 INHERITANCE **333**

10.1 Inheritance Hierarchies **334**

10.2 Implementing Derived Classes **338**
CE1 Private Inheritance 341
CE2 Replicating Base-Class Members 341
PT1 Use a Single Class for Variation in Values,
Inheritance for Variation in Behavior 342
ST1 Calling the Base-Class Constructor 342

10.3 Overriding Member Functions **343**
CE3 Forgetting the Base-Class Name 345

10.4 Virtual Functions and Polymorphism **346**
The Slicing Problem 346
Pointers to Base and Derived Classes 347
Virtual Functions 348
Polymorphism 349
PT2 Don't Use Type Tags 352
CE4 Slicing an Object 352
CE5 Failing to Override a Virtual Function 353
ST2 Virtual Self-Calls 354
HT1 Developing an Inheritance Hierarchy 354
WE1 Implementing an Employee Hierarchy for
Payroll Processing 359
C&S Who Controls the Internet? 360

APPENDIX A RESERVED WORD SUMMARY A-1
APPENDIX B OPERATOR SUMMARY A-3
APPENDIX C CHARACTER CODES A-5
APPENDIX D C++ LIBRARY SUMMARY A-8
APPENDIX E C++ LANGUAGE CODING
GUIDELINES A-11
APPENDIX F NUMBER SYSTEMS AND BIT AND SHIFT
OPERATIONS (E-TEXT ONLY)

GLOSSARY **G-1**
INDEX **I-1**
CREDITS **C-1**

ALPHABETICAL LIST OF SYNTAX BOXES

Assignment 30

C++ Program 12
Class Definition 295
Comparisons 67
Constructor with Base-Class Initializer 342

Defining an Array 181
Defining a Structure 251
Defining a Vector 213
Derived-Class Definition 340
Dynamic Memory Allocation 240

for Statement 106
Function Definition 145

if Statement 61
Input Statement 44

Member Function Definition 301

Output Statement 13

Pointer Syntax 226

Two-Dimensional Array Definition 207

Variable Definition 27

while Statement 97
Working with File Streams 262

CHAPTER	Common Errors	How Tos and Worked Examples
1 Introduction	Omitting Semicolons 13 Misspelling Words 15	Describing an Algorithm with Pseudocode 19 Writing an Algorithm for Tiling a Floor 21
2 Fundamental Data Types	Using Undefined Variables 33 Using Uninitialized Variables 33 Unintended Integer Division 39 Unbalanced Parentheses 40 Forgetting Header Files 40 Roundoff Errors 41	Computing Travel Time 48 Carrying out Computations 48 Computing the Cost of Stamps 51
3 Decisions	A Semicolon After the if Condition 63 Confusing = and == 68 Exact Comparison of Floating-Point Numbers 68 The Dangling else Problem 79 Combining Multiple Relational Operators 88 Confusing && and || Conditions 88	Implementing an if Statement 70 Extracting the Middle 72
4 Loops	Infinite Loops 100 Don't Think "Are We There Yet?" 101 Off-by-One Errors 101	Writing a Loop 123 Credit Card Processing 126 Manipulating the Pixels in an Image 129
5 Functions	Missing Return Value 149	Implementing a Function 151 Generating Random Passwords 152 Using a Debugger 152 Calculating a Course Grade 163 Thinking Recursively 173

Programming Tips		Special Topics		Computing & Society	
Backup Copies	10	Escape Sequences	13	Computers Are Everywhere	5
				Standards Organizations	7
Choose Descriptive Variable Names	33	Numeric Types in C++	34	The Pentium Floating-Point Bug	43
Do Not Use Magic Numbers	34	Numeric Ranges and Precisions	35	International Alphabets and Unicode	55
Spaces in Expressions	42	Defining Variables with auto	35		
		Casts	42		
		Combining Assignment and Arithmetic	42		
Brace Layout	63	The Conditional Operator	65	Dysfunctional Computerized Systems	72
Always Use Braces	64	Lexicographic Ordering of Strings	69	Artificial Intelligence	92
Tabs	64	The switch Statement	75		
Avoid Duplication in Branches	65	Short-Circuit Evaluation of Boolean Operators	89		
Compile with Zero Warnings	69	De Morgan's Law	89		
Hand-Tracing	79				
Make a Schedule and Make Time for Unexpected Problems	84				
Use for Loops for Their Intended Purpose Only	109	Clearing the Failure State	115	The First Bug	102
Choose Loop Bounds That Match Your Task	110	The Loop-and-a-Half Problem and the break Statement	116	Digital Piracy	138
Count Iterations	110	Redirection of Input and Output	116		
Flowcharts for Loops	111				
Function Comments	146	Function Declarations	150	The Explosive Growth of Personal Computers	174
Do Not Modify Parameter Variables	148	Constant References	170		
Keep Functions Short	161				
Tracing Functions	161				
Stubs	162				
Avoid Global Variables	165				
Prefer Return Values to Reference Parameters	169				

CHAPTER	Common Errors		How Tos and Worked Examples	
6 Arrays and Vectors	Bounds Errors	184	Working with Arrays	200
	Omitting the Column Size of a Two-Dimensional Array Parameter	212	Rolling the Dice	203
			A World Population Table	213
7 Pointers and Structures	Confusing Pointers with the Data to Which They Point	228	Working with Pointers	248
	Returning a Pointer to a Local Variable	234	Producing a Mass Mailing	249
	Dangling Pointers	242		
	Memory Leaks	243		
8 Streams	Mixing >> and getline Input	268	Processing Text Files	278
			Looking for for Duplicates	281
9 Classes	Forgetting a Semicolon	296	Implementing a Class	310
	Trying to Call a Constructor	306	Implementing a Bank Account Class	314
10 Inheritance	Private Inheritance	341	Developing an Inheritance Hierarchy	354
	Replicating Base-Class Members	341	Implementing an Employee Hierarchy for Payroll Processing	359
	Forgetting the Base-Class Name	345		
	Slicing an Object	352		
	Failing to Override a Virtual Function	353		

Programming Tips		Special Topics		Computing & Society	
Use Arrays for Sequences of Related Values	184	Sorting with the C++ Library	192	Computer Viruses	185
Prefer Vectors over Arrays	219	A Sorting Algorithm	192		
		Binary Search	193		
		Constant Array Parameters	198		
		The Range-Based for Loop	219		
Use a Separate Definition for Each Pointer Variable	229	Pointers and References	229	Embedded Systems	250
Program Clearly, Not Cleverly	234	Using a Pointer to Step Through an Array	233		
		Constant Pointers	235		
		Working with C Strings	238		
		Smart Pointers	256		
		Stream Failure Checking	269	Encryption Algorithms	277
		Unicode, UTF-8, and C++ Strings	272	Databases and Privacy	286
All Data Members Should Be Private; Most Member Functions Should Be Public	303	Overloading	306	Electronic Voting Machines	314
const Correctness	303	Initializer Lists	307	Open Source and Free Software	329
Make Parallel Vectors into Vectors of Objects	317	Universal and Uniform Initialization Syntax	308		
Use a Single Class for Variation in Values, Inheritance for Variation in Behavior	342	Calling the Base-Class Constructor	342	Who Controls the Internet?	360
		Virtual Self-Calls	354		

Variable and Constant Definitions

```
Type    Name        Initial value
  /      /              /
int cans_per_pack = 6;

const double CAN_VOLUME = 0.335;
```

Mathematical Operations

```
#include <cmath>
```

pow(x, y)	Raising to a power x^y
sqrt(x)	Square root $\sqrt{x}$
log10(x)	Decimal log $\log_{10}(x)$
abs(x)	Absolute value $|x|$
sin(x)	
cos(x)	Sine, cosine, tangent of x (x in radians)
tan(x)	

Selected Operators and Their Precedence

(See Appendix B for the complete list.)

[]	Array element access
++ -- !	Increment, decrement, Boolean *not*
* / %	Multiplication, division, remainder
+ -	Addition, subtraction
< <= > >=	Comparisons
== !=	Equal, not equal
&&	Boolean *and*
||	Boolean *or*
=	Assignment

Loop Statements

```
                Condition
                  /
while (balance < TARGET)
{
   year++;
   balance = balance * (1 + rate / 100);
}
```
Executed while condition is true

```
   Initialization  Condition  Update
       /              /          /
for (int i = 0; i < 10; i++)
{
   cout << i << endl;
}
```

Loop body executed at least once

```
do
{
   cout << "Enter a positive integer: ";
   cin >> input;
}
while (input <= 0);
```

Conditional Statement

```
              Condition
                /
if (floor >= 13)
{
   actual_floor = floor - 1;          Executed when
}                                      condition is true
else if (floor >= 0)    Second condition (optional)
{
   actual_floor = floor;
}
else
{                                      Executed when all
   cout << "Floor negative" << endl;   conditions are false
}                                      (optional)
```

String Operations

```
#include <string>
string s = "Hello";
int n = s.length(); // 5
string t = s.substr(1, 3); // "ell"
string c = s.substr(2, 1); // "l"
char ch = s[2]; // 'l'
for (int i = 0; i < s.length(); i++)
{
   string c = s.substr(i, 1);
   or char ch = s[i];
   Process c or ch
}
```

Function Definitions

```
   Return type        Parameter type and name
      /                    /          /
double cube_volume(double side_length)
{
   double vol = side_length * side_length * side_length;
   return vol;
}                        Exits function and returns result.

Reference parameter
                    /
void deposit(double& balance, double amount)
{
   balance = balance + amount;
}              Modifies supplied argument
```

Arrays

```
Element type    Length
    /            /
int numbers[5];
int squares[] = { 0, 1, 4, 9, 16 };
int magic_square[4][4] =
{
   { 16, 3, 2, 13 },
   { 5, 10, 11, 8 },
   { 9, 6, 7, 12 },
   { 4, 15, 14, 1 }
};

for (int i = 0; i < size; i++)
{
   Process numbers[i]
}
```

Vectors

```cpp
#include <vector>
```

Element type — Initial values (C++ 11)

```cpp
vector<int> values = { 0, 1, 4, 9, 16 };
```

Initially empty

```cpp
vector<string> names;
```

Add elements to the end

```cpp
names.push_back("Ann");
names.push_back("Cindy"); // names.size() is now 2

names.pop_back(); // Removes last element

names[0] = "Beth"; // Use [] for element access
```

Pointers

```cpp
int n = 10;
int* p = &n; // p set to address of n
*p = 11; // n is now 11
```

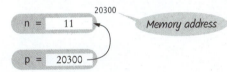

Memory address

```cpp
int a[5] = { 0, 1, 4, 9, 16 };
p = a; // p points to start of a
*p = 11; // a[0] is now 11
p++; // p points to a[1]
p[2] = 11; // a[3] is now 11
```

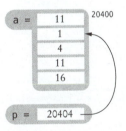

Input and Output

```cpp
#include <iostream>
cin >> x; // x can be int, double, string
cout << x;

while (cin >> x) { Process x }
if (cin.fail()) // Previous input failed


#include <fstream>
string filename = ...;
ifstream in(filename);
ofstream out("output.txt");

string line; getline(in, line);
char ch; in.get(ch);
```

Range-based for Loop

An array, vector, or other container (C++ 11)

```cpp
for (int v : values)
{
    cout << v << endl;
}
```

Output Manipulators

```cpp
#include <iomanip>
```

endl	Output new line
fixed	Fixed format for floating-point
setprecision(*n*)	Number of digits after decimal point for fixed format
setw(*n*)	Field width for the next item
left	Left alignment (use for strings)
right	Right alignment (default)
setfill(*ch*)	Fill character (default: space)

Class Definition

```cpp
class BankAccount
{
public:
    BankAccount(double amount);        // Constructor declaration
    void deposit(double amount);       // Member function declaration
    double get_balance() const;        // Accessor member function
    ...
private:                               // Data member
    double balance;
}

void BankAccount::deposit(double amount)    ⎤ Member function
{                                           ⎥ definition
    balance = balance + amount;             ⎦
}
```

Inheritance

Derived class   *Base class*

```cpp
class CheckingAccount : public BankAccount
{
public:                                    // Member function
    void deposit(double amount);           // overrides base class
private:                                   // Added data member
    int transactions;                      // in derived class
}

void CheckingAccount::deposit(double amount)
{                                          // Calls base class
    BankAccount::deposit(amount);          // member function
    transactions++;
}
```

CHAPTER 1

INTRODUCTION

© JanPietruszka/iStockphoto.

CHAPTER GOALS

To learn about the architecture of computers

To learn about machine languages and higher-level programming languages

To become familiar with your compiler

To compile and run your first C++ program

To recognize compile-time and run-time errors

To describe an algorithm with pseudocode

To understand the activity of programming

CHAPTER CONTENTS

1.1 WHAT IS PROGRAMMING? 2

1.2 THE ANATOMY OF A COMPUTER 3
C&S Computers Are Everywhere 5

1.3 MACHINE CODE AND PROGRAMMING LANGUAGES 5
C&S Standards Organizations 7

1.4 BECOMING FAMILIAR WITH YOUR PROGRAMMING ENVIRONMENT 7
PT1 Backup Copies 10

1.5 ANALYZING YOUR FIRST PROGRAM 11
SYN C++ Program 12
SYN Output Statement 13
CE1 Omitting Semicolons 13
ST1 Escape Sequences 13

1.6 ERRORS 14
CE2 Misspelling Words 15

1.7 PROBLEM SOLVING: ALGORITHM DESIGN 16
HT1 Describing an Algorithm with Pseudocode 19
WE1 Writing an Algorithm for Tiling a Floor 21

Just as you gather tools, study a project, and make a plan for tackling it, in this chapter you will gather up the basics you need to start learning to program. After a brief introduction to computer hardware, software, and programming in general, you will learn how to write and run your first C++ program. You will also learn how to diagnose and fix programming errors, and how to use pseudocode to describe an algorithm—a step-by-step description of how to solve a problem—as you plan your programs.

1.1 What Is Programming?

Computers execute very basic instructions in rapid succession.

You have probably used a computer for work or fun. Many people use computers for everyday tasks such as electronic banking or writing a term paper. Computers are good for such tasks. They can handle repetitive chores, such as totaling up numbers or placing words on a page, without getting bored or exhausted.

The flexibility of a computer is quite an amazing phenomenon. The same machine can balance your checkbook, print your term paper, and play a game. In contrast, other machines carry out a much narrower range of tasks; a car drives and a toaster toasts. Computers can carry out a wide range of tasks because they execute different programs, each of which directs the computer to work on a specific task.

A computer program is a sequence of instructions and decisions.

The computer itself is a machine that stores data (numbers, words, pictures), interacts with devices (the monitor, the sound system, the printer), and executes programs. A **computer program** tells a computer, in minute detail, the sequence of steps that are needed to fulfill a task. The physical computer and peripheral devices are collectively called the **hardware**. The programs the computer executes are called the **software**.

Today's computer programs are so sophisticated that it is hard to believe that they are composed of extremely primitive operations. A typical operation may be one of the following:

- Put a red dot at this screen position.
- Add up these two numbers.
- If this value is negative, continue the program at a certain instruction.

The computer user has the illusion of smooth interaction because a program contains a huge number of such operations, and because the computer can execute them at great speed.

Programming is the act of designing and implementing computer programs.

The act of designing and implementing computer programs is called *programming*. In this book, you will learn how to program a computer—that is, how to direct the computer to execute tasks.

To write a computer game with motion and sound effects or a word processor that supports fancy fonts and pictures is a complex task that requires a team of many highly skilled programmers. Your first programming efforts will be more mundane. The concepts and skills you learn in this book form an important foundation, and you should not be disappointed if your first programs do not rival the sophisticated software that is familiar to you. Actually, you will find that there is an immense thrill even in simple programming tasks. It is an amazing experience to see the computer precisely and quickly carry out a task that would take you hours of drudgery, to make small changes in a program that lead to immediate improvements, and to see the computer become an extension of your mental powers.

1.2 The Anatomy of a Computer

To understand the programming process, you need to have a rudimentary understanding of the building blocks that make up a computer. We will look at a personal computer. Larger computers have faster, larger, or more powerful components, but they have fundamentally the same design.

At the heart of the computer lies the **central processing unit** (CPU) (see Figure 1). It consists of a single *chip*, or a small number of chips. A computer chip (integrated circuit) is a component with a plastic or metal housing, metal connectors, and inside wiring made principally from silicon. For a CPU chip, the inside wiring is enormously complicated. For example, the Pentium chip (a popular CPU for personal computers at the time of this writing) is composed of several million structural elements, called *transistors*.

> The central processing unit (CPU) performs program control and data processing.

The CPU performs program control and data processing. That is, the CPU locates and executes the program instructions; it carries out arithmetic operations such as addition, subtraction, multiplication, and division; it fetches data from external memory or devices and stores data back.

> Storage devices include memory and secondary storage.

There are two kinds of storage. Primary storage, or memory, is made from electronic circuits that can store data, provided they are supplied with electric power. **Secondary storage**, usually a **hard disk** (see Figure 2) or a solid-state drive, provides slower and less expensive storage that persists without electricity. A hard disk consists of rotating platters, which are coated with a magnetic material. A solid-state drive uses electronic components that can retain information without power, and without moving parts.

© Amorphis/iStockphoto.

Figure 1   Central Processing Unit

Figure 2
A Hard Disk   © PhotoDisc, Inc./Getty Images.

Programs and data are typically stored on the hard disk and loaded into memory when the program starts. The program then updates the data in memory and writes the modified data back to the hard disk.

To interact with a human user, a computer requires peripheral devices. The computer transmits information (called *output*) to the user through a display screen, speakers, and printers. The user can enter information (called *input*) by using a keyboard or a pointing device such as a mouse.

Some computers are self-contained units, whereas others are interconnected through *networks*. Through the network cabling, the computer can read data and programs from central storage locations or send data to other computers. For the user of a networked computer it may not even be obvious which data reside on the computer itself and which are transmitted through the network.

Figure 3 gives a schematic overview of the architecture of a personal computer. Program instructions and data (such as text, numbers, audio, or video) reside in secondary storage or elsewhere on the network. When a program is started, its instructions are brought into memory, where the CPU can read them. The CPU reads and executes one instruction at a time. As directed by these instructions, the CPU reads data, modifies it, and writes it back to memory or secondary storage. Some program instructions will cause the CPU to place dots on the display screen or printer or to vibrate the speaker. As these actions happen many times over and at great speed, the human user will perceive images and sound. Some program instructions read user input from the keyboard, mouse, touch sensor, or microphone. The program analyzes the nature of these inputs and then executes the next appropriate instruction.

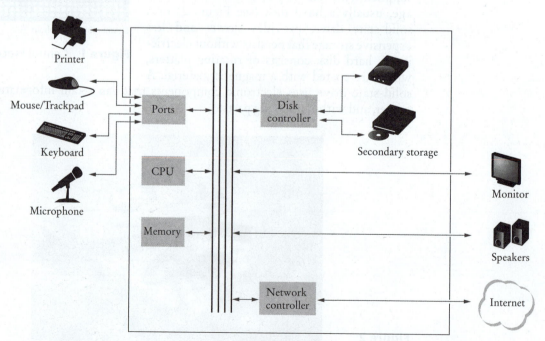

Figure 3 Schematic Design of a Personal Computer

Computing & Society 1.1 Computers Are Everywhere

When computers were first invented in the 1940s, a computer filled an entire room. Figure 4 shows the ENIAC (*electronic numerical integrator and computer*), completed in 1946 at the University of Pennsylvania. The ENIAC was used by the military to compute the trajectories of projectiles. Nowadays, computing facilities of search engines, Internet shops, and social networks fill huge buildings called data centers. At the other end of the spectrum, computers are all around us. Your cell phone has a computer inside, as do many credit cards and fare cards for public transit. A modern car has several computers—to control the engine, brakes, lights, and radio.

The advent of ubiquitous computing changed many aspects of our lives. Factories used to employ people to do repetitive assembly tasks that are today carried out by computer-controlled robots, operated by a few people who know how to work with those computers. Books, music, and movies nowadays are often consumed on computers, and computers are almost always involved in their production. The book that you are reading right now could not have been written without computers.

© Maurice Savage/Alamy Stock Photo.

This transit card contains a computer.

Knowing about computers and how to program them has become an essential skill in many careers. Engineers design computer-controlled cars and medical equipment that preserve lives. Computer scientists develop programs that help people come together to support social causes. For example, activists used social networks to share videos showing abuse by repressive regimes, and this information was instrumental in changing public opinion.

As computers, large and small, become ever more embedded in our everyday lives, it is increasingly important for everyone to understand how they work, and how to work with them. As you use this book to learn how to program a computer, you will develop a good understanding of computing fundamentals that will make you a more informed citizen and, perhaps, a computing professional.

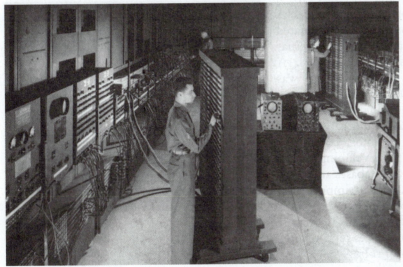

© UPPA/Photoshot.

Figure 4 The ENIAC

1.3 Machine Code and Programming Languages

On the most basic level, computer instructions are extremely primitive. The processor executes *machine instructions*. A typical sequence of machine instructions is

1. Move the contents of memory location 40000 into the CPU.
2. If that value is greater than 100, continue with the instruction that is stored in memory location 11280.

Actually, machine instructions are encoded as numbers so that they can be stored in memory. On a Pentium processor, this sequence of instruction is encoded as the sequence of numbers

Computer programs are stored as machine instructions in a code that depends on the processor type.

$$161\ 40000\ 45\ 100\ 127\ 11280$$

On a processor from a different manufacturer, the encoding would be different. When this kind of processor fetches this sequence of numbers, it decodes them and executes the associated sequence of commands.

How can we communicate the command sequence to the computer? The simplest method is to place the actual numbers into the computer memory. This is, in fact, how the very earliest computers worked. However, a long program is composed of thousands of individual commands, and it is a tedious and error-prone affair to look up the numeric codes for all commands and place the codes manually into memory. As already mentioned, computers are really good at automating tedious and error-prone activities. It did not take long for computer scientists to realize that the computers themselves could be harnessed to help in the programming process.

Computer scientists devised **high-level programming languages** that allow programmers to describe tasks, using a **syntax** that is more closely related to the problems to be solved. In this book, we will use the C++ programming language, which was developed by Bjarne Stroustrup in the 1980s.

C++ is a general-purpose language that is in widespread use for systems and embedded programming.

Over the years, C++ has grown by the addition of many features. A standardization process culminated in the publication of the international C++ standard in 1998. A minor update to the standard was issued in 2003. A major revision came to fruition in 2011, followed by updates in 2014 and 2017. At this time, C++ is the most commonly used language for developing system software such as databases and operating systems. Just as importantly, C++ is commonly used for programming "embedded systems", computers that control devices such as automobile engines or robots.

© Courtesy of Bjarne Stroustrup.

Bjarne Stroustrup

Here is a typical statement in C++:

```
if (int_rate > 100) { cout << "Interest rate error"; }
```

High-level programming languages are independent of the processor.

This means, "If the interest rate is over 100, display an error message". A special computer program, a **compiler**, translates this high-level description into machine instructions for a particular processor.

High-level languages are independent of the underlying hardware. C++ instructions work equally well on an Intel Pentium and a processor in a cell phone. Of course, the compiler-generated machine instructions are different, but the programmer who uses the compiler need not worry about these differences.

Computing & Society 1.2   Standards Organizations

Two standards organizations, the American National Standards Institute (ANSI) and the International Organization for Standardization (ISO), have jointly developed the definitive standard for the C++ language.

Why have standards? You encounter the benefits of standardization every day. When you buy a light bulb, you can be assured that it fits in the socket without having to measure the socket at home and the bulb in the store. In fact, you may have experienced how painful the lack of standards can be if you have ever purchased a flashlight with nonstandard bulbs. Replacement bulbs for such a flashlight can be difficult and expensive to obtain.

The ANSI and ISO standards organizations are associations of industry professionals who develop standards for everything from car tires and credit card shapes to programming languages. Having a standard for a programming language such as C++ means that you can take a program that you developed on one system with one manufacturer's compiler to a different system and be assured that it will continue to work.

© Denis Vorob'yev/iStockphoto.

1.4 Becoming Familiar with Your Programming Environment

Set aside some time to become familiar with the programming environment that you will use for your class work.

Many students find that the tools they need as programmers are very different from the software with which they are familiar. You should spend some time making yourself familiar with your programming environment. Because computer systems vary widely, this book can give only an outline of the steps you need to follow. It is a good idea to participate in a hands-on lab, or to ask a knowledgeable friend to give you a tour.

Step 1   Start the C++ development environment.

Computer systems differ greatly in this regard. On many computers there is an **integrated development environment** in which you can write and test your programs. On other computers you first launch an **editor,** a program that functions like a word processor, in which you can enter your C++ instructions; then open a *console window* and type commands to execute your program. Other programming environments are online. In such an environment, you write programs in a web browser. The programs are then executed on a remote machine, and the results are displayed in the web browser window. You need to find out how to get started with your environment.

Step 2   Write a simple program.

The traditional choice for the very first program in a new programming language is a program that displays a simple greeting: "Hello, World!". Let us follow that tradition. Here is the "Hello, World!" program in C++:

```cpp
#include <iostream>

using namespace std;

int main()
{
```

```
        cout << "Hello, World!" << endl;
        return 0;
}
```

We will examine this program in the next section.

An editor is a program for entering and modifying text, such as a C++ program.

No matter which programming environment you use, you begin your activity by typing the program statements into an editor window.

Create a new file and call it hello.cpp, using the steps that are appropriate for your environment. (If your environment requires that you supply a project name in addition to the file name, use the name hello for the project.) Enter the program instructions *exactly* as they are given above. Alternatively, locate an electronic copy of the program in the source files for this book and paste it into your editor. (You can download the full set of files for this book from its companion site at wiley.com/go/bclo3.)

C++ is case sensitive. You must be careful about distinguishing between upper- and lowercase letters.

As you write this program, pay careful attention to the various symbols, and keep in mind that C++ is **case sensitive**. You must enter upper- and lowercase letters exactly as they appear in the program listing. You cannot type MAIN or Endl. If you are not careful, you will run into problems—see Common Error 1.2.

Step 3 Compile and run the program.

The compiler translates C++ programs into machine code.

The process for building and running a C++ program depends greatly on your programming environment. In some integrated development environments, you simply push a button. In other environments, you may have to type commands. When you run the test program, the message

```
Hello, World!
```

will appear somewhere on the screen (see Figures 5 and 6).

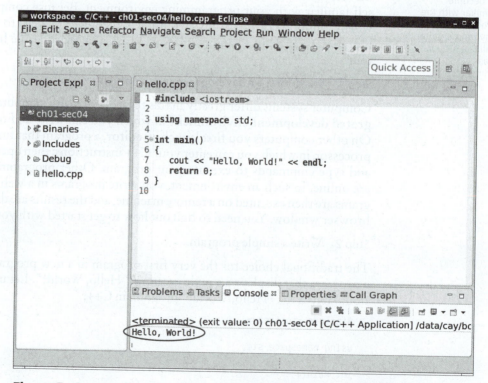

Figure 5 Running the hello Program in an Integrated Development Environment

```
Terminal                                                    _ □ ×
File  Edit  View  Terminal  Help
~$ cd cs1/bookcode/ch01
~/cs1/bookcode/ch01$ g++ -o hello hello.cpp
~/cs1/bookcode/ch01$ ./hello
Hello, World!
~/cs1/bookcode/ch01$ []
```

Figure 6   Compiling and Running the `hello` Program in a Console Window

> The linker combines machine code with library code into an executable program.

It is useful to know what goes on behind the scenes when your program gets built. First, the compiler translates the C++ **source code** (that is, the statements that you wrote) into machine instructions. The **machine code** contains only the translation of the code that you wrote. That is not enough to actually run the program. To display a string on a window, quite a bit of low-level activity is necessary. The implementors of your C++ development environment provided a library that includes the definition of cout and its functionality. A **library** is a collection of code that has been programmed and translated by someone else, ready for you to use in your program. (More complicated programs are built from more than one machine code file and more than one library.) A program called the **linker** takes your machine code and the necessary parts from the C++ library and builds an **executable file**. (Figure 7 gives an overview of these steps.) The executable file is usually called `hello.exe` or `hello`, depending on your computer system. You can run the executable program even after you exit the C++ development environment.

Step 4   Organize your work.

As a programmer, you write programs, try them out, and improve them. You store your programs in *files*. Files have names, and the rules for legal names differ from one system to another. Some systems allow spaces in file names; others don't. Some distinguish between upper- and lowercase letters; others don't. Most C++ compilers require that C++ files end in an **extension** `.cpp`, `.cxx`, `.cc`, or `.C`; for example, `demo.cpp`.

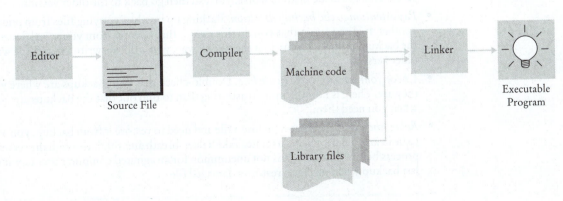

Editor → Source File → Compiler → Machine code → Library files → Linker → Executable Program

Figure 7   From Source Code to Executable Program

Files are stored in **folders** or **directories**. A folder can contain files as well as other folders, which themselves can contain more files and folders (see Figure 8). This hierarchy can be quite large, and you need not be concerned with all of its branches.

However, you should create folders for organizing your work. It is a good idea to make a separate folder for your programming class. Inside that folder, make a separate folder for each assignment.

Some programming environments place your programs into a default location if you don't specify a folder yourself. In that case, you need to find out where those files are located.

Be sure that you understand where your files are located in the folder hierarchy. This information is essential when you submit files for grading, and for making *backup copies*.

You will spend many hours creating and improving C++ programs. It is easy to delete a file by accident, and occasionally files are lost because of a computer malfunction. To avoid the frustration of recreating lost files, get in the habit of making backup copies of your work on a memory stick or on another computer.

> Develop a strategy for keeping backup copies of your work before disaster strikes.

```
📁 home
▼ 📁 cay
  ▼ 📁 cs1
    ▼ 📁 homework1
        📄 face.cpp
    ▼ 📁 textbook
      ▼ 📁 ch01
        ▼ 📁 sec04
            📄 hello
            📄 hello.cpp
      ▼ 📁 ch02
        ▼ 📁 how_to_1
            📄 vending.cpp
```

Figure 8 A Folder Hierarchy

Programming Tip 1.1
Backup Copies

Backing up files on a memory stick is an easy and convenient storage method for many people. Another increasingly popular form of backup is Internet file storage. Here are a few pointers to keep in mind.

© Tatiana Popova/iStockphoto.

- *Back up often.* Backing up a file takes only a few seconds, and you will hate yourself if you have to spend many hours recreating work that you could have saved easily. I recommend that you back up your work once every thirty minutes.

- *Rotate backups.* Use more than one directory for backups, and rotate them. That is, first back up to the first directory. Then back up to the second directory. Then use the third, and then go back to the first. That way you always have three recent backups. If your recent changes made matters worse, you can then go back to the older version.

- *Pay attention to the backup direction.* Backing up involves copying files from one place to another. It is important that you do this right—that is, copy from your work location to the backup location. If you do it the wrong way, you will overwrite a newer file with an older version.

- *Check your backups once in a while.* Double-check that your backups are where you think they are. There is nothing more frustrating than to find out that the backups are not there when you need them.

- *Relax, then restore.* When you lose a file and need to restore it from backup, you are likely to be in an unhappy, nervous state. Take a deep breath and think through the recovery process before you start. It is not uncommon for an agitated computer user to wipe out the last backup when trying to restore a damaged file.

1.5 Analyzing Your First Program

© Amanda Rohde/iStockphoto.

In this section, we will analyze the first C++ program in detail. Here again is the source code:

sec05/hello.cpp

```
1  #include <iostream>
2
3  using namespace std;
4
5  int main()
6  {
7     cout << "Hello, World!" << endl;
8     return 0;
9  }
```

The first line,

```
#include <iostream>
```

tells the compiler to include a service for "stream input/output". You will learn in Chapter 8 what a stream is. For now, you should simply remember to add this line into all programs that perform input or output.

The next line,

```
using namespace std;
```

tells the compiler to use the "standard namespace". Namespaces are a mechanism for avoiding naming conflicts in large programs. You need not be concerned about namespaces. For the programs that you will be writing in this book, you will always use the standard namespace. Simply add `using namespace std;` at the top of every program that you write, just below the `#include` directives.

The construction

```
int main()
{
   . . .
   return 0;
}
```

defines a *function* called `main` that "returns" an "integer" (that is, a whole number without a fractional part, called `int` in C++) with value 0. This value indicates that the program finished successfully. A **function** is a collection of programming instructions that carry out a particular task. Every C++ program must have a `main` function. Most C++ programs contain other functions besides `main`, but it will take us until Chapter 5 to discuss functions and return values.

Every C++ program contains a function called main.

For now, it is a good idea to consider all these parts as the "plumbing" that is necessary to write a simple program. Simply place the code that you want to execute inside the braces of the `main` function. (The basic structure of a C++ program is shown in Syntax 1.1.)

Syntax 1.1 C++ Program

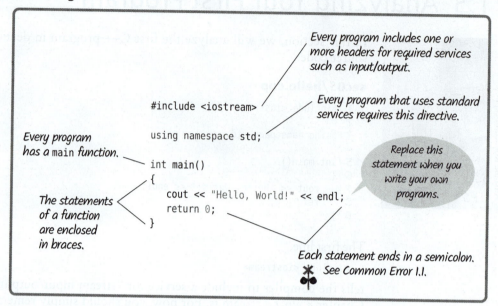

Every program includes one or more headers for required services such as input/output.

Every program that uses standard services requires this directive.

Every program has a main function.

The statements of a function are enclosed in braces.

Replace this statement when you write your own programs.

```cpp
#include <iostream>

using namespace std;

int main()
{
    cout << "Hello, World!" << endl;
    return 0;
}
```

Each statement ends in a semicolon.
✖ See Common Error 1.1.

Use cout and the << operator to display values on the screen.

To display values on the screen, you use an entity called cout and the << operator (sometimes called the *insertion* operator). For example, the statement

```cpp
cout << 39 + 3;
```

displays the number 42.

The statement

Enclose text strings in quotation marks.

```cpp
cout << "Hello";
```

displays the **string** Hello. A string is a sequence of characters. You must enclose the contents of a string inside quotation marks so that the compiler knows you literally mean the text "Hello" and not a function with the same name.

You can send more than one item to cout. Use a << before each one of them. For example,

Use + to add two numbers and * to multiply two numbers.

```cpp
cout << "The answer is " << 6 * 7;
```

displays The answer is 42 (in C++, the * denotes multiplication).

The endl symbol denotes an *end of line* marker. When this marker is sent to cout, the cursor is moved to the first column in the next screen row. If you don't use an end of line marker, then the next displayed item will simply follow the current string on the same line. In this program we only printed one item, but in general we will want to print multiple items, and it is a good habit to end all lines of output with an end of line marker.

Send endl to cout to end a line of displayed output.

Finally, note that the output and return statements end in a semicolon, just as every English sentence ends in a period.

End each statement with a semicolon.

Syntax 1.2 Output Statement

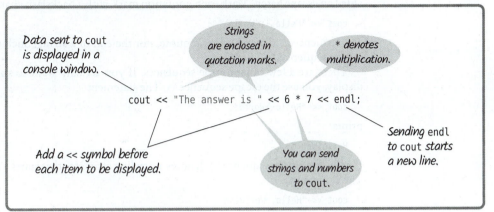

Common Error 1.1

Omitting Semicolons

In C++, statements such as output or return statements end in a semicolon. Forgetting to type a semicolon is a common error. It confuses the compiler because the compiler uses the semicolon to find where one statement ends and the next one starts. The compiler does not use line ends or closing braces to recognize the ends of statements. For example, the compiler considers

```
cout << "Hello, World!" << endl
return 0;
```

a single statement, as if you had written

```
cout << "Hello, World!" << endl return 0;
```

and then it doesn't understand that statement, because it does not expect the word return in the middle of an output command. The remedy is simple. Just scan every statement for a terminating semicolon, just as you would check that every English sentence ends in a period.

Sometimes, the error message that flags the missing semicolon is displayed in the following line. When you see such a message, be sure to check the preceding line as well.

Special Topic 1.1

Escape Sequences

How can you display a string containing quotation marks, such as

```
Hello, "World"
```

You can't use

```
cout << "Hello, "World"";
```

As soon as the compiler reads "Hello, ", it thinks the string is finished, and then it gets all confused about World. Compilers have a one-track mind, and if a simple analysis of the input doesn't make sense to them, they just refuse to go on, and they report an error. In contrast, a human would probably realize that the second and third quotation marks were supposed to be part of the string.

Well, how do we then display quotation marks on the screen? The designers of C++ provided an escape hatch. Mark each quotation mark with a backslash character (\), like this:

```
cout << "Hello, \"World\"";
```

The sequence \" denotes a literal quote, not the end of a string. Such a sequence is called an **escape sequence**.

There are a few other escape sequences. If you actually want to show a backslash on the display, you use the escape sequence \\. The statement

```
cout << "Hello\\World";
```

prints

```
Hello\World
```

Finally, the escape sequence \n denotes a **newline** character that starts a new line on the screen. The command

```
cout << "Hello, World!\n";
```

has the same effect as

```
cout << "Hello, World!" << endl;
```

1.6 Errors

Programming languages follow very strict conventions. When you talk to another person, and you scramble or omit a word or two, your conversation partner will usually still understand what you have to say. But when you make an error in a C++ program, the compiler will not try to guess what you meant. (This is actually a good thing. If the compiler were to guess wrongly, the resulting program would do the wrong thing—quite possibly with disastrous effects.) In this section, you will learn how to cope with errors in your program.

Experiment a little with the `hello.cpp` program. What happens if you make a typing error such as

© Martin Carlsson/iStockphoto.

Programmers spend a fair amount of time fixing compile-time and run-time errors.

```
cot << "Hello, World!" << endl;
cout << "Hello, World! << endl;
cout << "Hollo, World!" << endl;
```

A compile-time error is a violation of the programming language rules that is detected by the compiler.

In the first case, the compiler will complain that it has no clue what you mean by cot. The exact wording of the error message is dependent on the compiler, but it might be something like "Undefined symbol cot". This is a **compile-time error** or **syntax error**. Something is wrong according to the language rules, and the compiler finds it. When the compiler finds one or more errors, it will not translate the program to machine code, and as a consequence there is no program to run. You must fix the error and compile again. It is common to go through several rounds of fixing compile-time errors before compilation succeeds for the first time.

If the compiler finds an error, it will not simply stop and give up. It will try to report as many errors as it can find, so you can fix them all at once. Sometimes, however, one error throws it off track. This is likely to happen with the error in the second line. Because the programmer forgot the closing quote, the compiler will keep looking for the end of the string. In such cases, it is common for the compiler to emit bogus error reports for neighboring lines. You should fix only those error messages that make sense to you and then recompile.

The error in the third line is of a different kind. The program will compile and run, but its output will be wrong. It will print

```
Hollo, World!
```

This is a **run-time error**. The program is syntactically correct and does something, but it doesn't do what it is supposed to do. The compiler cannot find the error, and it must be flushed out when the program runs, by testing it and carefully looking at its output. Because run-time errors are caused by logical flaws in the program, they are often called **logic errors**. Some kinds of run-time errors are so severe that they generate an **exception**: a signal from the processor that aborts the program with an error message. For example, if your program includes the statement cout << 1 / 0; your program may terminate with a "divide by zero" exception.

During program development, errors are unavoidable. Once a program is longer than a few lines, it requires superhuman concentration to enter it correctly without slipping up once. You will find yourself omitting semicolons or quotes more often than you would like, but the compiler will track down these problems for you.

Run-time errors are more troublesome. The compiler will not find them—in fact, the compiler will cheerfully translate any program as long as its syntax is correct—but the resulting program will do something wrong. It is the responsibility of the program author to test the program and find any run-time errors. Program testing is an important topic that you will encounter many times in this book.

> A run-time error causes a program to take an action that the programmer did not intend.

> The programmer is responsible for inspecting and testing the program to guard against run-time errors.

Common Error 1.2
Misspelling Words

If you accidentally misspell a word, strange things may happen, and it may not always be completely obvious from the error messages what went wrong. Here is a good example of how simple spelling errors can cause trouble:

```cpp
#include <iostream>

using namespace std;

int Main()
{
    cout << "Hello, World!" << endl;
    return 0;
}
```

This code defines a function called Main. The compiler will not consider this to be the same as the main function, because Main starts with an uppercase letter and the C++ language is **case sensitive**. Upper- and lowercase letters are considered to be completely different from each other, and to the compiler Main is no better match for main than rain. The compiler will compile your Main function, but when the linker is ready to build the executable file, it will complain about the missing main function and refuse to link the program. Of course, the message "missing main function" should give you a clue where to look for the error.

If you get an error message that seems to indicate that the compiler is on the wrong track, it is a good idea to check for spelling and capitalization. In C++, most names use only lowercase letters. If you misspell the name of a symbol (for example out instead of cout), the compiler will complain about an "undefined symbol" (or, on some systems, an "undeclared identifier" or "not declared in this scope"). This error message is usually a good clue that you made a spelling error.

1.7 Problem Solving: Algorithm Design

You will soon learn how to program calculations and decision making in C++. But before we look at the mechanics of implementing computations in the next chapter, let's consider how you can describe the steps that are necessary for finding the solution to a problem.

1.7.1 The Algorithm Concept

You may have run across advertisements that encourage you to pay for a computerized service that matches you up with a love partner. Think how this might work. You fill out a form and send it in. Others do the same. The data are processed by a computer program. Is it reasonable to assume that the computer can perform the task of finding the best match for you? Suppose your younger brother, not the computer, had all the forms on his desk. What instructions could you give him? You can't say, "Find the best-looking person who likes inline skating and browsing the Internet". There is no objective standard for good looks, and your brother's opinion (or that

© mammamaart/iStockphoto.

Finding the perfect partner is not a problem that a computer can solve.

of a computer program analyzing the photos of prospective partners) will likely be different from yours. If you can't give written instructions for someone to solve the problem, there is no way the computer can magically find the right solution. The computer can only do what you tell it to do. It just does it faster, without getting bored or exhausted.

For that reason, a computerized match-making service cannot guarantee to find the optimal match for you. Instead, you may be presented with a set of potential partners who share common interests with you. That is a task that a computer program can solve.

In order for a computer program to provide an answer to a problem that computes an answer, it must follow a sequence of steps that is

- Unambiguous
- Executable
- Terminating

The step sequence is *unambiguous* when there are precise instructions for what to do at each step and where to go next. There is no room for guesswork or personal opinion. A step is *executable* when it can be carried out in practice. For example, a computer can list all people that share your hobbies, but it can't predict who will be your life-long partner. Finally, a sequence of steps is *terminating* if it will eventually come to an end. A program that keeps working without delivering an answer is clearly not useful.

A sequence of steps that is unambiguous, executable, and terminating is called an **algorithm**. Although there is no algorithm for finding a partner, many problems do have algorithms for solving them. The next section gives an example.

An algorithm for solving a problem is a sequence of steps that is unambiguous, executable, and terminating.

© Claudiad/iStockphoto.

An algorithm is a recipe for finding a solution.

1.7.2 An Algorithm for Solving an Investment Problem

Consider the following investment problem:

> You put $10,000 into an account that earns 5 percent interest per year. How many years does it take for the account balance to be double the original?

Could you solve this problem by hand? Sure, you could. You figure out the balance as follows:

year	interest	balance
0		10000
1	10000.00 x 0.05 = 500.00	10000.00 + 500.00 = 10500.00
2	10500.00 x 0.05 = 525.00	10500.00 + 525.00 = 11025.00
3	11025.00 x 0.05 = 551.25	11025.00 + 551.25 = 11576.25
4	11576.25 x 0.05 = 578.81	11576.25 + 578.81 = 12155.06

You keep going until the balance is at least $20,000. Then the last number in the year column is the answer.

Of course, carrying out this computation is intensely boring to you or your younger brother. But computers are very good at carrying out repetitive calculations quickly and flawlessly. What is important to the computer is a description of the steps for finding the solution. Each step must be clear and unambiguous, requiring no guesswork. Here is such a description:

Set year to 0, balance to 10000.

year	interest	balance
0		10000

While the balance is less than $20,000
*   Add 1 to the year.*
*   Set the interest to balance x 0.05 (i.e., 5 percent interest).*
*   Add the interest to the balance.*

year	interest	balance
0		10000
1	500.00	10500.00
14	942.82	19799.32
(15)	989.96	20789.28

Report year as the answer.

These steps are not yet in a language that a computer can understand, but you will soon learn how to formulate them in C++. This informal description is called **pseudocode**. We examine the rules for writing pseudocode in the next section.

1.7.3 Pseudocode

Pseudocode is an informal description of a sequence of steps for solving a problem.

There are no strict requirements for pseudocode because it is read by human readers, not a computer program. Here are the kinds of pseudocode statements and how we will use them in this book:

- Use statements such as the following to describe how a value is set or changed:

  total cost = purchase price + operating cost
  Multiply the balance value by 1.05.
  Remove the first and last character from the word.

- Describe decisions and repetitions as follows:

  If total cost 1 < total cost 2
  While the balance is less than $20,000
  For each picture in the sequence

  Use indentation to indicate which statements should be selected or repeated:

  For each car
  *   operating cost = 10 x annual fuel cost*
  *   total cost = purchase price + operating cost*

  Here, the indentation indicates that both statements should be executed for each car.

- Indicate results with statements such as:

  Choose car2.
  Report year as the answer.

1.7.4 From Algorithms to Programs

In Section 1.7.2, we developed pseudocode for finding how long it takes to double an investment. Let's double-check that the pseudocode represents an algorithm; that is, that it is unambiguous, executable, and terminating.

Our pseudocode is unambiguous. It simply tells how to update values in each step. The pseudocode is executable because we use a fixed interest rate. Had we said to use the actual interest rate that will be charged in years to come, and not a fixed rate of 5 percent per year, the instructions would not have been executable. There is no way for anyone to know what the interest rate will be in the future. It requires a bit of thought to see that the steps are terminating: With every step, the balance goes up by at least $500, so eventually it must reach $20,000.

Therefore, we have found an algorithm to solve our investment problem, and we know we can find the solution by programming a computer. The existence of an algorithm is an essential prerequisite for programming a task. You need to first discover and describe an algorithm for the task before you start programming (see Figure 9). In the chapters that follow, you will learn how to express algorithms in the C++ language.

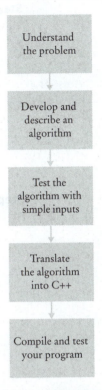

Figure 9   The Software Development Process

HOW TO 1.1

Describing an Algorithm with Pseudocode

This is the first of many "How To" sections in this book that give you step-by-step procedures for carrying out important tasks in developing computer programs.

Before you are ready to write a program in C++, you need to develop an algorithm—a method for arriving at a solution for a particular problem. Describe the algorithm in pseudocode—a sequence of precise steps formulated in English. To illustrate, we'll devise an algorithm for this problem:

Problem Statement   You have the choice of buying one of two cars. One is more fuel efficient than the other, but also more expensive. You know the price and fuel efficiency (in miles per gallon, mpg) of both cars. You plan to keep the car for ten years. Assume a price of $4 per gallon of gas and usage of 15,000 miles per year. You will pay cash for the car and not worry about financing costs. Which car is the better deal?

© dlewis33/Getty Images.

Step 1   Determine the inputs and outputs.

In our sample problem, we have these inputs:

- *purchase price1* and *fuel efficiency1*, the price and fuel efficiency (in mpg) of the first car
- *purchase price2* and *fuel efficiency2*, the price and fuel efficiency of the second car

We simply want to know which car is the better buy. That is the desired output.

Step 2 Break down the problem into smaller tasks.

For each car, we need to know the total cost of driving it. Let's do this computation separately for each car. Once we have the total cost for each car, we can decide which car is the better deal.

> The total cost for each car is *purchase price + operating cost.*

We assume a constant usage and gas price for ten years, so the operating cost depends on the cost of driving the car for one year.

> The operating cost is *10 x annual fuel cost.*
> The annual fuel cost is *price per gallon x annual fuel consumed.*

The annual fuel consumed is *annual miles driven / fuel efficiency.* For example, if you drive the car for 15,000 miles and the fuel efficiency is 15 miles/gallon, the car consumes 1,000 gallons.

Step 3 Describe each subtask in pseudocode.

In your description, arrange the steps so that any intermediate values are computed before they are needed in other computations. For example, list the step

> *total cost = purchase price + operating cost*

after you have computed *operating cost.*

Here is the algorithm for deciding which car to buy:

> *For each car, compute the total cost as follows:*
>   *annual fuel consumed = annual miles driven / fuel efficiency*
>   *annual fuel cost = price per gallon x annual fuel consumed*
>   *operating cost = 10 x annual fuel cost*
>   *total cost = purchase price + operating cost*
> *If total cost of car1 < total cost of car2*
>   *Choose car1.*
> *Else*
>   *Choose car2.*

Step 4 Test your pseudocode by working a problem.

We will use these sample values:

> Car 1: $25,000, 50 miles/gallon
> Car 2: $20,000, 30 miles/gallon

Here is the calculation for the cost of the first car:

> *annual fuel consumed = annual miles driven / fuel efficiency = 15000 / 50 = 300*
> *annual fuel cost = price per gallon x annual fuel consumed = 4 x 300 = 1200*
> *operating cost = 10 x annual fuel cost = 10 x 1200 = 12000*
> *total cost = purchase price + operating cost = 25000 + 12000 = 37000*

Similarly, the total cost for the second car is $40,000. Therefore, the output of the algorithm is to choose car 1.

The following Worked Example demonstrates how to use the concepts in this chapter and the steps in the How To to solve another problem. In this case, you will see how to develop an algorithm for laying tile in an alternating pattern of colors. You should read the Worked Example to review what you have learned, and for help in tackling another problem.

In future chapters, Worked Examples are indicated by a brief description of the problem tackled in the example, plus a reminder to view it in your eText or download it from the book's companion Web site at wiley.com/go/bclo3. You will find any code related to the Worked Example included with the book's companion code for the chapter. When you see the Worked Example description, go to the example and view the code to learn how the problem was solved.

WORKED EXAMPLE 1.1

Writing an Algorithm for Tiling a Floor

Problem Statement Your task is to tile a rectangular bathroom floor with alternating black and white tiles measuring 4 × 4 inches. The floor dimensions, measured in inches, are multiples of 4.

Step 1 Determine the inputs and outputs.

The inputs are the floor dimensions (length × width), measured in inches. The output is a tiled floor.

Step 2 Break down the problem into smaller tasks.

A natural subtask is to lay one row of tiles. If you can solve that task, then you can solve the problem by laying one row next to the other, starting from a wall, until you reach the opposite wall.

How do you lay a row? Start with a tile at one wall. If it is white, put a black one next to it. If it is black, put a white one next to it. Keep going until you reach the opposite wall. The row will contain *width / 4* tiles.

© rban/iStockphoto.

Step 3 Describe each subtask in pseudocode.

In the pseudocode, you want to be more precise about exactly where the tiles are placed.

> *Place a black tile in the northwest corner.*
> *While the floor is not yet filled, repeat the following steps:*
>   *Repeat this step width / 4 − 1 times:*
>   *If the previously placed tile was white*
>   *Pick a black tile.*
>   *Else*
>   *Pick a white tile.*
>   *Place the picked tile east of the previously placed tile.*
>   *Locate the tile at the beginning of the row that you just placed. If there is space to the south, place a tile of the opposite color below it.*

Step 4 Test your pseudocode by working a problem.

Suppose you want to tile an area measuring 20 × 12 inches.
  The first step is to place a black tile in the northwest corner.

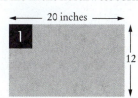

Next, alternate four tiles until reaching the east wall. *(width / 4 − 1 = 20 / 4 − 1 = 4)*

There is room to the south. Locate the tile at the beginning of the completed row. It is black. Place a white tile south of it.

Complete the row.

1	2	3	4	5
6	7	8	9	10

There is still room to the south. Locate the tile at the beginning of the completed row. It is white. Place a black tile south of it.

1	2	3	4	5
6	7	8	9	10
11				

Complete the row.

1	2	3	4	5
6	7	8	9	10
11	12	13	14	15

Now the entire floor is filled, and you are done.

CHAPTER SUMMARY

Define "computer program" and programming.

- Computers execute very basic instructions in rapid succession.
- A computer program is a sequence of instructions and decisions.
- Programming is the act of designing and implementing computer programs.

Describe the components of a computer.

- The central processing unit (CPU) performs program control and data processing.
- Storage devices include memory and secondary storage.

Describe the process of translating high-level languages to machine code.

- Computer programs are stored as machine instructions in a code that depends on the processor type.
- C++ is a general-purpose language that is in widespread use for systems and embedded programming.
- High-level programming languages are independent of the processor.

Become familiar with your C++ programming environment.

- Set aside some time to become familiar with the programming environment that you will use for your class work.
- An editor is a program for entering and modifying text, such as a C++ program.
- C++ is case sensitive. You must be careful about distinguishing between upper- and lowercase letters.
- The compiler translates C++ programs into machine code.
- The linker combines machine code with library code into an executable program.

- Develop a strategy for keeping backup copies of your work before disaster strikes.

Describe the building blocks of a simple program.

- Every C++ program contains a function called main.
- Use cout and the << operator to display values on the screen.
- Enclose text strings in quotation marks.
- Use + to add two numbers and * to multiply two numbers.
- Send endl to cout to end a line of displayed output.
- End each statement with a semicolon.

Classify program errors as compile-time and run-time errors.

- A compile-time error is a violation of the programming language rules that is detected by the compiler.
- A run-time error causes a program to take an action that the programmer did not intend.
- The programmer is responsible for inspecting and testing the program to guard against run-time errors.

Write pseudocode for simple algorithms.

- An algorithm for solving a problem is a sequence of steps that is unambiguous, executable, and terminating.
- Pseudocode is an informal description of a sequence of steps for solving a problem.

CHAPTER 2

FUNDAMENTAL DATA TYPES

CHAPTER GOALS

To be able to define and initialize variables and constants

To understand the properties and limitations of integer and floating-point numbers

To write arithmetic expressions and assignment statements in C++

To appreciate the importance of comments and good code layout

To create programs that read and process input, and display the results

To process strings, using the standard C++ string type

© samxmeg/iStockphoto.

CHAPTER CONTENTS

2.1 VARIABLES 26

SYN Variable Definition 27

SYN Assignment 30

CE1 Using Undefined Variables 33

CE2 Using Uninitialized Variables 33

PT1 Choose Descriptive Variable Names 33

PT2 Do Not Use Magic Numbers 34

ST1 Numeric Types in C++ 34

ST2 Numeric Ranges and Precisions 35

ST3 Defining Variables with auto 35

2.2 ARITHMETIC 36

CE3 Unintended Integer Division 39

CE4 Unbalanced Parentheses 40

CE5 Forgetting Header Files 40

CE6 Roundoff Errors 41

PT3 Spaces in Expressions 42

ST4 Casts 42

ST5 Combining Assignment and Arithmetic 42

C&S The Pentium Floating-Point Bug 43

2.3 INPUT AND OUTPUT 44

SYN Input Statement 44

2.4 PROBLEM SOLVING: FIRST DO IT BY HAND 47

WE1 Computing Travel Time 48

HT1 Carrying out Computations 48

WE2 Computing the Cost of Stamps 51

2.5 STRINGS 51

C&S International Alphabets and Unicode 55

Nanjing

503

506 Gate Chang

Kaohsiung

Singapore   49 Boarding

Shanghai/P   40 Boarding

Singapore   46

Taipei   512

JieyangChaost 25 Est 11

510

Numbers and character strings (such as the ones on this display board) are important data types in any C++ program. In this chapter, you will learn how to work with numbers and text, and how to write simple programs that perform useful tasks with them.

2.1 Variables

When your program carries out computations, you will want to store values so that you can use them later. In a C++ program, you use *variables* to store values. In this section, you will learn how to define and use variables.

To illustrate the use of variables, we will develop a program that solves the following problem. Soft drinks are sold in cans and bottles. A store offers a six-pack of 12-ounce cans for the same price as a two-liter bottle. Which should you buy? (Twelve fluid ounces equal approximately 0.355 liters.)

In our program, we will define variables for the number of cans per pack and for the volume of each can. Then we will compute the volume of a six-pack in liters and print out the answer.

cans: © blackred/iStockphoto. bottle: © travismanley/iStockphoto.

What contains more soda? A six-pack of 12-ounce cans or a two-liter bottle?

2.1.1 Variable Definitions

The following statement defines a variable named cans_per_pack:

```
int cans_per_pack = 6;
```

A **variable** is a storage location in a computer program. Each variable has a name and holds a value.

A variable is similar to a parking space in a parking garage. The parking space has an identifier (such as "J053"), and it can hold a vehicle. A variable has a name (such as cans_per_pack), and it can hold a value (such as 6).

> A variable is a storage location with a name.

Like a variable in a computer program, a parking space has an identifier and contents.

Javier Larrea/Age Fotostock.

When defining a variable, you usually specify an initial value.

When defining a variable, you also specify the type of its values.

When defining a variable, you usually want to **initialize** it. That is, you specify the value that should be stored in the variable. Consider again this variable definition:

```
int cans_per_pack = 6;
```

The variable cans_per_pack is initialized with the value 6.

Like a parking space that is restricted to a certain type of vehicle (such as a compact car, motorcycle, or electric vehicle), a variable in C++ stores data of a specific **type**. C++ supports quite a few data types: numbers, text strings, files, dates, and many others. You must specify the type whenever you define a variable (see Syntax 2.1).

Syntax 2.1   Variable Definition

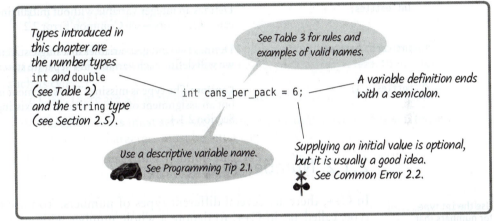

Types introduced in this chapter are the number types int and double (see Table 2) and the string type (see Section 2.5).

See Table 3 for rules and examples of valid names.

`int cans_per_pack = 6;`

A variable definition ends with a semicolon.

Use a descriptive variable name. See Programming Tip 2.1.

Supplying an initial value is optional, but it is usually a good idea.
✱ See Common Error 2.2.

The cans_per_pack variable is an **integer**, a whole number without a fractional part. In C++, this type is called int. (See the next section for more information about number types in C++.)

Note that the type comes *before* the variable name:

```
int cans_per_pack = 6;
```

Each parking space is suitable for a particular type of vehicle, just as each variable holds a value of a particular type.

© Ingenui/iStockphoto.

2.1.4 The Assignment Statement

You use the **assignment statement** to place a new value into a variable. Here is an example:

```
cans_per_pack = 8;
```

The left-hand side of an assignment statement consists of a variable. The right-hand side is an expression that has a value. That value is stored in the variable, overwriting its previous contents.

There is an important difference between a variable definition and an assignment statement:

```
int cans_per_pack = 6; // Variable definition
. . .
cans_per_pack = 8; // Assignment statement
```

The first statement is the *definition* of cans_per_pack. It is an instruction to create a new variable of type int, to give it the name cans_per_pack, and to initialize it with 6. The second statement is an *assignment statement:* an instruction to replace the contents of the *existing* variable cans_per_pack with another value.

Syntax 2.2 **Assignment**

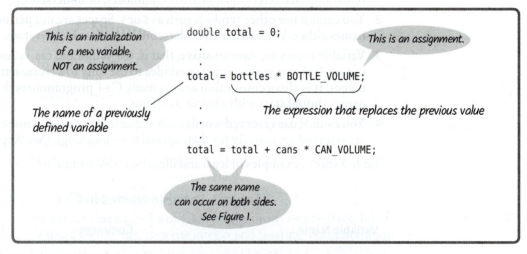

The = sign doesn't mean that the left-hand side is *equal* to the right-hand side. The expression on the right is evaluated, and its value is placed into the variable on the left.

Do not confuse this *assignment operation* with the = used in algebra to denote *equality*. The assignment operator is an instruction to do something, namely place a value into a variable. The mathematical equality states the fact that two values are equal.

For example, in C++, it is perfectly legal to write

```
total_volume = total_volume + 2;
```

It means to look up the value stored in the variable total_volume, add 2 to it, and place the result back into total_volume. (See Figure 1.) The net effect of executing this statement is to increment total_volume by 2. For example, if total_volume was 2.13 before execution of the statement, it is set to 4.13 afterwards. Of course, in mathematics it would make no sense to write that $x = x + 2$. No value can equal itself plus 2.

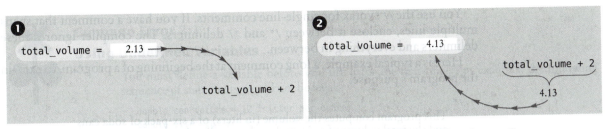

Figure 1 Executing the Assignment total_volume = total_volume + 2

2.1.5 Constants

You cannot change the value of a variable that is defined as const.

When a variable is defined with the reserved word const, its value can never change. Constants are commonly written using capital letters to distinguish them visually from regular variables:

```
const double BOTTLE_VOLUME = 2;
```

It is good programming style to use named constants in your program to explain the meanings of numeric values. For example, compare the statements

```
double total_volume = bottles * 2;
```

and

```
double total_volume = bottles * BOTTLE_VOLUME;
```

A programmer reading the first statement may not understand the significance of the number 2. The second statement, with a named constant, makes the computation much clearer.

2.1.6 Comments

Use comments to add explanations for humans who read your code. The compiler ignores comments.

As your programs get more complex, you should add **comments**, explanations for human readers of your code. Here is an example:

```
const double CAN_VOLUME = 0.355; // Liters in a 12-ounce can
```

This comment explains the significance of the value 0.355 to a human reader. The compiler does not process comments at all. It ignores everything from a // **delimiter** to the end of the line.

Just as a television commentator explains the news, you use comments in your program to explain its behavior.

© jgroup/iStockphoto.

Programming Tip 2.2
Do Not Use Magic Numbers

A **magic number** is a numeric constant that appears in your code without explanation. For example,

```
total_volume = bottles * 2;
```

Why 2? Are bottles twice as voluminous as cans? No, the reason is that every bottle contains 2 liters. Use a named constant to make the code self-documenting:

```
const double BOTTLE_VOLUME = 2;
total_volume = bottles * BOTTLE_VOLUME;
```

© FinnBrandt/iStockphoto.

There is another reason for using named constants. Suppose circumstances change, and the bottle volume is now 1.5 liters. If you used a named constant, you make a single change, and you are done. Otherwise, you have to look at every value of 2 in your program and ponder whether it means a bottle volume, or something else. In a program that is more than a few pages long, that is incredibly tedious and error-prone.

Even the most reasonable cosmic constant is going to change one day. You think there are 365 days per year? Your customers on Mars are going to be pretty unhappy about your silly prejudice. Make a constant

```
const int DAYS_PER_YEAR = 365;
```

Special Topic 2.1
Numeric Types in C++

In addition to the int and double types, C++ has several other numeric types.

C++ has two floating-point types. The float type uses half the storage of the double type that we use in this book, but it can only store 6–7 digits. Many years ago, when computers had far less memory than they have today, float was the standard type for floating-point computations, and programmers would indulge in the luxury of "double precision" only when they needed the additional digits. Today, the float type is rarely used.

By the way, these numbers are called "floating-point" because of their internal representation in the computer. Consider numbers 29600, 2.96, and 0.0296. They can be represented in a very similar way: namely, as a sequence of the significant digits—296—and an indication of the position of the decimal point. When the values are multiplied or divided by 10, only the position of the decimal point changes; it "floats". Computers use base 2, not base 10, but the principle is the same.

In addition to the int type, C++ has integer types short, long, and long long. For each integer type, there is an unsigned equivalent. For example, the short type typically has a range from −32,768 to 32,767, whereas unsigned short has a range from 0 to 65,535. These strange-looking limits are the result of the use of binary numbers in computers. A short value uses 16 binary digits, which can encode $2^{16} = 65,536$ values. Keep in mind that the ranges for integer types are not standardized, and they differ among compilers. Table 4 contains typical values.

	Table 4 Number Types	
Type	Typical Range	Typical Size
int	−2,147,483,648 ... 2,147,483,647 (about 2 billion)	4 bytes
unsigned	0 ... 4,294,967,295	4 bytes

Table 4 Number Types		
Type	Typical Range	Typical Size
short	−32,768 … 32,767	2 bytes
unsigned short	0 … 65,535	2 bytes
long long	−9,223,372,036,854,775,808 … 9,223,372,036,854,775,807	8 bytes
long	Depending on the compiler, the same as int or long long	4 or 8 bytes
double	The double-precision floating-point type, with a range of about $\pm 10^{308}$ and about 15 significant decimal digits	8 bytes
float	The single-precision floating-point type, with a range of about $\pm 10^{38}$ and about 7 significant decimal digits	4 bytes

Special Topic 2.2

Numeric Ranges and Precisions

Because numbers are represented in the computer with a limited number of digits, they cannot represent arbitrary integer or floating-point numbers.

The int type has a *limited range:* On most platforms, it can represent numbers up to a little more than two billion. For many applications, this is not a problem, but you cannot use an int to represent the world population.

If a computation yields a value that is outside the int range, the result *overflows*. No error is displayed. Instead, the result is truncated to fit into an int, yielding a useless value. For example,

```
int one_billion = 1000000000;
cout << 3 * one_billion << endl;
```

displays −1294967296.

In situations such as this, you can switch to double values. However, read Common Error 2.6 for more information about a related issue: roundoff errors.

Special Topic 2.3

Defining Variables with auto

Instead of providing a type for a variable, you can use the reserved word auto. Then the type is automatically deduced from the type of the initial value. For example,

```
auto cans = 6; // This variable has type int
const auto CAN_VOLUME = 0.355; // This constant has type double
```

For simple types such as int or double, it is better to use the explicit type in the variable definition. The auto reserved word is useful to avoid complex types that can be automatically determined.

2.2 Arithmetic

In the following sections, you will learn how to carry out arithmetic and mathematical calculations in C++.

2.2.1 Arithmetic Operators

© hocus-focus/iStockphoto.

C++ supports the same four basic arithmetic operations as a calculator—addition, subtraction, multiplication, and division—but it uses different symbols for multiplication and division.

You must write a * b to denote multiplication. Unlike in mathematics, you cannot write a b, a · b, or a × b. Similarly, division is always indicated with a /, never a ÷ or a fraction bar.

For example, $\dfrac{a+b}{2}$ becomes (a + b) / 2.

Parentheses are used just as in algebra: to indicate in which order the subexpressions should be computed. For example, in the expression (a + b) / 2, the sum a + b is computed first, and then the sum is divided by 2. In contrast, in the expression

    a + b / 2

Use * for multiplication and / for division.

only b is divided by 2, and then the sum of a and b / 2 is formed. Just as in regular algebraic notation, multiplication and division have a *higher precedence* than addition and subtraction. For example, in the expression a + b / 2, the / is carried out first, even though the + operation occurs further to the left. If both arguments of an arithmetic operation are integers, the result is an integer. If one or both arguments are floating-point numbers, the result is a floating-point number. For example, 4 * 0.5 is 2.0.

2.2.2 Increment and Decrement

The ++ operator adds 1 to a variable; the -- operator subtracts 1.

Changing a variable by adding or subtracting 1 is so common that there is a special shorthand for it, namely

    counter++;
    counter--;

The ++ increment operator gave the C++ programming language its name. C++ is the incremental improvement of the C language.

2.2.3 Integer Division and Remainder

If both arguments of / are integers, the remainder is discarded.

Division works as you would expect, as long as at least one of the numbers involved is a floating-point number. That is, 7.0 / 4.0, 7 / 4.0, and 7.0 / 4 all yield 1.75. However, if *both* numbers are integers, then the result of the division is always an integer, with the remainder discarded. That is,

    7 / 4

evaluates to 1 because 7 divided by 4 is 1 with a remainder of 3 (which is discarded). This can be a source of subtle programming errors—see Common Error 2.3.

If you are interested in the remainder only, use the % operator:

```
7 % 4
```

is 3, the remainder of the **integer division** of 7 by 4. The % symbol has no analog in algebra. It was chosen because it looks similar to /, and the remainder operation is related to division. The operator is called **modulus**. (Some people call it *modulo* or *mod*.) It has no relationship with the percent operation that you find on some calculators.

Here is a typical use for the integer / and % operations. Suppose you have an amount of pennies in a piggybank:

```
int pennies = 1729;
```

You want to determine the value in dollars and cents. You obtain the dollars through an integer division by 100.

```
int dollars = pennies / 100;  // Sets dollars to 17
```

The integer division discards the remainder. To obtain the remainder, use the % operator:

```
int cents = pennies % 100;  // Sets cents to 29
```

© Michael Flippo/iStockphoto.

Another common use of the % operator is to check whether a number is even or odd. If a number n is even, then n % 2 is zero.

Integer division and the % operator yield the dollar and cent values of a piggybank full of pennies.

Table 5 Integer Division and Remainder

Expression (where n = 1729)	Value	Comment
n % 10	9	n % 10 is always the last digit of n.
n / 10	172	This is always n without the last digit.
n % 100	29	The last two digits of n.
n / 10.0	172.9	Because 10.0 is a floating-point number, the fractional part is not discarded.
-n % 10	-9	Because the first argument is negative, the remainder is also negative.
n % 2	1	n % 2 is 0 if n is even, 1 or –1 if n is odd.

2.2.4 Converting Floating-Point Numbers to Integers

When a floating-point value is assigned to an integer variable, the fractional part is discarded:

```
double price = 2.55;
int dollars = price; // Sets dollars to 2
```

Assigning a floating-point variable to an integer drops the fractional part.

Discarding the fractional part is not always what you want. Often, you want to round to the *nearest* integer. To round a positive floating-point value to the nearest integer, add 0.5 and then convert to an integer:

```
int dollars = price + 0.5; // Rounds to the nearest integer
```

In our example, adding 0.5 turns all values above 2.5 into values above 3. In particular, 2.55 is turned into 3.05, which is then truncated to 3. (For a negative floating-point value, you subtract 0.5.)

Because truncation is a potential cause for errors, your compiler may issue a warning that assigning a floating-point value to an integer variable is unsafe. See Special Topic 2.4 on how to avoid this warning.

2.2.5 Powers and Roots

In C++, there are no symbols for powers and roots. To compute them, you must call **functions**. To take the square root of a number, you use the sqrt function. For example, $\sqrt{x}$ is written as sqrt(x). To compute x^n, you write pow(x, n).

The C++ library defines many mathematical functions such as sqrt (square root) and pow (raising to a power).

To use the sqrt and pow functions, you must place the line #include <cmath> at the top of your program file. The header file <cmath> is a standard C++ header that is available with all C++ systems, as is <iostream>.

As you can see, the effect of the /, sqrt, and pow operations is to flatten out mathematical terms. In algebra, you use fractions, exponents, and roots to arrange expressions in a compact two-dimensional form. In C++, you have to write all expressions in a linear arrangement. For example, the mathematical expression

$$b \times \left(1 + \frac{r}{100}\right)^n$$

becomes

```
b * pow(1 + r / 100, n)
```

Figure 2 shows how to analyze such an expression.

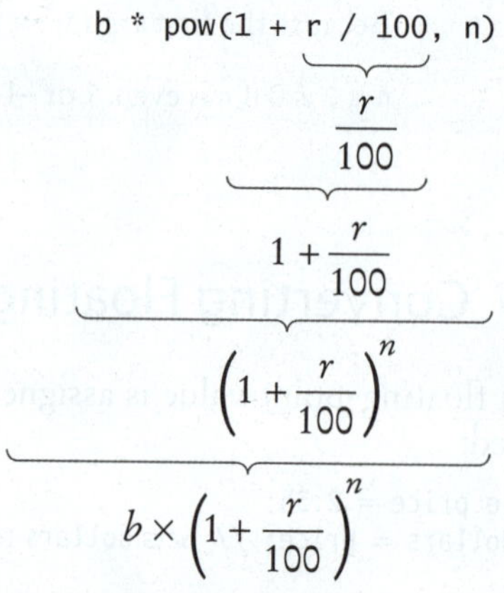

Figure 2 Analyzing an Expression

Table 6 Arithmetic Expressions

Mathematical Expression	C++ Expression	Comments
$\dfrac{x + y}{2}$	`(x + y) / 2`	The parentheses are required; `x + y / 2` computes $x + \dfrac{y}{2}$.
$\dfrac{xy}{2}$	`x * y / 2`	Parentheses are not required; operators with the same precedence are evaluated left to right.
$\left(1 + \dfrac{r}{100}\right)^n$	`pow(1 + r / 100, n)`	Remember to add `#include <cmath>` to the top of your program.
$\sqrt{a^2 + b^2}$	`sqrt(a * a + b * b)`	`a * a` is simpler than `pow(a, 2)`.
$\dfrac{i + j + k}{3}$	`(i + j + k) / 3.0`	If i, j, and k are integers, using a denominator of 3.0 forces floating-point division.

Table 7 shows additional functions that are declared in the <cmath> header. Inputs and outputs are floating-point numbers.

Table 7 Other Mathematical Functions

Function	Description
`sin(x)`	sine of x (x in radians)
`cos(x)`	cosine of x
`tan(x)`	tangent of x
`log(x)`	(natural log) $\ln(x), x > 0$
`log10(x)`	(decimal log) $\log_{10}(x), x > 0$
`abs(x)`	absolute value $|x|$

EXAMPLE CODE   See sec02 of your companion code for a program that gives examples of working with numbers in C++.

Common Error 2.3

Unintended Integer Division

It is unfortunate that C++ uses the same symbol, namely /, for both integer and floating-point division. These are really quite different operations. It is a common error to use integer division by accident. Consider this segment that computes the average of three integers:

```
cout << "Please enter your last three test scores: ";
int s1;
int s2;
int s3;
cin >> s1 >> s2 >> s3;
```

```
double average = (s1 + s2 + s3) / 3; // Error
cout << "Your average score is " << average << endl;
```

What could be wrong with that? Of course, the average of s1, s2, and s3 is

$$\frac{s1+s2+s3}{3}$$

Here, however, the / does not mean division in the mathematical sense. It denotes integer division because both s1 + s2 + s3 and 3 are integers. For example, if the scores add up to 14, the average is computed to be 4, the result of the integer division of 14 by 3. That integer 4 is then moved into the floating-point variable average. The remedy is to make the numerator or denominator into a floating-point number:

```
double total = s1 + s2 + s3;
double average = total / 3;
```

or

```
double average = (s1 + s2 + s3) / 3.0;
```

Common Error 2.4

Unbalanced Parentheses

Consider the expression

```
(-(b * b - 4 * a * c) / (2 * a)
```

What is wrong with it? Count the parentheses. There are three (and two). The parentheses are *unbalanced*. This kind of typing error is very common with complicated expressions. Now consider this expression.

© Croko/iStockphoto.

```
-(b * b - (4 * a * c))) / (2 * a
```

This expression has three (and three), but it still is not correct. In the middle of the expression,

```
-(b * b - (4 * a * c))) / (2 * a
                    ↑
```

there are only two (but three), which is an error. In the middle of an expression, the count of (must be greater than or equal to the count of), and at the end of the expression the two counts must be the same.

Here is a simple trick to make the counting easier without using pencil and paper. It is difficult for the brain to keep two counts simultaneously. Keep only one count when scanning the expression. Start with 1 at the first opening parenthesis, add 1 whenever you see an opening parenthesis, and subtract one whenever you see a closing parenthesis. Say the numbers aloud as you scan the expression. If the count ever drops below zero, or is not zero at the end, the parentheses are unbalanced. For example, when scanning the previous expression, you would mutter

```
-(b * b - (4 * a * c ) ) ) / (2 * a
 1          2          1 0 −1
```

and you would find the error.

Common Error 2.5

Forgetting Header Files

Every program that carries out input or output needs the <iostream> header. If you use mathematical functions such as sqrt, you need to include <cmath>. If you forget to include the appropriate header file, the compiler will not know symbols such as cout or sqrt. If the compiler complains about an undefined function or symbol, check your header files.

Sometimes you may not know which header file to include. Suppose you want to compute the absolute value of an integer using the abs function. As it happens, this version of abs is not defined in the <cmath> header but in <cstdlib>. How can you find the correct header file? You need to locate the documentation of the abs function, preferably using the online help of your development environment or a reference site on the Internet such as http://cplusplus.com (see Figure 3). The documentation includes a short description of the function and the name of the header file that you must include.

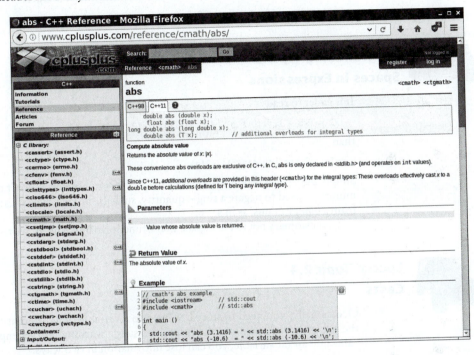

Figure 3 Online Documentation

Common Error 2.6

Roundoff Errors

Roundoff errors are a fact of life when calculating with floating-point numbers. You probably have encountered that phenomenon yourself with manual calculations. If you calculate 1/3 to two decimal places, you get 0.33. Multiplying again by 3, you obtain 0.99, not 1.00.

In the processor hardware, numbers are represented in the binary number system, not in decimal. You still get roundoff errors when binary digits are lost. They just may crop up at different places than you might expect. Here is an example.

```
#include <iostream>

using namespace std;

int main()
{
    double price = 4.35;
    int cents = 100 * price; // Should be 100 * 4.35 = 435
    cout << cents << endl; // Prints 434!
```

```
        return 0;
    }
```

Of course, one hundred times 4.35 is 435, but the program prints 434.

Most computers represent numbers in the binary system. In the binary system, there is no exact representation for 4.35, just as there is no representation for 1/3 in the decimal system. The representation used by the computer is just a little less than 4.35, so 100 times that value is just a little less than 435. When a floating-point value is converted to an integer, the entire fractional part, which is almost 1, is thrown away, and the integer 434 is stored in cents. The remedy is to add 0.5 in order to round to the nearest integer:

```
int cents = 100 * price + 0.5;
```

Programming Tip 2.3

Spaces in Expressions

It is easier to read

```
x1 = (-b + sqrt(b * b - 4 * a * c)) / (2 * a);
```

than

```
x1=(-b+sqrt(b*b-4*a*c))/(2*a);
```

Simply put spaces around all operators + - * / % =. However, don't put a space after a *unary* minus: a – used to negate a single quantity, such as -b. That way, it can be easily distinguished from a *binary* minus, as in a - b.

It is customary not to put a space after a function name. That is, write sqrt(x) and not sqrt (x).

Special Topic 2.4

Casts

Occasionally, you need to store a value into a variable of a different type. Whenever there is the risk of *information loss*, the compiler issues a warning. For example, if you store a double value into an int variable, you can lose information in two ways:

- The fractional part is lost.
- The magnitude may be too large.

For example,

```
int n = 1.0E100; // NO
```

is not likely to work, because 10^{100} is larger than the largest representable integer.

Nevertheless, sometimes you do want to convert a floating-point value into an integer value. If you are prepared to lose the fractional part and you know that this particular floating-point number is not larger than the largest possible integer, then you can turn off the warning by using a **cast**. A cast is a conversion from one type (such as double) to another type (such as int) that is not safe in general, but that you know to be safe in a particular circumstance. You express a cast in C++ as follows:

```
int cents = static_cast<int>(100 * price + 0.5);
```

Special Topic 2.5

Combining Assignment and Arithmetic

In C++, you can combine arithmetic and assignment. For example, the instruction

```
total += cans * CAN_VOLUME;
```

is a shortcut for

```
total = total + cans * CAN_VOLUME;
```

Similarly,

```
total *= 2;
```

is another way of writing

```
total = total * 2;
```

Many programmers find this a convenient shortcut. If you like it, go ahead and use it in your own code. For simplicity, we won't use it in this book, though.

Computing & Society 2.1 The Pentium Floating-Point Bug

In 1994, Intel Corporation released what was then its most powerful processor, the Pentium. Unlike previous generations of its processors, it had a very fast floating-point unit. Intel's goal was to compete aggressively with the makers of higher-end processors for engineering workstations. The Pentium was a huge success immediately.

In the summer of 1994, Dr. Thomas Nicely of Lynchburg College, Virginia, ran an extensive set of computations to analyze the sums of reciprocals of certain sequences of prime numbers. The results were not always what his theory predicted, even after he took into account the inevitable roundoff errors. Then Dr. Nicely noted that the same program did produce the correct results when running on the slower 486 processor that preceded the Pentium in Intel's lineup. This should not have happened. The optimal round-off behavior of floating-point calculations were standardized by the Institute for Electrical and Electronic Engineers (IEEE) and Intel claimed to adhere to the IEEE standard in both the 486 and the Pentium processors. Upon further checking, Dr. Nicely discovered that there was a very small set of numbers for which the product of two numbers was computed differently on the two processors. For example,

$$4,195,835 - \left(\left(4,195,835 / 3,145,727 \right) \times 3,145,727 \right)$$

is mathematically equal to 0, and it did compute as 0 on a 486 processor. On his Pentium processor the result was 256.

As it turned out, Intel had independently discovered the bug in its testing and had started to produce chips that fixed it. The bug was caused by an error in a table that was used to speed up the processor's floating-point multiplication algorithm. Intel determined that the problem was exceedingly rare. They claimed that under normal use, a typical consumer would only notice the problem once every 27,000 years. Unfortunately for Intel, Dr. Nicely had not been a normal user.

Now Intel had a real problem on its hands. It figured that the cost of replacing all Pentium processors that it had

sold so far would cost a great deal of money. Intel already had more orders for the chip than it could produce, and it would be particularly galling to have to give out the scarce chips as free replacements instead of selling them. Intel's management decided to punt and initially offered to replace the processors only for those customers who could prove that their work required absolute precision in mathematical calculations. Naturally, that did not go over well with the hundreds of thousands of customers who had paid retail prices of $700 and more for a Pentium chip and did not want to live with the nagging feeling that perhaps, one day, their income tax program would produce a faulty return. Ultimately, Intel caved in to public demand and replaced all defective chips, at a cost of about 475 million dollars.

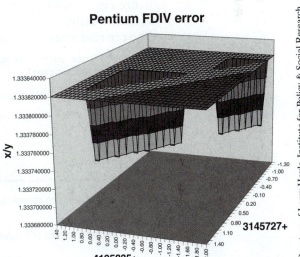

This graph shows a set of numbers for which the original Pentium processor obtained the wrong quotient.

Courtesy of Larry Hoyle, Institute for Policy & Social Research, University of Kansas.

2.3 Input and Output

In the following sections, you will see how to read user input and how to control the appearance of the output that your programs produce.

2.3.1 Input

In this section, you will see how to place user input into a variable. Consider for example the volume1.cpp program in Section 2.1.6. Rather than assuming that the price for the two-liter bottle and the six-pack of cans are identical, we can ask the program user for the prices.

When a program asks for user input, it should first print a message that tells the user which input is expected. Such a message is called a **prompt**.

```
cout << "Please enter the number of bottles: "; // Display prompt
```

Do not add an endl after the prompt. You want the input to appear after the colon, not on the following line.

Next, the program issues a command to read the input. The cin object reads input from the console window. You use the >> operator (sometimes called the *extraction* operator) to place an input value into a variable, like this:

Use the >> operator to read a value and place it in a variable.

```
int bottles;
cin >> bottles;
```

When the program executes the input statement, it waits for the user to provide input. The user also needs to press the Enter key so that the program accepts the input. After the user supplies the input, the number is placed into the bottles variable, and the program continues.

Note that in this code segment, there was no need to initialize the bottles variable because it is being filled by the very next statement. As a rule of thumb, you should initialize a variable when you declare it *unless* it is filled in an input statement that follows immediately.

You can read more than one value in a single input statement:

```
cout << "Please enter the number of bottles and cans: ";
cin >> bottles >> cans;
```

The user can supply both inputs on the same line:

```
Please enter the number of bottles and cans: 2 6
```

Syntax 2.3 Input Statement

Display a prompt in the console window.

```
cout << "Enter the number of bottles: ";
```

Define a variable to hold the input value. — int bottles;

cin >> bottles;

Don't use endl here.

The program waits for user input, then places the input into the variable.

Alternatively, the user can press the Enter key after each input:

```
Please enter the number of bottles and cans: 2
6
```

2.3.2 Formatted Output

When you print the result of a computation, you often want some control over its appearance. For example, when you print an amount in dollars and cents, you usually want it to be rounded to two significant digits. That is, you want the output to look like

```
Price per ounce: 0.04
```

instead of

```
Price per ounce: 0.0409722
```

The following command instructs cout to use two digits after the decimal point for all floating-point numbers:

```
cout << fixed << setprecision(2);
```

> You use manipulators to specify how values should be formatted.

This command does not produce any output; it just manipulates cout so that it will change the output format. The values fixed and setprecision are called *manipulators*. We will discuss manipulators in detail in Chapter 8. For now, just remember to include the statement given above whenever you want currency values displayed neatly.

To use manipulators, you must include the <iomanip> header in your program:

```
#include <iomanip>
```

You can combine the manipulators and the values to be displayed into a single statement:

```
cout << fixed << setprecision(2)
   << "Price per ounce: "
   << price_per_ounce << endl;
```

There is another manipulator that is sometimes handy. When you display several rows of data, you usually want the columns to line up.

You use the setw manipulator to set the *width* of the next output field. The width is the total number of characters used for showing the value, including digits, the

You use manipulators to line up your output in neat columns.

© Koele/iStockphoto.

decimal point, and spaces. Controlling the width is important when you want columns of numbers to line up.

For example, if you want a number to be printed in a column that is eight characters wide, you use

```
cout << setw(8) << price_per_ounce;
```

This command prints the value `price_per_ounce` in a field of width 8, for example

```
                0 . 0 4
```

(where each ■ represents a space).

There is a notable difference between the `setprecision` and `setw` manipulators. Once you set the precision, that value is used for all floating-point numbers in that statement. But the width affects only the *next* value. Subsequent values are formatted without added spaces.

Our next example program will prompt for the price of a six-pack and the volume of each can, then print out the price per ounce. The program puts to work what you just learned about reading input and formatting output.

sec03/volume2.cpp

```
1   #include <iostream>
2   #include <iomanip>
3
4   using namespace std;
5
6   int main()
7   {
8      // Read price per pack
9
10        cout << "Please enter the price for a six-pack: ";
11        double pack_price;
12        cin >> pack_price;
13
14        // Read can volume
15
16        cout << "Please enter the volume for each can (in ounces): ";
17        double can_volume;
18        cin >> can_volume;
19
20        // Compute pack volume
21
22        const double CANS_PER_PACK = 6;
23        double pack_volume = can_volume * CANS_PER_PACK;
24
25        // Compute and print price per ounce
26
27        double price_per_ounce = pack_price / pack_volume;
28
29        cout << fixed << setprecision(2);
30        cout << "Price per ounce: " << price_per_ounce << endl;
31
32        return 0;
33  }
```

Program Run

```
Please enter the price for a six-pack: 2.95
Please enter the volume for each can (in ounces): 12
Price per ounce: 0.04
```

Table 8 Formatting Output

Output Statement	Output	Comment
`cout << 12.345678;`	12.3457	By default, a number is printed with 6 significant digits.

`cout << fixed`
`    << setprecision(2)`
`    << 12.3;`
	12.30	Use the fixed and setprecision manipulators to control the number of digits after the decimal point.

`cout << ":" << setw(6)` `    << 12;`	: 12	Four spaces are printed before the number, for a total width of 6 characters.
`cout << ":" << setw(2)` `    << 123;`	:123	If the width not sufficient, it is ignored.
`cout << setw(6)` `    << ":" << 12;`	:12	The width only refers to the next item. Here, the : is preceded by five spaces.

2.4 Problem Solving: First Do It By Hand

A very important step for developing an algorithm is to first carry out the computations *by hand*. If you can't compute a solution yourself, it's unlikely that you'll be able to write a program that automates the computation.

To illustrate the use of hand calculations, consider the following problem.

A row of black and white tiles needs to be placed along a wall. For aesthetic reasons, the architect has specified that the first and last tile shall be black.

Your task is to compute the number of tiles needed and the gap at each end, given the space available and the width of each tile.

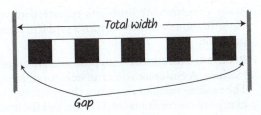

To make the problem more concrete, let's assume the following dimensions:

> Pick concrete values for a typical situation to use in a hand calculation.

- Total width: 100 inches
- Tile width: 5 inches

The obvious solution would be to fill the space with 20 tiles, but that would not work—the last tile would be white.

Instead, look at the problem this way: The first tile must always be black, and then we add some number of white/black pairs:

The first tile takes up 5 inches, leaving 95 inches to be covered by pairs. Each pair is 10 inches wide. Therefore the number of pairs is 95 / 10 = 9.5. However, we need to discard the fractional part because we can't have fractions of tile pairs.

Therefore, we will use 9 tile pairs or 18 tiles, together with the initial black tile. Altogether, we require 19 tiles.

The tiles span $19 \times 5 = 95$ inches, leaving a total gap of $100 - 19 \times 5 = 5$ inches. The gap should be evenly distributed at both ends. At each end, the gap is $(100 - 19 \times 5) / 2 = 2.5$ inches.

This computation gives us enough information to devise an algorithm with arbitrary values for the total width and tile width.

number of pairs = integer part of (total width - tile width) / (2 x tile width)
number of tiles = 1 + 2 x number of pairs
gap at each end = (total width - number of tiles x tile width) / 2

As you can see, doing a hand calculation gives enough insight into the problem that it becomes easy to develop an algorithm.

EXAMPLE CODE   See sec04 of your companion code for a program that implements this algorithm.

WORKED EXAMPLE 2.1
Computing Travel Time

Learn how to develop a hand calculation to compute the time that a robot requires to retrieve an item from rocky terrain. See your E-Text or visit wiley.com/go/bclo3.

Courtesy of NASA.

HOW TO 2.1
Carrying out Computations

Many programming problems require that you carry out arithmetic computations. This How To shows you how to turn a problem statement into pseudocode and, ultimately, a C++ program.

Problem Statement   Suppose you are asked to write a program that simulates a vending machine. A customer selects an item for purchase and inserts a bill into the vending machine. The vending machine dispenses the purchased item and gives change. We will assume that all item prices are multiples of 25 cents, and the machine gives all change in dollar coins and quarters. Your task is to compute how many coins of each type to return.

Step 1   Understand the problem: What are the inputs? What are the desired outputs?

In this problem, there are two inputs:
- The denomination of the bill that the customer inserts
- The price of the purchased item

There are two desired outputs:

- The number of dollar coins that the machine returns
- The number of quarters that the machine returns

Step 2   Work out examples by hand.

Let's assume that a customer purchased an item that cost $2.25 and inserted a $5 bill. The customer is due $2.75, or two dollar coins and three quarters.

That is easy for you to see, but how can a C++ program come to the same conclusion? The computation is simpler if you work in pennies, not dollars. The change due the customer is 275 pennies. Dividing by 100 yields 2, the number of dollars. Dividing the remainder (75) by 25 yields 3, the number of quarters.

Step 3   Write pseudocode for computing the answers.

In the previous step, you worked out a specific instance of the problem. You now need to come up with a method that works in general.

Given an arbitrary item price and payment, how can you compute the change due in coins? First, compute the change due in pennies:

change due = 100 x bill value - item price in pennies

To get the dollars, divide by 100 and discard the remainder:

dollar coins = change due / 100 (without remainder)

The remaining amount due can be computed in two ways. If you are familiar with the modulus operator, you can simply compute

change due = change due % 100

Alternatively, subtract the penny value of the dollar coins from the change due:

change due = change due - 100 x dollar coins

To get the quarters due, divide by 25:

quarters = change due / 25

Step 4   Define the variables and constants that you need, and specify their types.

Here, we have five variables:

- `bill_value`
- `item_price`
- `change_due`
- `dollar_coins`
- `quarters`

A vending machine takes bills and gives change in coins.

Jupiter Images/Getty Images.

Should we introduce constants to explain 100 and 25 as PENNIES_PER_DOLLAR and PENNIES_PER_QUARTER? Doing so will make it easier to convert the program to international markets, so we will take this step.

It is very important that change_due and PENNIES_PER_DOLLAR are of type int because the computation of dollar_coins uses integer division. Similarly, the other variables are integers.

Step 5 Turn the pseudocode into C++ statements.

If you did a thorough job with the pseudocode, this step should be easy. Of course, you have to know how to express mathematical operations (such as powers or integer division) in C++.

```
change_due = PENNIES_PER_DOLLAR * bill_value - item_price;
dollar_coins = change_due / PENNIES_PER_DOLLAR;
change_due = change_due % PENNIES_PER_DOLLAR;
quarters = change_due / PENNIES_PER_QUARTER;
```

Step 6 Provide input and output.

Before starting the computation, we prompt the user for the bill value and item price:

```
cout << "Enter bill value (1 = $1 bill, 5 = $5 bill, etc.): ";
cin >> bill_value;
cout << "Enter item price in pennies: ";
cin >> item_price;
```

When the computation is finished, we display the result. For extra credit, we use the setw manipulator to make sure that the output lines up neatly.

```
cout << "Dollar coins: " << setw(6) << dollar_coins << endl
     << "Quarters:     " << setw(6) << quarters << endl;
```

Step 7 Include the required headers and provide a main function.

We need the <iostream> header for all input and output. Because we use the setw manipulator, we also require <iomanip>. This program does not use any special mathematical functions. Therefore, we do not include the <cmath> header.

In the main function, you need to define constants and variables (Step 4), carry out computations (Step 5), and provide input and output (Step 6). Clearly, you will want to first get the input, then do the computations, and finally show the output. Define the constants at the beginning of the function, and define each variable just before it is needed.

Here is the complete program:

how_to_1/vending.cpp

```
1   #include <iostream>
2   #include <iomanip>
3
4   using namespace std;
5
6   int main()
7   {
8      const int PENNIES_PER_DOLLAR = 100;
9      const int PENNIES_PER_QUARTER = 25;
10
11     cout << "Enter bill value (1 = $1 bill, 5 = $5 bill, etc.): ";
12     int bill_value;
13     cin >> bill_value;
14     cout << "Enter item price in pennies: ";
15     int item_price;
16     cin >> item_price;
17
18     int change_due = PENNIES_PER_DOLLAR * bill_value - item_price;
19     int dollar_coins = change_due / PENNIES_PER_DOLLAR;
```

```
20    change_due = change_due % PENNIES_PER_DOLLAR;
21    int quarters = change_due / PENNIES_PER_QUARTER;
22
23    cout << "Dollar coins: " << setw(6) << dollar_coins << endl
24       << "Quarters:      " << setw(6) << quarters << endl;
25
26    return 0;
27 }
```

Program Run

```
Enter bill value (1 = $1 bill, 5 = $5 bill, etc.): 5
Enter item price in pennies: 225
Dollar coins:      2
Quarters:          3
```

WORKED EXAMPLE 2.2

Computing the Cost of Stamps

Learn how to use arithmetic functions to simulate a stamp vending machine. See your E-Text or visit wiley.com/go.bclo3.

2.5 Strings

Strings are sequences of characters.

Many programs process text, not numbers. Text consists of **characters**: letters, numbers, punctuation, spaces, and so on. A **string** is a sequence of characters. For example, the string "Harry" is a sequence of five characters.

© essxboy/iStockphoto.

2.5.1 The string Type

You can define variables that hold strings.

```
string name = "Harry";
```

The string type is a part of the C++ standard. To use it, simply include the header file, <string>:

```
#include <string>
```

We distinguish between string *variables* (such as the variable name defined above) and string *literals* (character sequences enclosed in quotes, such as "Harry"). The string stored in a string variable can change. A string literal denotes a particular string, just as a number literal (such as 2) denotes a particular number.

Unlike number variables, string variables are guaranteed to be initialized even if you do not supply an initial value. By default, a string variable is set to an empty string: a string containing no characters. An empty string literal is written as "". The definition

```
string response;
```

has the same effect as

```
string response = "";
```

2.5.2 Concatenation

Use the + operator to *concatenate* strings; that is, to put them together to yield a longer string.

Given two strings, such as "Harry" and "Morgan", you can **concatenate** them to one long string. The result consists of all characters in the first string, followed by all characters in the second string. In C++, you use the + operator to concatenate two strings. For example,

```
string fname = "Harry";
string lname = "Morgan";
string name = fname + lname;
```

results in the string

```
"HarryMorgan"
```

What if you'd like the first and last name separated by a space? No problem:

```
string name = fname + " " + lname;
```

This statement concatenates three strings: fname, the string literal " ", and lname. The result is

```
"Harry Morgan"
```

2.5.3 String Input

You can read a string from the console:

```
cout << "Please enter your name: ";
string name;
cin >> name;
```

When a string is read with the >> operator, only one word is placed into the string variable. For example, suppose the user types

```
Harry Morgan
```

as the response to the prompt. This input consists of two words. After the call cin >> name, the string "Harry" is placed into the variable name. Use another input statement to read the second word.

2.5.4 String Functions

The length member function yields the number of characters in a string.

The number of characters in a string is called the *length* of the string. For example, the length of "Harry" is 5. You can compute the length of a string with the length function. Unlike the sqrt or pow function, the length function is invoked with the **dot notation**.

That is, you write the string whose length you want, then a period, then the name of the function, followed by parentheses:

```
int n = name.length();
```

Many C++ functions require you to use this dot notation, and you must memorize (or look up) which do and which don't. These functions are called **member functions**. We say that the member function length is *invoked on* the variable name.

Once you have a string, you can extract substrings by using the substr member function. The member function call

```
s.substr(start, length)
```

returns a string that is made from the characters in the string s, starting at character start, and containing length characters. Here is an example:

```
string greeting = "Hello, World!";
string sub = greeting.substr(0, 5);
// sub is "Hello"
```

The substr operation makes a string that consists of five characters taken from the string greeting. Indeed, "Hello" is a string of length 5 that occurs inside greeting. A curious aspect of the substr operation is the starting position. Starting position 0 means "start at the beginning of the string". The first position in a string is labeled 0, the second one 1, and so on. For example, here are the position numbers in the greeting string:

```
H  e  l  l  o  ,     W  o  r  l  d  !
0  1  2  3  4  5  6  7  8  9  10 11 12
```

The position number of the last character (12) is always one less than the length of the string.

Let's figure out how to extract the substring "World". Count characters starting at 0, not 1. You find that W, the 8th character, has position number 7. The string you want is 5 characters long. Therefore, the appropriate substring command is

```
string w = greeting.substr(7, 5);
```

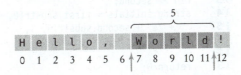

If you omit the length, you get all characters from the given position to the end of the string. For example,

```
greeting.substr(7)
```

is the string "World!" (including the exclamation point).

In a string that contains characters other than the English alphabet, digits, and punctuation marks, a character may take up more than a single char value. We will discuss this issue further in Chapter 8.

Here is a simple program that puts these concepts to work. The program asks for your name and that of your significant other. It then prints out your initials.

The operation `first.substr(0, 1)` makes a string consisting of one character, taken from the start of `first`. The program does the same for `second`. Then it concatenates the resulting one-character strings with the string literal `"&"` to get a string of length 3, the `initials` string. (See Figure 4.)

© Rich Legg/iStockphoto.

Initials are formed from the first letter of each name.

first = `R o d o l f o`
           0 1 2 3 4 5 6

second = `S a l l y`
          0 1 2 3 4

initials = `R & S`
          0 1 2

Figure 4 Building the `initials` String

sec05/initials.cpp

```cpp
1  #include <iostream>
2  #include <string>
3
4  using namespace std;
5
6  int main()
7  {
8     cout << "Enter your first name: ";
9     string first;
10    cin >> first;
11    cout << "Enter your significant other's first name: ";
12    string second;
13    cin >> second;
14    string initials = first.substr(0, 1)
15       + "&" + second.substr(0, 1);
16    cout << initials << endl;
17
18    return 0;
19 }
```

Program Run

```
Enter your first name: Rodolfo
Enter your significant other's first name: Sally
R&S
```

Table 9 String Operations

Statement	Result	Comment
`string str = "C";` `str = str + "++";`	str is set to "C++"	When applied to strings, + denotes concatenation.
🚫 `string str = "C" + "++";`	**Error**	**Error:** You cannot concatenate two string literals.

`cout << "Enter name: ";`
`cin >> name;`
(User input: Harry Morgan)
	name contains "Harry"	The >> operator places the next word into the string variable.

`cout << "Enter name: ";`
`cin >> name >> last_name;`
(User input: Harry Morgan)
	name contains "Harry", last_name contains "Morgan"	Use multiple >> operators to read more than one word.

`string greeting = "H & S";` `int n = greeting.length();`	n is set to 5	Each space counts as one character.
`string str = "Sally";` `string str2 = str.substr(1, 3);`	str2 is set to "all"	Extracts the substring of length 3 starting at position 1. (The initial position is 0.)
`string str = "Sally";` `string str2 = str.substr(1);`	str2 is set to "ally"	If you omit the length, all characters from the position until the end are included.
`string a = str.substr(0, 1);`	a is set to the initial letter in str	Extracts the substring of length 1 starting at position 0.
`string b = str.substr(str.length() - 1);`	b is set to the last letter in str	The last letter has position `str.length() - 1`. We need not specify the length.

Computing & Society 2.2 International Alphabets and Unicode

The English alphabet is pretty simple: upper- and lowercase *a* to *z*. Other European languages have accent marks and special characters. For example, German has three so-called *umlaut* characters, ä, ö, ü, and a *double-s* character ß. These are not optional frills; you couldn't write a page of German text without using these characters a few times. German keyboards have keys for these characters.

This poses a problem for computer users and designers. The American standard character encoding (called ASCII, for American Standard Code for Information Interchange) specifies 128 codes: 52 upper- and lowercase characters, 10 digits, 32 typographical symbols, and 34 control characters (such as space, newline, and 32 others for controlling printers and other devices). The umlaut and double-s are

© pvachier/iStockphoto.

The German Keyboard Layout

not among them. Some German data processing systems replace seldom-used ASCII characters with German letters: [\ ] { | } ~ are replaced with Ä Ö Ü ä ö ü ß. While most people can live without these characters, C++ programmers definitely cannot. Other encoding schemes take advantage of the fact that one byte can encode 256 different characters, of which only 128 are standardized by ASCII. Unfortunately, there are multiple incompatible standards for such encodings, resulting in a certain amount of aggravation among European computer users.

Many countries don't use the Roman script at all. Russian, Greek, Hebrew, Arabic, and Thai letters, to name just a few, have completely different shapes. To complicate matters, Hebrew and Arabic are typed from right to left. Each of these alphabets has between 30 and 100 letters, and the countries using them have established encoding standards for them.

The situation is much more dramatic in languages that use the Chinese script: the Chinese dialects, Japanese, and Korean. The Chinese script is not alphabetic but *ideographic.* A character represents an idea or thing. Most words are made up of one, two, or three of these ideographic characters. (Over 50,000 ideographs are known, of which about 20,000 are in active use.) Therefore, two bytes are needed to encode them. China, Taiwan, Japan, and Korea have incompatible encoding standards for them. (Japanese and Korean writing uses a mixture of native syllabic and Chinese ideographic characters.)

The inconsistencies among character encodings have been a major nuisance for international electronic communication and for software manufacturers vying for a global market. Starting in 1988, a consortium of hardware and software manufacturers developed a uniform 21-**bit** encoding scheme called **Unicode** that is capable of encoding text in essentially all written languages of the world. About 100,000 characters have been given codes, including more than 70,000 Chinese, Japanese, and Korean ideographs. Even extinct languages, such as Egyptian hieroglyphs, have been included in Unicode.

© Joel Carillet/iStockphoto.

Hebrew, Arabic, and English

© Saipg/iStockphoto.

The Chinese Script

CHAPTER SUMMARY

Write variable definitions in C++.

- A variable is a storage location with a name.
- When defining a variable, you usually specify an initial value.
- When defining a variable, you also specify the type of its values.
- Use the `int` type for numbers that cannot have a fractional part.
- Use the `double` type for floating-point numbers.
- By convention, variable names should start with a lowercase letter.
- An assignment statement stores a new value in a variable, replacing the previously stored value.
- The assignment operator = does *not* denote mathematical equality.

- You cannot change the value of a variable that is defined as `const`.
- Use comments to add explanations for humans who read your code. The compiler ignores comments.

Use the arithmetic operations in C++.

- Use `*` for multiplication and `/` for division.
- The `++` operator adds 1 to a variable; the `--` operator subtracts 1.
- If both arguments of `/` are integers, the remainder is discarded.
- The `%` operator computes the remainder of an integer division.
- A common use of the `%` operator is to check whether a number is even or odd.
- Assigning a floating-point variable to an integer drops the fractional part.
- The C++ library defines many mathematical functions such as `sqrt` (square root) and `pow` (raising to a power).

Write programs that read user input and write formatted output.

- Use the `>>` operator to read a value and place it in a variable.
- You use manipulators to specify how values should be formatted.

Carry out hand calculations when developing an algorithm.

- Pick concrete values for a typical situation to use in a hand calculation.

Write programs that process strings.

- Strings are sequences of characters.
- Use the `+` operator to *concatenate* strings; that is, put them together to yield a longer string.
- The `length` member function yields the number of characters in a string.
- A member function is invoked using the dot notation.
- Use the `substr` member function to extract a substring of a string.

CHAPTER 3

DECISIONS

© zennie/iStockphoto.

CHAPTER GOALS

To be able to implement decisions
   using if statements

To learn how to compare integers,
   floating-point numbers, and strings

To understand the Boolean data type

To develop strategies for validating user input

CHAPTER CONTENTS

3.1   THE IF STATEMENT   60
SYN   if Statement 61
CE1   A Semicolon After the if Condition 63
PT1   Brace Layout 63
PT2   Always Use Braces 64
PT3   Tabs 64
PT4   Avoid Duplication in Branches 65
ST1   The Conditional Operator 65

**3.2   COMPARING NUMBERS AND
      STRINGS**   66
SYN   Comparisons 67
CE2   Confusing = and == 68
CE3   Exact Comparison of Floating-Point
      Numbers 68
PT5   Compile with Zero Warnings 69
ST2   Lexicographic Ordering of Strings 69
HT1   Implementing an if Statement 70
WE1   Extracting the Middle 72
C&S   Dysfunctional Computerized Systems 72

3.3   MULTIPLE ALTERNATIVES   73
ST3   The switch Statement 75

3.4   NESTED BRANCHES   76
CE4   The Dangling else Problem 79
PT6   Hand-Tracing 79

**3.5   PROBLEM SOLVING:
      FLOWCHARTS**   81

3.6   PROBLEM SOLVING: TEST CASES   83
PT7   Make a Schedule and Make Time for
      Unexpected Problems 84

**3.7   BOOLEAN VARIABLES AND
      OPERATORS**   85
CE5   Combining Multiple Relational
      Operators 88
CE6   Confusing && and || Conditions 88
ST4   Short-Circuit Evaluation of Boolean
      Operators 89
ST5   De Morgan's Law 89

**3.8   APPLICATION: INPUT
      VALIDATION**   90
C&S   Artificial Intelligence 92

One of the essential features of computer programs is their ability to make decisions. Like a train that changes tracks depending on how the switches are set, a program can take different actions, depending on inputs and other circumstances.

In this chapter, you will learn how to program simple and complex decisions. You will apply what you learn to the task of checking user input.

3.1 The if Statement

The if statement allows a program to carry out different actions depending on the nature of the data to be processed.

The if statement is used to implement a decision. When a condition is fulfilled, one set of statements is executed. Otherwise, another set of statements is executed (see Syntax 3.1).

Here is an example using the if statement. In many countries, the number 13 is considered unlucky. Rather than offending superstitious tenants, building owners sometimes skip the thirteenth floor; floor 12 is immediately followed by floor 14. Of course, floor 13 is not usually left empty or, as some conspiracy theorists believe, filled with secret offices and research labs. It is simply called floor 14. The computer that controls the building elevators needs to compensate for this foible and adjust all floor numbers above 13.

Let's simulate this process in C++. We will ask the user to type in the desired floor number and then compute the actual floor. When the input is above 13, then we need to decrement the input to obtain the actual floor.

© DrGrounds/iStockphoto.

This elevator panel "skips" the thirteenth floor. The floor is not actually missing—the computer that controls the elevator adjusts the floor numbers above 13.

An if statement is like a fork in the road. Depending upon a decision, different parts of the program are executed.

© Media Bakery.

For example, if the user provides an input of 20, the program determines the actual floor as 19. Otherwise, we simply use the supplied floor number.

```
int actual_floor;

if (floor > 13)
{
   actual_floor = floor - 1;
}
else
{
   actual_floor = floor;
}
```

The flowchart in Figure 1 shows the branching behavior.

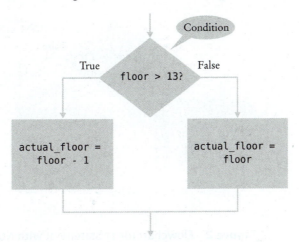

Figure 1   Flowchart for if Statement

Syntax 3.1   if Statement

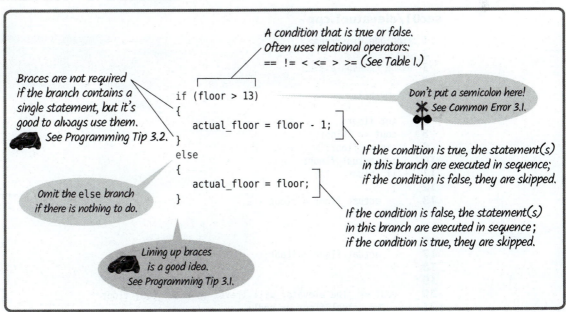

In our example, each branch of the if statement contains a single statement. You can include as many statements in each branch as you like. Sometimes, it happens that there is nothing to do in the else branch of the statement. In that case, you can omit it entirely, such as in this example:

```
int actual_floor = floor;

if (floor > 13)
{
   actual_floor--;
} // No else needed
```

See Figure 2 for the flowchart.

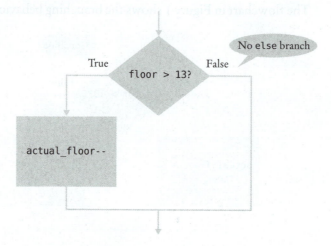

Figure 2 Flowchart for if Statement with No else Branch

The following program puts the if statement to work. This program asks for the desired floor and then prints out the actual floor.

sec01/elevator1.cpp

```
1   #include <iostream>
2
3   using namespace std;
4
5   int main()
6   {
7      int floor;
8      cout << "Floor: ";
9      cin >> floor;
10     int actual_floor;
11     if (floor > 13)
12     {
13        actual_floor = floor - 1;
14     }
15     else
16     {
17        actual_floor = floor;
18     }
19
20     cout << "The elevator will travel to the actual floor "
21        << actual_floor << endl;
```

```
22
23     return 0;
24 }
```

Program Run

```
Floor: 20
The elevator will travel to the actual floor 19
```

Common Error 3.1

A Semicolon After the `if` Condition

The following code fragment has an unfortunate error:

```
if (floor > 13) ; // ERROR
{
    floor--;
}
```

There should be no semicolon after the `if` condition. The compiler interprets this statement as follows: If `floor` is greater than 13, execute the statement that is denoted by a single semicolon, that is, the do-nothing statement. The statement enclosed in braces is no longer a part of the `if` statement. It is always executed. Even if the value of `floor` is not above 13, it is decremented.

Placing a semicolon after the `else` reserved word is also wrong:

```
if (floor > 13)
{
    actual_floor = floor - 1;
}
else ;
{
    actual_floor = floor;
}
```

In this case, the do-nothing statement is executed if `floor > 13` is not fulfilled. This is the end of the `if` statement. The next statement, enclosed in braces, is executed in both cases; that is, `actual_floor` is always set to `floor`.

Programming Tip 3.1

Brace Layout

Programmers vary in how they align braces in their code. In this book, we follow the simple rule of making { and } line up.

```
if (floor > 13)
{
    floor--;
}
```

This style makes it easy to spot matching braces.

Some programmers put the opening brace on the same line as the `if`:

```
if (floor > 13) {
    floor--;
}
```

© Timothy Large/iStockphoto.

Properly lining up your code makes your programs easier to read.

This style makes it harder to match the braces, but it saves a line of code, allowing you to view more code on the screen without scrolling. There are passionate advocates of both styles.

It is important that you pick a layout style and stick with it consistently within a given programming project. Which style you choose may depend on your personal preference or a coding style guide that you need to follow.

Programming Tip 3.2
Always Use Braces

When a branch of an if statement consists of a single statement, you need not use braces. For example, the following is legal:

```
if (floor > 13)
    floor--;
```

However, it is a good idea to always include the braces:

```
if (floor > 13)
{
    floor--;
}
```

The braces makes your code easier to read, and you are less likely to make errors such as the one described in Common Error 3.1.

Programming Tip 3.3
Tabs

Block-structured code has the property that nested statements are indented by one or more levels:

```
int main()
{
|   int floor;
|   . . .
|   if (floor > 13)
|   {
|   |   floor--;
|   }   |
|   . . .
|   return 0;
}   |   |
0   1   2     Indentation level
```

How do you move the cursor from the leftmost column to the appropriate indentation level? A perfectly reasonable strategy is to hit the space bar a sufficient number of times. However, many programmers use the Tab key instead. A tab moves the cursor to the next indentation level.

While the Tab *key* is nice, some editors use *tab characters* for alignment, which is not so nice. Tab characters can lead to problems when you send your file to another person or a printer. There is no universal agreement on the width of a tab character, and some software will ignore tabs altogether. It is therefore best to save your files with spaces instead of tabs. Most editors have a setting to automatically convert all tabs to spaces. Look at the documentation of your development environment to find out how to activate this useful setting.

© Vincent LaRussa/John Wiley & Sons, Inc.

You use the Tab key to move the cursor to the next indentation level.

Programming Tip 3.4

Avoid Duplication in Branches

Look to see whether you *duplicate code* in each branch. If so, move it out of the `if` statement. Here is an example of such duplication:

```cpp
if (floor > 13)
{
   actual_floor = floor - 1;
   cout << "Actual floor: " << actual_floor << endl;
}
else
{
   actual_floor = floor;
   cout << "Actual floor: " << actual_floor << endl;
}
```

The output statement is exactly the same in both branches. This is not an error—the program will run correctly. However, you can simplify the program by moving the duplicated statement, like this:

```cpp
if (floor > 13)
{
   actual_floor = floor - 1;
}
else
{
   actual_floor = floor;
}
cout << "Actual floor: " << actual_floor << endl;
```

Removing duplication is particularly important when programs are maintained for a long time. When there are two sets of statements with the same effect, it can easily happen that a programmer modifies one set but not the other.

Special Topic 3.1

The Conditional Operator

C++ has a *conditional operator* of the form

condition ? *value*$_1$: *value*$_2$

The value of that expression is either *value*$_1$ if the test passes or *value*$_2$ if it fails. For example, we can compute the actual floor number as

```cpp
actual_floor = floor > 13 ? floor - 1 : floor;
```

which is equivalent to

```cpp
if (floor > 13)
{
   actual_floor =  floor - 1;
}
else
{
   actual_floor = floor;
}
```

You can use the conditional operator anywhere that a value is expected, for example:

```cpp
cout << "Actual floor: " << (floor > 13 ? floor - 1 : floor);
```

We don't use the conditional operator in this book, but it is a convenient construct that you will find in many C++ programs.

3.2 Comparing Numbers and Strings

Relational operators (< <= > >= == !=) are used to compare numbers and strings.

Every if statement contains a *condition*. In many cases, the condition involves comparing two values. For example, in the previous examples we tested floor > 13. The comparison > is called a **relational operator**. C++ has six relational operators (see Table 1).

As you can see, only two C++ relational operators (> and <) look as you would expect from the mathematical notation. Computer keyboards do not have keys for ≥, ≤, or ≠, but the >=, <=, and != operators are easy to remember because they look similar. The == operator is initially confusing to most newcomers to C++. In C++, = already has a meaning, namely assignment.

© arturbo/iStockphoto.

In C++, you use a relational operator to check whether one value is greater than another.

The == operator denotes equality testing:

```
floor = 13; // Assign 13 to floor
if (floor == 13)  // Test whether floor equals 13
```

You must remember to use == inside tests and to use = outside tests. (See Common Error 3.2 for more information.)

Table 1 Relational Operators		
C++	Math Notation	Description
>	>	Greater than
>=	≥	Greater than or equal
<	<	Less than
<=	≤	Less than or equal
==	=	Equal
!=	≠	Not equal

You can compare strings as well:

```
if (input == "Quit") . . .
```

Use != to check whether two strings are different. In C++, letter case matters. For example, "Quit" and "quit" are not the same string.

Syntax 3.2 Comparisons

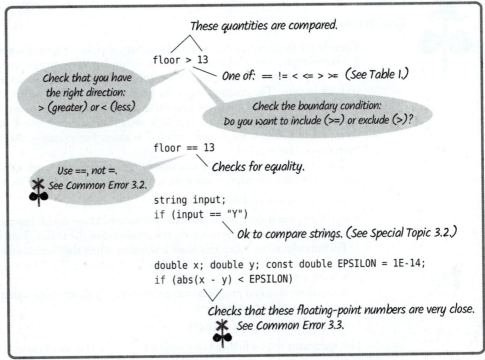

These quantities are compared.

```
floor > 13
```

Check that you have the right direction: > (greater) or < (less)

One of: == != < <= > >= (See Table 1.)

Check the boundary condition: Do you want to include (>=) or exclude (>)?

```
floor == 13
```

Checks for equality.

Use ==, not =.
✖ See Common Error 3.2.

```
string input;
if (input == "Y")
```

Ok to compare strings. (See Special Topic 3.2.)

```
double x; double y; const double EPSILON = 1E-14;
if (abs(x - y) < EPSILON)
```

Checks that these floating-point numbers are very close.
✖ See Common Error 3.3.

EXAMPLE CODE See sec02 of your companion code for a program that compares numbers and strings.

Table 2 summarizes how to use relational operators in C++.

Expression	Value	Comment
3 <= 4	true	3 is less than 4; <= tests for "less than or equal".
🚫 3 =< 4	**Error**	The "less than or equal" operator is <=, not =<. The "less than" symbol comes first.
3 > 4	false	> is the opposite of <=.
4 < 4	false	The left-hand side must be strictly smaller than the right-hand side.
4 <= 4	true	Both sides are equal; <= tests for "less than or equal".
3 == 5 - 2	true	== tests for equality.
3 != 5 - 1	true	!= tests for inequality. It is true that 3 is not 5 – 1.
🚫 3 = 6 / 2	**Error**	Use == to test for equality.
1.0 / 3.0 == 0.333333333	false	Although the values are very close to one another, they are not exactly equal. See Common Error 3.3.
🚫 "10" > 5	**Error**	You cannot compare a string to a number.

Table 2 Relational Operator Examples

Common Error 3.2

Confusing = and ==

The rule for the correct usage of = and == is very simple: In tests, always use == and never use =. If it is so simple, why can't the compiler be helpful and flag any errors?

Actually, the C++ language allows the use of = inside tests. To understand this, we have to go back in time. The creators of C, the predecessor to C++, were very frugal. They did not want to have special values true and false. Instead, they allowed any numeric value inside a condition, with the convention that 0 denotes false and any non-0 value denotes true. Furthermore, in C and C++ assignments have values. For example, the value of the assignment expression floor = 13 is 13.

These two features—namely that numbers can be used as truth values and that assignments are expressions with values—conspire to make a horrible pitfall. The test

```
if (floor = 13) // ERROR
```

is legal C++, but it does not test whether floor and 13 are equal. Instead, the code sets floor to 13, and because that value is not zero, the condition of the if statement is always fulfilled.

Fortunately, most compilers issue a warning when they encounter such a statement. You should take such warnings seriously. (See Programming Tip 3.5 for more advice about compiler warnings.)

Some shell-shocked programmers are so nervous about using = that they use == even when they want to make an assignment:

```
floor == floor - 1; // ERROR
```

This statement tests whether floor equals floor - 1. It doesn't do anything with the outcome of the test, but that is not an error. Some compilers will warn that "the code has no effect", but others will quietly accept the code.

Common Error 3.3

Exact Comparison of Floating-Point Numbers

Floating-point numbers have only a limited precision, and calculations can introduce roundoff errors. You must take these inevitable roundoffs into account when comparing floating-point numbers. For example, the following code multiplies the square root of 2 by itself. Ideally, we expect to get the answer 2:

© caracterdesign/iStockphoto.

Take limited precision into account when comparing floating-point numbers.

```
double r = sqrt(2.0);
if (r * r == 2)
{
   cout << "sqrt(2) squared is 2" << endl;
}
else
{
   cout << "sqrt(2) squared is not 2 but "
      << setprecision(18) << r * r << endl;
}
```

This program displays

```
sqrt(2) squared is not 2 but 2.00000000000000044
```

It does not make sense in most circumstances to compare floating-point numbers exactly. Instead, we should test whether they are *close enough*. That is, the magnitude of their difference should be less than some threshold. Mathematically, we would write that *x* and *y* are close enough if

$$|x - y| < \varepsilon$$

for a very small number, ε. ε is the Greek letter epsilon, a letter used to denote a very small quantity. It is common to set ε to 10^{-14} when comparing double numbers:

```
const double EPSILON = 1E-14;
double r = sqrt(2.0);
if (abs(r * r - 2) < EPSILON)
{
    cout << "sqrt(2) squared is approximately 2";
}
```

Include the `<cmath>` header when you use the abs function.

Programming Tip 3.5
Compile with Zero Warnings

There are two kinds of messages that the compiler gives you: *errors* and *warnings*. Error messages are fatal; the compiler will not translate a program with one or more errors. Warning messages are advisory; the compiler will translate the program, but there is a good chance that the program will not do what you expect it to do.

It is a good idea to learn how to activate warnings with your compiler, and to write code that emits no warnings at all. For example, consider the test

```
if (floor = 13)
```

One C++ compiler emits a curious warning message: "Suggest parentheses around assignment used as truth value". Sadly, the message is misleading because it was not written for students. Nevertheless, such a warning gives you another chance to look at the offending statement and fix it, in this case, by replacing the = with an ==.

In order to make warnings more visible, many compilers require you to take some special action. This might involve clicking a checkbox in an integrated environment or supplying a special option on the command line. Ask your instructor or lab assistant how to turn on warnings for your compiler.

Special Topic 3.2
Lexicographic Ordering of Strings

If you compare strings using < <= > >=, they are compared in "lexicographic" order. This ordering is very similar to the way in which words are sorted in a dictionary.

For example, consider this code fragment.

```
string name = "Tom";
if (name < "Dick") . . .
```

The condition is not fulfilled, because in the dictionary Dick comes before Tom. There are a few differences between the ordering in a dictionary and in C++. In C++:

Corbis Digital Stock.

To see which of two terms comes first in the dictionary, consider the first letter in which they differ.

- All uppercase letters come before the lowercase letters. For example, "Z" comes before "a".

- The space character comes before all printable characters.

- Numbers come before letters.
- For the ordering of punctuation marks, see Appendix C.

Lexicographic order is used to compare strings.

When comparing two strings, the first letters of each word are compared, then the second letters, and so on, until one of the strings ends or a letter pair doesn't match.

If one of the strings ends, the longer string is considered the "larger" one. For example, compare "car" with "cart". The first three letters match, and we reach the end of the first string. Therefore "car" comes before "cart" in lexicographic ordering.

When you reach a mismatch, the string containing the "larger" character is considered "larger". For example, let's compare "cat" with "cart". The first two letters match. Since t comes after r, the string "cat" comes after "cart" in the lexicographic ordering.

Letters r comes
match before t

Lexicographic Ordering

HOW TO 3.1

Implementing an if Statement

This How To walks you through the process of implementing an if statement. We will illustrate the steps with the following example problem:

Problem Statement The university bookstore has a Kilobyte Day sale every October 24, giving an 8 percent discount on all computer accessory purchases if the price is less than $128, and a 16 percent discount if the price is at least $128. Write a program that asks the cashier for the original price and then prints the discounted price.

Step 1 Decide upon the branching condition.

In our sample problem, the obvious choice for the condition is:

original price < 128?

That is just fine, and we will use that condition in our solution.

But you could equally well come up with a correct solution if you chose the opposite condition: Is the original price at least (≥) $128? You might choose this condition if you put yourself into the position of a shopper who wants to know when the bigger discount applies.

© MikePanic/iStockphoto.

Sales discounts are often higher for expensive products. Use the if statement to implement such a decision.

Step 2 Give pseudocode for the work that needs to be done when the condition is true.

In this step, you list the action or actions that are taken in the "positive" branch. The details depend on your problem. You may want to print a message, compute values, or even exit the program.

In our example, we need to apply an 8 percent discount:

discounted price = 0.92 × original price

Step 3 Give pseudocode for the work (if any) that needs to be done when the condition is *not* true.

What do you want to do in the case that the condition of Step 1 is not fulfilled? Sometimes, you want to do nothing at all. In that case, use an if statement without an else branch.

In our example, the condition tested whether the price was less than $128. If that condition is *not* true, the price is at least $128, so the higher discount of 16 percent applies to the sale:

discounted price = 0.84 x original price

Step 4   Double-check relational operators.

First, be sure that the test goes in the right *direction*. It is a common error to confuse > and <. Next, consider whether you should use the < operator or its close cousin, the <= operator.

What should happen if the original price is exactly $128? Reading the problem carefully, we find that the lower discount applies if the original price is *less than* $128, and the higher discount applies when it is *at least* $128. A price of $128 should therefore *not* fulfill our condition, and we must use <, not <=.

Step 5   Remove duplication.

Check which actions are common to both branches, and move them outside. (See Programming Tip 3.4.)

In our example, we have two statements of the form

discounted price = ___ x original price

They only differ in the discount rate. It is best to just set the rate in the branches, and to do the computation afterwards:

If original price < 128
*   discount rate = 0.92*
Else
*   discount rate = 0.84*
discounted price = discount rate x original price

Step 6   Test both branches.

Formulate two test cases, one that fulfills the condition of the if statement, and one that does not. Ask yourself what should happen in each case. Then follow the pseudocode and act each of them out.

In our example, let us consider two scenarios for the original price: $100 and $200. We expect that the first price is discounted by $8, the second by $32.

When the original price is 100, then the condition 100 < 128 is true, and we get

discount rate = 0.92
discounted price = 0.92 x 100 = 92

When the original price is 200, then the condition 200 < 128 is false, and

discount rate = 0.84
discounted price = 0.84 x 200 = 168

In both cases, we get the expected answer.

Step 7   Assemble the if statement in C++.

Type the skeleton

```
if ()
{
}
else
{
}
```

and fill it in, as shown in Syntax 3.1. Omit the else branch if it is not needed.

In our example, the completed statement is

```
if (original_price < 128)
{
    discount_rate = 0.92;
}
else
{
    discount_rate = 0.84;
}
discounted_price = discount_rate * original_price;
```

EXAMPLE CODE   See how_to_1 of your companion code for a program that calculates a discounted price.

WORKED EXAMPLE 3.1

Extracting the Middle

Learn how to extract the middle character from a string, or the two middle characters if the length of the string is even. See your E-Text or visit wiley.com/go/bclo3.

Computing & Society 3.1   Dysfunctional Computerized Systems

Making decisions is an essential part of any computer program. Nowhere is this more obvious than in a computer system that helps sort luggage at an airport. After scanning the luggage identification codes, the system sorts the items and routes them to different conveyor belts. Human operators then place the items onto trucks. When the city of Denver built a huge airport to replace an outdated and congested facility, the luggage system contractor went a step further. The new system was designed to replace the human operators with robotic carts. Unfortunately, the system plainly did not work. It was plagued by mechanical problems, such as luggage falling onto the tracks and jamming carts. Equally frustrating were the software glitches. Carts would uselessly accumulate at some locations when they were needed elsewhere.

The airport had been scheduled to open in 1993, but without a functioning luggage system, the opening was delayed for over a year while the contractor tried to fix the problems. The contractor never succeeded, and ultimately a manual system was installed. The delay cost the city and airlines close to a billion dollars, and the contractor, once the leading luggage systems vendor in the United States, went bankrupt.

Clearly, it is very risky to build a large system based on a technology that has never been tried on a smaller scale. In 2013, the rollout of universal healthcare in the United States was put in jeopardy by a dysfunctional web site for selecting insurance plans. The system promised an insurance shopping experience similar to booking airline flights. But, the HealthCare.gov site didn't simply present the available insurance plans. It also had to check the income level of each applicant and use that information to determine the subsidy level. That task turned out to be quite a bit harder than checking whether a credit card had sufficient credit to pay for an airline ticket. The Obama administration would have been well advised to design a signup process that did not rely on an untested computer program.

Lyn Alweis/Contributor/Getty Images.

The Denver airport originally had a fully automatic system for moving luggage, replacing human operators with robotic carts. Unfortunately, the system never worked and was dismantled before the airport was opened.

3.3 Multiple Alternatives

Multiple alternatives are required for decisions that have more than two cases.

In Section 3.1, you saw how to program a two-way branch with an `if` statement. In many situations, there are more than two cases. In this section, you will see how to implement a decision with multiple alternatives. For example, consider a program that displays the effect of an earthquake, as measured by the Richter scale (see Table 3).

Table 3 Richter Scale	
Value	**Effect**
8	Most structures fall
7	Many buildings destroyed
6	Many buildings considerably damaged, some collapse
4.5	Damage to poorly constructed buildings

The Richter scale is a measurement of the strength of an earthquake. Every step in the scale, for example from 6.0 to 7.0, signifies a tenfold increase in the strength of the quake.

In this case, there are five branches: one each for the four descriptions of damage, and one for no destruction.

You use multiple `if` statements to implement multiple alternatives, like this:

© kevinruss/iStockphoto.

The 1989 Loma Prieta earthquake that damaged the Bay Bridge in San Francisco and destroyed many buildings measured 7.1 on the Richter scale.

```
if (richter >= 8.0)
{
   cout << "Most structures fall";
}
else if (richter >= 7.0)
{
   cout << "Many buildings destroyed";
}
else if (richter >= 6.0)
{
   cout << "Many buildings considerably damaged, "
      << "some collapse";
}
else if (richter >= 4.5)
{
   cout << "Damage to poorly constructed buildings";
}
else
{
   cout << "No destruction of buildings";
}
```

As soon as one of the four tests succeeds, the effect is displayed, and no further tests are attempted. If none of the four cases applies, the final `else` clause applies, and a default message is printed. Figure 3 shows the flowchart for this multiple-branch statement.

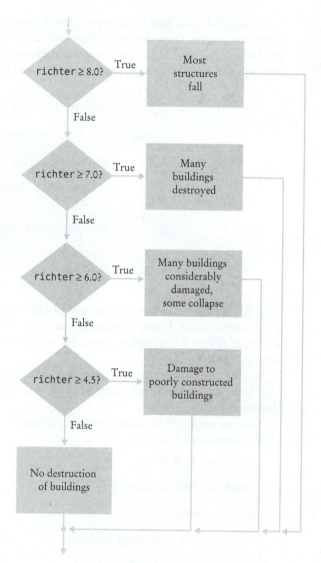

Figure 3 Multiple Alternatives

Here you must sort the conditions and test against the largest cutoff first. Suppose we reverse the order of tests:

```
if (richter >= 4.5) // Tests in wrong order
{
   cout << "Damage to poorly constructed buildings";
}
else if (richter >= 6.0)
{
   cout << "Many buildings considerably damaged, some collapse";
}
else if (richter >= 7.0)
{
```

```
      cout << "Many buildings destroyed";
   }
   else if (richter >= 8.0)
   {
      cout << "Most structures fall";
   }
```

When using multiple if statements, pay attention to the order of the conditions.

This does not work. Suppose the value of richter is 7.1. That value is at least 4.5, matching the first case. The other tests will never be attempted.

In this example, it is also important that we use a sequence of else if clauses, not just multiple independent if statements. Consider this sequence of independent tests:

```
   if (richter >= 8.0) // Didn't use else
   {
      cout << "Most structures fall";
   }
   if (richter >= 7.0)
   {
      cout << "Many buildings destroyed";
   }
   if (richter >= 6.0)
   {
      cout << "Many buildings considerably damaged, some collapse";
   }
   if (richter >= 4.5)
   {
      cout << "Damage to poorly constructed buildings";
   }
```

Now the alternatives are no longer exclusive. If richter is 7.1, then the last *three* tests all match, and three messages are printed.

EXAMPLE CODE See sec03 of your companion code for the full program that prints earthquake descriptions.

Special Topic 3.3

The switch Statement

A sequence of if statements that compares a *single integer value* against several *constant* alternatives can be implemented as a switch statement. For example,

```
int digit;
. . .
switch (digit)
{
   case 1: digit_name = "one"; break;
   case 2: digit_name = "two"; break;
   case 3: digit_name = "three"; break;
   case 4: digit_name = "four"; break;
   case 5: digit_name = "five"; break;
   case 6: digit_name = "six"; break;
   case 7: digit_name = "seven"; break;
   case 8: digit_name = "eight"; break;
   case 9: digit_name = "nine"; break;
   default: digit_name = ""; break;
}
```

© travelpixpro/iStockphoto.

The switch *statement lets you choose from a fixed set of alternatives.*

sec04/tax.cpp

```
1   #include <iostream>
2   #include <string>
3
4   using namespace std;
5
6   int main()
7   {
8      const double RATE1 = 0.10;
9      const double RATE2 = 0.25;
10     const double RATE1_SINGLE_LIMIT = 32000;
11     const double RATE1_MARRIED_LIMIT = 64000;
12
13     double tax1 = 0;
14     double tax2 = 0;
15
16     double income;
17     cout << "Please enter your income: ";
18     cin >> income;
19
20     cout << "Please enter s for single, m for married: ";
21     string marital_status;
22     cin >> marital_status;
23
24     if (marital_status == "s")
25     {
26        if (income <= RATE1_SINGLE_LIMIT)
27        {
28           tax1 = RATE1 * income;
29        }
30        else
31        {
32           tax1 = RATE1 * RATE1_SINGLE_LIMIT;
33           tax2 = RATE2 * (income - RATE1_SINGLE_LIMIT);
34        }
35     }
36     else
37     {
38        if (income <= RATE1_MARRIED_LIMIT)
39        {
40           tax1 = RATE1 * income;
41        }
42        else
43        {
44           tax1 = RATE1 * RATE1_MARRIED_LIMIT;
45           tax2 = RATE2 * (income - RATE1_MARRIED_LIMIT);
46        }
47     }
48
49     double total_tax = tax1 + tax2;
50
51     cout << "The tax is $" << total_tax << endl;
52     return 0;
53  }
```

Program Run

```
Please enter your income: 80000
Please enter s for single, m for married: m
The tax is $10400
```

Common Error 3.4

The Dangling else Problem

When an if statement is nested inside another if statement, the following error may occur.

```
double shipping_charge = 5.00; // $5 inside continental U.S.
if (country == "USA")
   if (state == "HI")
      shipping_charge = 10.00; // Hawaii is more expensive
else // Pitfall!
   shipping_charge = 20.00; // As are foreign shipments
```

The indentation level seems to suggest that the else is grouped with the test country == "USA". Unfortunately, that is not the case. The compiler ignores all indentation and matches the else with the preceding if. That is, the code is actually

```
double shipping_charge = 5.00; // $5 inside continental U.S.
if (country == "USA")
   if (state == "HI")
      shipping_charge = 10.00; // Hawaii is more expensive
   else // Pitfall!
      shipping_charge = 20.00; // As are foreign shipments
```

That isn't what you want. You want to group the else with the first if.

The ambiguous else is called a *dangling* else. You can avoid this pitfall if you *always use braces*, as recommended in Programming Tip 3.2:

```
double shipping_charge = 5.00; // $5 inside continental U.S.
if (country == "USA")
{
   if (state == "HI")
   {
      shipping_charge = 10.00; // Hawaii is more expensive
   }
}
else
{
   shipping_charge = 20.00; // As are foreign shipments
}
```

Programming Tip 3.6

Hand-Tracing

A very useful technique for understanding whether a program works correctly is called *hand-tracing*. You simulate the program's activity on a sheet of paper. You can use this method with pseudocode or C++ code.

Get an index card, a cocktail napkin, or whatever sheet of paper is within reach. Make a column for each variable. Have the program code ready. Use a marker, such as a paper clip, to mark the current statement. In your mind, execute statements one at a time. Every time the value of a variable changes, cross out the old value and write the new value below the old one.

For example, let's trace the tax program with the data from the program run in Section 3.4.

© thomasd007/iStockphoto.

Hand-tracing helps you understand whether a program works correctly.

Make a list of the test cases and the expected outputs:

Test Case		Expected Output	Comment
30,000	s	3,000	10% bracket
72,000	s	13,200	3,200 + 25% of 40,000
50,000	m	5,000	10% bracket
104,000	m	16,400	6,400 + 25% of 40,000
32,000	s	3,200	boundary case
0		0	boundary case

When you develop a set of test cases, it is helpful to have a flowchart of your program (see Section 3.5). Check off each branch that has a test case. Include **boundary test cases** for each decision. For example, if a decision checks whether an input is less than 100, test with an input of 100.

It is always a good idea to design test cases *before* starting to code. Working through the test cases gives you a better understanding of the algorithm that you are about to implement.

> It is a good idea to design test cases before implementing a program.

Programming Tip 3.7
Make a Schedule and Make Time for Unexpected Problems

Commercial software is notorious for being delivered later than promised. For example, Microsoft originally promised that its Windows Vista operating system would be available late in 2003, then in 2005, then in March 2006; it finally was released in January 2007. Some of the early promises might not have been realistic. It was in Microsoft's interest to let prospective customers expect the imminent availability of the product. Had customers known the actual delivery date, they might have switched to a different product in the meantime. Undeniably, though, Microsoft had not anticipated the full complexity of the tasks it had set itself to solve.

Microsoft can delay the delivery of its product, but it is likely that you cannot. As a student or a programmer, you are expected to manage your time wisely and to finish your assignments on time. You can probably do simple programming exercises the night before the due date, but an assignment that looks twice as hard may well take four times as long, because more things can go wrong. You should therefore make a schedule whenever you start a programming project.

First, estimate realistically how much time it will take you to:

- Design the program logic.
- Develop test cases.
- Type in the program and fix syntax errors.
- Test and debug the program.

For example, for the income tax program I might estimate an hour for the design; 30 minutes for developing test cases; an hour for data entry and fixing syntax errors; and an hour for testing and debugging. That is a total of 3.5 hours. If I work two hours a day on this project, it will take me almost two days.

Then think of things that can go wrong. Your computer might break down. You might be stumped by a problem with the computer system.

Bananastock/Media Bakery.

Make a schedule for your programming work and build in time for problems.

(That is a particularly important concern for beginners. It is *very* common to lose a day over a trivial problem just because it takes time to track down a person who knows the magic command to overcome it.) As a rule of thumb, *double* the time of your estimate. That is, you should start four days, not two days, before the due date. If nothing went wrong, great; you have the program done two days early. When the inevitable problem occurs, you have a cushion of time that protects you from embarrassment and failure.

3.7 Boolean Variables and Operators

Sometimes, you need to evaluate a logical condition in one part of a program and use it elsewhere. To store a condition that can be true or false, you use a *Boolean variable*. Boolean variables are named after the mathematician George Boole (1815–1864), a pioneer in the study of logic.

> The Boolean type bool has two values, false and true.

In C++, the `bool` data type represents the Boolean type. Variables of type `bool` can hold exactly two values, denoted `false` and `true`. These values are not strings or integers; they are special values, just for Boolean variables.

Here is a definition of a Boolean variable:

```
bool failed = true;
```

You can use the value later in your program to make a decision:

```
if (failed) // Only executed if failed has been set to true
{
    . . .
}
```

Jon Patton/E+/iStockphoto.

A Boolean variable is also called a flag because it can be either up (true) or down (false).

When you make complex decisions, you often need to combine Boolean values. An operator that combines Boolean conditions is called a **Boolean operator**. In C++, the `&&` operator (called *and*) yields `true` only when *both* conditions are true. The `||` operator (called *or*) yields the result `true` if *at least one* of the conditions is true.

Suppose you write a program that processes temperature values, and you want to test whether a given temperature corresponds to liquid water. (At sea level, water freezes at 0 degrees Celsius and boils at 100 degrees.) Water is liquid if the temperature is greater than zero *and* less than 100:

```
if (temp > 0 && temp < 100) { cout << "Liquid"; }
```

At this geyser in Iceland, you can see ice, liquid water, and steam.

© toos/iStockphoto.

4.3 The for Loop

The for loop is used when a value runs from a starting point to an ending point with a constant increment or decrement.

It often happens that you want to execute a sequence of statements a given number of times. You can use a while loop that is controlled by a counter, as in the following example:

```
counter = 1; // Initialize the counter
while (counter <= 10) // Check the counter
{
    cout << counter << endl;
    counter++; // Update the counter
}
```

Because this loop type is so common, there is a special form for it, called the for loop (see Syntax 4.2).

```
for (counter = 1; counter <= 10; counter++)
{
    cout << counter << endl;
}
```

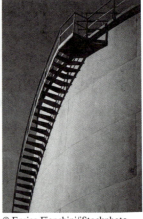

© Enrico Fianchini/iStockphoto.

You can visualize the for *loop as an orderly sequence of steps.*

Some people call this loop *count-controlled*. In contrast, the while loop of the preceding section can be called an *event-controlled* loop because it executes until an event occurs (for example, when the balance reaches the target). Another commonly-used term for a count-controlled loop is *definite*. You know from the outset that the loop body will be executed a definite number of times—ten times in our example. In contrast, you do not know how many iterations it takes to accumulate a target balance. Such a loop is called *indefinite*.

Syntax 4.2 for Statement

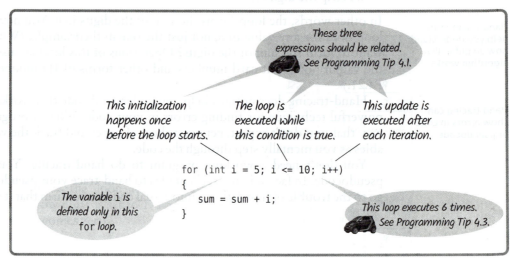

The for loop neatly groups the initialization, condition, and update expressions together. However, it is important to realize that these expressions are *not* executed together (see Figure 3).

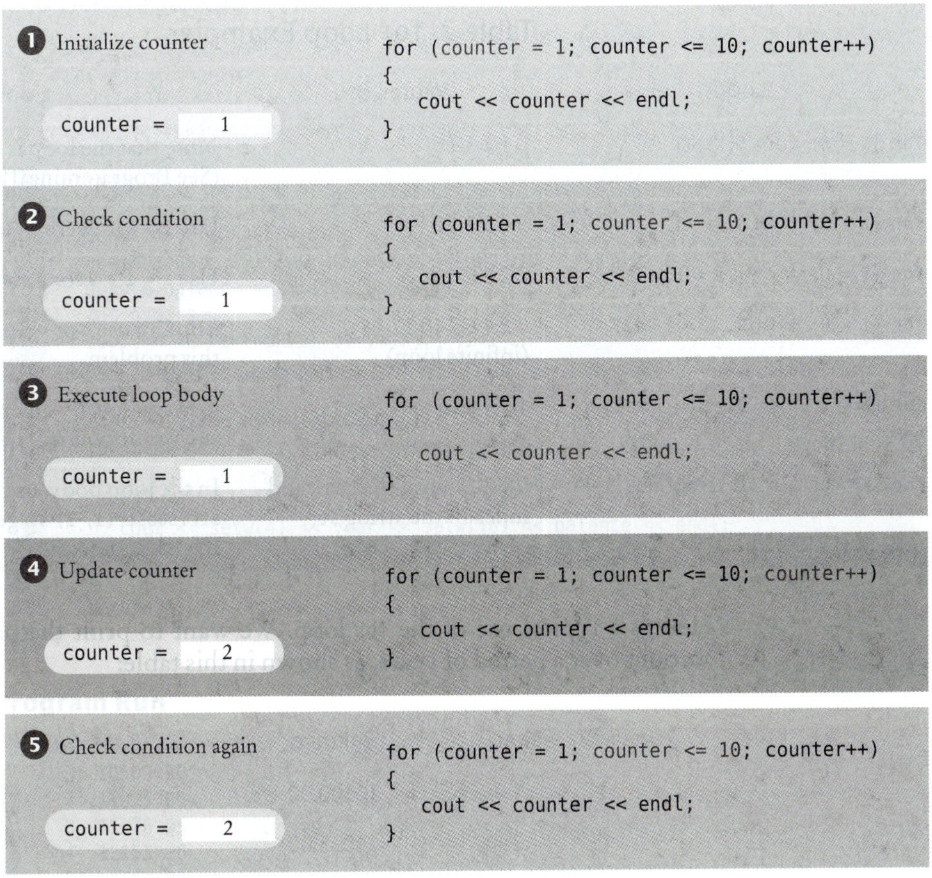

1 Initialize counter

```
for (counter = 1; counter <= 10; counter++)
{
    cout << counter << endl;
}
```

counter = 1

2 Check condition

```
for (counter = 1; counter <= 10; counter++)
{
    cout << counter << endl;
}
```

counter = 1

3 Execute loop body

```
for (counter = 1; counter <= 10; counter++)
{
    cout << counter << endl;
}
```

counter = 1

4 Update counter

```
for (counter = 1; counter <= 10; counter++)
{
    cout << counter << endl;
}
```

counter = 2

5 Check condition again

```
for (counter = 1; counter <= 10; counter++)
{
    cout << counter << endl;
}
```

counter = 2

Figure 3 Execution of a for Loop

- The initialization is executed once, before the loop is entered. **1**
- The condition is checked before each iteration. **2** **5**
- The update is executed after each iteration. **4**

A for loop can count down instead of up:

```
for (counter = 10; counter >= 0; counter--) . . .
```

The increment or decrement need not be in steps of 1:

```
for (counter = 0; counter <= 10; counter = counter + 2) . . .
```

So far, we assumed that the counter variable had already been defined before the for loop. Alternatively, you can define a variable in the loop initialization. Such a variable is defined *only* in the loop:

```
for (int counter = 1; counter <= 10; counter++)
{
    . . .
} // counter no longer defined here
```

See Table 2 for additional variations.

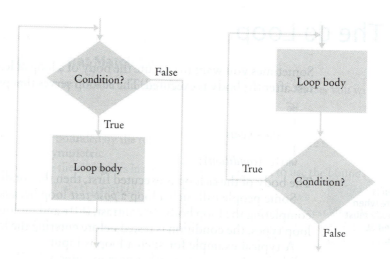

As described in Section 3.5, you want to avoid "spaghetti code" in your flowcharts. For loops, that means that you never want to have an arrow that points inside a loop body.

4.5 Processing Input

In the following sections, you will learn how to read and process a sequence of input values.

4.5.1 Sentinel Values

A sentinel value denotes the end of a data set, but it is not part of the data.

Whenever you read a sequence of inputs, you need to have some method of indicating the end of the sequence. Sometimes you are lucky and no input value can be zero. Then you can prompt the user to keep entering numbers, or 0 to finish the sequence. If zero is allowed but negative numbers are not, you can use –1 to indicate termination. A value that serves as a signal for termination is called a **sentinel**.

Let's put this technique to work in a program that computes the average of a set of salary values. In our sample program, we will use –1 as a sentinel. An employee would surely not work for a negative salary, but there may be volunteers who work for free.

Inside the loop, we read an input. If the input is not –1, we process it. In order to compute the average, we need the total sum of all salaries, and the number of inputs.

© Rhoberazzi/iStockphoto.

In the military, a sentinel guards a border or passage. In computer science, a sentinel value denotes the end of an input sequence or the border between input sequences.

```
while (. . .)
{
   cin >> salary;
```

```
   if (salary != -1)
   {
      sum = sum + salary;
      count++;
   }
}
```

We stay in the loop while the sentinel value is not detected.

```
while (salary != -1)
{
   . . .
}
```

There is just one problem: When the loop is entered for the first time, no data value has been read. Be sure to initialize salary with some value other than the sentinel:

```
double salary = 0; // Any value other than –1 will do
```

Alternatively, use a do loop

```
do
{
   . . .
}
while (salary != -1)
```

The following program reads inputs until the user enters the sentinel, and then computes and prints the average.

sec05/sentinel.cpp

```
1  #include <iostream>
2
3  using namespace std;
4
5  int main()
6  {
7     double sum = 0;
8     int count = 0;
9     double salary = 0;
10    cout << "Enter salaries, -1 to finish: ";
11    while (salary != -1)
12    {
13       cin >> salary;
14       if (salary != -1)
15       {
16          sum = sum + salary;
17          count++;
18       }
19    }
20    if (count > 0)
21    {
22       double average = sum / count;
23       cout << "Average salary: " << average << endl;
24    }
25    else
26    {
27       cout << "No data" << endl;
28    }
29    return 0;
30 }
```

Program Run

```
Enter salaries, -1 to finish: 10 10 40 -1
Average salary: 20
```

4.5.2 Reading Until Input Fails

Numeric sentinels only work if there is some restriction on the input. In many cases, though, there isn't. Suppose you want to compute the average of a data set that may contain 0 or negative values. Then you cannot use 0 or –1 to indicate the end of the input.

In such a situation, you can read input data until input fails. As you have seen in Section 3.8, the condition

```
cin.fail()
```

is true if the preceding input has failed. For example, suppose that the input was read with these statements:

```
double value;
cin >> value;
```

If the user enters a value that is not a number (such as Q), then the input fails.

We now encounter an additional complexity. You only know that input failed after you have entered the loop and attempted to read it. To remember the failure, use a Boolean variable:

You can use a Boolean variable to control a loop. Set the variable before entering the loop, then set it to the opposite to leave the loop.

```
cout << "Enter values, Q to quit: ";
bool done = false;
while (!done)
{
   cin >> value;
   if (cin.fail())
   {
      done = true;
   }
   else
   {
      Process value.
   }
}
```

Some programmers dislike the introduction of a Boolean variable to control a loop. Special Topic 4.2 shows an alternative mechanism for leaving a loop. However, when reading input, there is an easier way. The expression

```
cin >> value
```

can be used in a condition. It evaluates to true if cin has *not* failed after reading value. Therefore, you can read and process a set of inputs with the following loop:

```
cout << "Enter values, Q to quit: ";
while (cin >> value)
{
   Process value.
}
```

This loop is suitable for processing a single sequence of inputs. You will learn more about reading inputs in Chapter 8.

EXAMPLE CODE   See sec05 of your companion code for a program that uses a Boolean variable to control a loop.

Special Topic 4.1
Clearing the Failure State

When an input operation has failed, all further input operations also fail. Consider the doloop.cpp program in Section 4.4 in which a user is prompted to enter a value that is not negative. Suppose the user enters a value that is not an integer, such as the string zero.

Then the operation

```
cin >> value;
```

sets cin to the failed state. If you want to give the user another chance to enter a value, you need to *clear* the failed state, by calling the clear member function. You also need to read and discard the offending item:

```
cin.clear();
string item;
cin >> item;
```

Now the user can try again. Here is an improved version of the do loop:

```
do
{
    cout << "Enter a number >= 0: ";
    cin >> value;

    if (cin.fail())
    {
        // Clear the failed state
        cin.clear();
        // Read and discard the item
        string item;
        cin >> item;
        // Set to an invalid input
        value = -1;
    }
}
while (value < 0);
```

Note that we set value to an invalid input if the input was not a number, in order to enter the loop once more.

Here is another situation in which you need to clear the failed state. Suppose you read two number sequences, each of which has a letter as a sentinel. You read the first sequence:

```
cout << "Enter values, Q to quit.\n";
while (cin >> values)
{
    Process input.
}
```

Suppose the user has entered 30 10 5 Q. The input of Q has caused the failure. Because only successfully processed characters are removed from the input, the Q character is still present. Clear the stream and read the sentinel into a string variable:

```
cin.clear();
string sentinel;
cin >> sentinel;
```

Now you can go on and read more inputs.

Special Topic 4.2

The Loop-and-a-Half Problem and the break Statement

Some programmers dislike loops that are controlled by a Boolean variable, such as:

```
bool done = false;
while (!done)
{
    cin >> value;
    if (cin.fail())
    {
        done = true;
    }
    else
    {
        Process value.
    }
}
```

The actual test for loop termination is in the middle of the loop, not at the top. This is called a **loop and a half** because one must go halfway into the loop before knowing whether one needs to terminate.

As an alternative, you can use the break reserved word:

```
while (true)
{
    cin >> value;
    if (cin.fail()) { break; }
    Process value.
}
```

The break statement breaks out of the enclosing loop, independent of the loop condition.

In the loop-and-a-half case, break statements can be beneficial. But it is difficult to lay down clear rules as to when they are safe and when they should be avoided. We do not use the break statement in this book.

Special Topic 4.3

Redirection of Input and Output

Consider the sentinel.cpp program that computes the average value of an input sequence. If you use such a program, then it is quite likely that you already have the values in a file, and it seems a shame that you have to type them all in again. The command line interface of your operating system provides a way to link a file to the input of a program, as if all the characters in the file had actually been typed by a user. If you type

```
sentinel < numbers.txt
```

the program is executed. Its input instructions no longer expect input from the keyboard. All input commands get their input from the file numbers.txt. This process is called *input redirection*.

> Use input redirection to read input from a file. Use output redirection to capture program output in a file.

Input redirection is an excellent tool for testing programs. When you develop a program and fix its bugs, it is boring to keep entering the same input every time you run the program. Spend a few minutes putting the inputs into a file, and use redirection.

You can also redirect output. In this program, that is not terribly useful. If you run

```
sentinel < numbers.txt > output.txt
```

the file output.txt contains the input prompts and the output, such as

```
Enter salaries, -1 to finish:
Average salary: 15
```

However, redirecting output is obviously useful for programs that produce lots of output. You can print the file containing the output or edit it before you turn it in for grading.

4.6 Problem Solving: Storyboards

When you design a program that interacts with a user, you need to make a plan for that interaction. What information does the user provide, and in which order? What information will your program display, and in which format? What should happen when there is an error? When does the program quit?

A storyboard consists of annotated sketches for each step in an action sequence.

This planning is similar to the development of a movie or a computer game, where *storyboards* are used to plan action sequences. A storyboard is made up of panels that show a sketch of each step. Annotations explain what is happening and note any special situations. Storyboards are also used to develop software—see Figure 6.

Developing a storyboard helps you understand the inputs and outputs that are required for a program.

Making a storyboard is very helpful when you begin designing a program. You need to ask yourself which information you need in order to compute the answers that the program user wants. You need to decide how to present those answers. These are important considerations that you want to settle before you design an algorithm for computing the answers.

Let's look at a simple example. We want to write a program that helps users with questions such as "How many tablespoons are in a pint?" or "How many inches are 30 centimeters?"

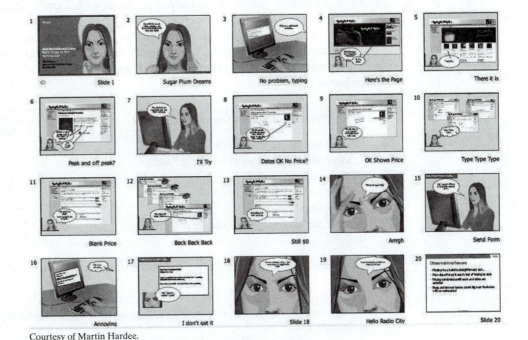

Courtesy of Martin Hardee.

Figure 6   Storyboard for the Design of a Web Application

What information does the user provide?

- The quantity and unit to convert from
- The unit to convert to

What if there is more than one quantity? A user may have a whole table of centimeter values that should be converted into inches.

What if the user enters units that our program doesn't know how to handle, such as ångström?

What if the user asks for impossible conversions, such as inches to gallons?

Let's get started with a storyboard panel. It is a good idea to write the user inputs in a different color. (Underline them if you don't have a color pen handy.)

Converting a Sequence of Values

What unit do you want to convert from? cm
What unit do you want to convert to? in
Enter values, terminated by zero ————— *Allows conversion of multiple values*
30
30 cm = 11.81 in ——
100   ———— *Format makes clear what got converted*
100 cm = 39.37 in
0
What unit do you want to convert from?

The storyboard shows how we deal with a potential confusion. A user who wants to know how many inches are 30 centimeters may not read the first prompt carefully and specify inches. But then the output is "30 in = 76.2 cm", alerting the user to the problem.

The storyboard also raises an issue. How is the user supposed to know that "cm" and "in" are valid units? Would "centimeter" and "inches" also work? What happens when the user enters a wrong unit? Let's make another storyboard to demonstrate error handling.

Handling Unknown Units (needs improvement)

What unit do you want to convert from? cm
What unit do you want to convert to? inches
Sorry, unknown unit.
What unit do you want to convert to? inch
Sorry, unknown unit.
What unit do you want to convert to? grr

To eliminate frustration, it is better to list the units that the user can supply.

From unit (in, ft, mi, mm, cm, m, km, oz, lb, g, kg, tsp, tbsp, pint, gal): cm
To unit: in ——
              ———— *No need to list the units again*

We switched to a shorter prompt to make room for all the unit names. Exercise R4.24 explores a different alternative.

There is another issue that we haven't addressed yet. How does the user quit the program? The first storyboard gives the impression that the program will go on forever.

We can ask the user after seeing the sentinel that terminates an input sequence.

Exiting the Program

From unit (in, ft, mi, mm, cm, m, km, oz, lb, g, kg, tsp, tbsp, pint, gal): cm
To unit: in
Enter values, terminated by zero
30
30 cm = 11.81 in ——————————— *Sentinel triggers the prompt to exit*
0
More conversions (y, n)? n
(Program exits)

As you can see from this case study, a storyboard is essential for developing a working program. You need to know the flow of the user interaction in order to structure your program.

4.7 Common Loop Algorithms

In the following sections, we discuss some of the most common algorithms that are implemented as loops. You can use them as starting points for your loop designs.

4.7.1 Sum and Average Value

Computing the sum of a number of inputs is a very common task. Keep a *running total:* a variable to which you add each input value. Of course, the total should be initialized with 0.

```
double total = 0;
double input;
while (cin >> input)
{
    total = total + input;
}
```

To compute an average, count how many values you have, and divide by the count. Be sure to check that the count is not zero.

> To compute an average, keep a total and a count of all values.

```
double total = 0;
int count = 0;
double input;
while (cin >> input)
{
    total = total + input;
    count++;
}
double average = 0;
if (count > 0) { average = total / count; }
```

4.7.2 Counting Matches

You often want to know how many values fulfill a particular condition. For example, you may want to count how many spaces are in a string. Keep a counter, a variable that is initialized with 0 and incremented whenever there is a match.

> To count values that fulfill a condition, check all values and increment a counter for each match.

```
int spaces = 0;
for (int i = 0; i < str.length(); i++)
{
    string ch = str.substr(i, 1);
    if (ch == " ")
    {
        spaces++;
    }
}
```

For example, if str is the string "My Fair Lady", spaces is incremented twice (when i is 2 and 7).

Note that the spaces variable is declared outside the loop. We want the loop to update a single variable. The ch variable is declared inside the loop. A separate variable is created for each iteration and removed at the end of each loop iteration.

This loop can also be used for scanning inputs. The following loop reads text, a word at a time, and counts the number of words with at most three letters:

```
int short_words = 0;
string input;
while (cin >> input)
{
    if (input.length() <= 3)
    {
        short_words++;
    }
}
```

© Hiob/iStockphoto.

In a loop that counts matches, a counter is incremented whenever a match is found.

4.7.3 Finding the First Match

> If your goal is to find a match, exit the loop when the match is found

When you count the values that fulfill a condition, you need to look at all values. However, if your task is to find a match, then you can stop as soon as the condition is fulfilled.

Here is a loop that finds the first space in a string. Because we do not visit all elements in the string, a while loop is a better choice than a for loop:

```
bool found = false;
int position = 0;
while (!found && position < str.length())
{
    string ch = str.substr(position, 1);
    if (ch == " ") { found = true; }
```

© drflet/iStockphoto.

When searching, you look at items until a match is found.

```
    else { position++; }
}
```

If a match was found, then `found` is `true` and `position` is the index of the first match. If the loop did not find a match, then `found` remains `false` after the end of the loop.

Note that the variable `position` is declared *outside* the `while` loop because you may want to use it after the loop has finished.

4.7.4 Prompting Until a Match is Found

In the preceding example, we searched a string for a character that matches a condition. You can apply the same process for user input. Suppose you are asking a user to enter a positive value < 100. Keep asking until the user provides a correct input:

```
bool valid = false;
double input;
while (!valid)
{
    cout << "Please enter a positive value < 100: ";
    cin >> input;
    if (0 < input && input < 100) { valid = true; }
    else { cout << "Invalid input." << endl; }
}
```

Note that the variable `input` is declared *outside* the `while` loop because you will want to use the input after the loop has finished. If it had been declared inside the loop body, you would not be able to use it outside the loop.

4.7.5 Maximum and Minimum

To find the largest value, update the largest value seen so far whenever you see a larger one.

To compute the largest value in a sequence, keep a variable that stores the largest element that you have encountered, and update it when you find a larger one:

```
double largest;
cin >> largest;
double input;
while (cin >> input)
{
    if (input > largest)
    {
        largest = input;
    }
}
```

This algorithm requires that there is at least one input.

To compute the smallest value, simply reverse the comparison:

```
double smallest;
cin >> smallest;
double input;
while (cin >> input)
{
```

© CEFutcher/iStockphoto.

To find the height of the tallest bus rider, remember the largest value so far, and update it whenever you see a taller one.

```
if (input < smallest)
{
    smallest = input;
}
}
```

4.7.6 Comparing Adjacent Values

When processing a sequence of values in a loop, you sometimes need to compare a value with the value that just preceded it. For example, suppose you want to check whether a sequence of inputs contains adjacent duplicates such as 1 7 2 9 9 4 9.

Now you face a challenge. Consider the typical loop for reading a value:

```
double input;
while (cin >> input)
{
    // Now input contains the current input
    . . .
}
```

To compare adjacent inputs, store the preceding input in a variable.

How can you compare the current input with the preceding one? At any time, input contains the current input, overwriting the previous one.

The answer is to store the previous input, like this:

```
double input;
double previous;
while (cin >> input)
{
    if (input == previous) { cout << "Duplicate input" << endl; }
    previous = input;
}
```

One problem remains. When the loop is entered for the first time, previous has not yet been set. You can solve this problem with an initial input operation outside the loop:

```
double input;
double previous;
cin >> previous;
while (cin >> input)
{
    if (input == previous) { cout << "Duplicate input" << endl; }
    previous = input;
}
```

When comparing adjacent values, store the previous value in a variable. © tingberg/iStockphoto.

EXAMPLE CODE   See sec07 of your companion code for a program that demonstrates common loop algorithms.

HOW TO 4.1

Writing a Loop

This How To walks you through the process of implementing a loop statement. We will illustrate the steps with the following example problem:

Problem Statement Read twelve temperature values (one for each month), and display the number of the month with the highest temperature. For example, according to `http://worldclimate.com`, the average maximum temperatures for Death Valley are (in order by month):

18.2 22.6 26.4 31.1 36.6 42.2
45.7 44.5 40.2 33.1 24.2 17.6

In this case, the month with the highest temperature (45.7 degrees Celsius) is July, and the program should display 7.

© Stevegeer/iStockphoto.

Step 1 Decide what work must be done *inside* the loop.

Every loop needs to do some kind of repetitive work, such as

- Reading another item.
- Updating a value (such as a bank balance or total).
- Incrementing a counter.

If you can't figure out what needs to go inside the loop, start by writing down the steps that you would take if you solved the problem by hand. For example, with the temperature reading problem, you might write

> *Read the first value.*
> *Read the second value.*
> *If the second value is higher than the first value*
>   *Set highest temperature to the second value.*
>   *Set highest month to 2.*
> *Read the next value.*
> *If the value is higher than the first and second values*
>   *Set highest temperature to the value.*
>   *Set highest month to 3.*
> *Read the next value.*
> *If the value is higher than the highest temperature seen so far*
>   *Set highest temperature to the value.*
>   *Set highest month to 4.*
>
>   . . .

Now look at these steps and reduce them to a set of *uniform* actions that can be placed into the loop body. The first action is easy:

> *Read the next value.*

The next action is trickier. In our description, we used tests "higher than the first", "higher than the first and second", "higher than the highest temperature seen so far". We need to settle on one test that works for all iterations. The last formulation is the most general.

Similarly, we must find a general way of setting the highest month. We need a variable that stores the current month, running from 1 to 12. Then we can formulate the second loop action:

If the value is higher than the highest temperature
    Set highest temperature to the value.
    Set highest month to current month.

Altogether our loop is

While . . .
    Read the next value.
    If the value is higher than the highest temperature
        Set the highest temperature to the value.
        Set highest month to current month.
    Increment current month.

Step 2   Specify the loop condition.

What goal do you want to reach in your loop? Typical examples are:

- Has the counter reached the final value?
- Have you read the last input value?
- Has a value reached a given threshold?

In our example, we simply want the current month to reach 12.

Step 3   Determine the loop type.

We distinguish between two major loop types. A *count-controlled* loop is executed a definite number of times. In an *event-controlled* loop, the number of iterations is not known in advance—the loop is executed until some event happens.

Count-controlled loops can be implemented as for statements. For other loops, consider the loop condition. Do you need to complete one iteration of the loop body before you can tell when to terminate the loop? In that case, choose a do loop. Otherwise, use a while loop.

Sometimes, the condition for terminating a loop changes in the middle of the loop body. In that case, you can use a Boolean variable that specifies when you are ready to leave the loop. Such a variable is called a **flag**. Follow this pattern:

```
bool done = false;
while (!done)
{
    Do some work.
    If all work has been completed
    {
        done = true;
    }
    else
    {
        Do more work.
    }
}
```

In summary,

- If you know in advance how many times a loop is repeated, use a for loop.
- If the loop body must be executed at least once, use a do loop.
- Otherwise, use a while loop.

In our example, we read 12 temperature values. Therefore, we choose a for loop.

Step 4 Set up variables for entering the loop for the first time.

List all variables that are used and updated in the loop, and determine how to initialize them. Commonly, counters are initialized with 0 or 1, totals with 0.

In our example, the variables are

current month
highest value
highest month

We need to be careful how we set up the highest temperature value. We can't simply set it to 0. After all, our program needs to work with temperature values from Antarctica, all of which may be negative.

A good option is to set the highest temperature value to the first input value. Of course, then we need to remember to only read in another 11 values, with the current month starting at 2.

We also need to initialize the highest month with 1. After all, in an Australian city, we may never find a month that is warmer than January.

Step 5 Process the result after the loop has finished.

In many cases, the desired result is simply a variable that was updated in the loop body. For example, in our temperature program, the result is the highest month. Sometimes, the loop computes values that contribute to the final result. For example, suppose you are asked to average the temperatures. Then the loop should compute the sum, not the average. After the loop has completed, you are ready to compute the average: divide the sum by the number of inputs.

Here is our complete loop:

Read value.
highest temperature = value
highest month = 1
For current month from 2 to 12
    Read next value.
    If the value is higher than the highest temperature
        Set highest temperature to the value.
        Set highest month to current month.

Step 6 Trace the loop with typical examples.

Hand-trace your loop code, as described in Section 4.2. Choose example values that are not too complex—executing the loop 3–5 times is enough to check for the most common errors. Pay special attention when entering the loop for the first and last time.

Sometimes, you want to make a slight modification to make tracing feasible. For example, when hand-tracing the investment doubling problem, use an interest rate of 20 percent rather than 5 percent. When hand-tracing the temperature loop, use 4 data values, not 12.

Let's say the data are 22.6 36.6 44.5 24.2. Here is the walkthrough:

current month	current value	highest month	highest value
		~~1~~	~~22.6~~
~~2~~	36.6	~~2~~	~~36.6~~
~~3~~	44.5	3	44.5
4	24.2		

The trace demonstrates that *highest month* and *highest value* are properly set.

Step 7 Implement the loop in C++.

Here's the loop for our example. Exercise E4.4 asks you to complete the program.

```cpp
double highest_value;
cin >> highest_value;
int highest_month = 1;
for (int current_month = 2; current_month <= 12; current_month++)
{
   double next_value;
   cin >> next_value;
   if (next_value > highest_value)
   {
      highest_value = next_value;
      highest_month = current_month;
   }
}
cout << highest_month << endl;
```

WORKED EXAMPLE 4.1
Credit Card Processing

Learn how to use a loop to remove spaces from a credit card number. See your E-Text or visit wiley.com/go/bclo3.

© MorePixels/iStockphoto.

4.8 Nested Loops

When the body of a loop contains another loop, the loops are nested. A typical use of nested loops is printing a table with rows and columns.

In Section 3.4, you saw how to nest two if statements. Similarly, complex iterations sometimes require a **nested loop**: a loop inside another loop statement. When processing tables, nested loops occur naturally. An outer loop iterates over all rows of the table. An inner loop deals with the columns in the current row.

In this section you will see how to print a table. For simplicity, we will simply print powers x^n, as in the table below.

Here is the pseudocode for printing the table:

Print table header.
For x from 1 to 10
    Print table row.
    Print endl.

How do you print a table row? You need to print a value for each exponent. This requires a second loop:

For n from 1 to 4
    Print x^n.

This loop must be placed inside the preceding loop.

x^1	x^2	x^3	x^4
1	1	1	1
2	4	8	16
3	9	27	81
...	...	...	...
10	100	1000	10000

The hour and minute displays in a digital clock are an example of nested loops. The hours loop 12 times, and for each hour, the minutes loop 60 times.

© davejkahn/iStockphoto.

We say that the inner loop is *nested* inside the outer loop (see Figure 7).

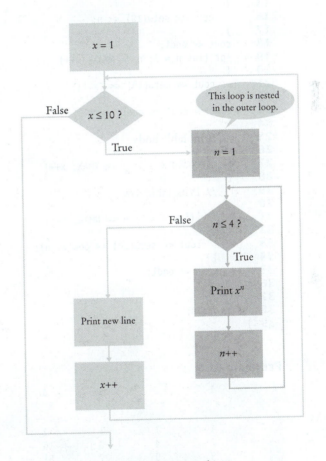

Figure 7 Flowchart of a Nested Loop

There are 10 rows in the outer loop. For each x, the program prints four columns in the inner loop. Thus, a total of $10 \times 4 = 40$ values are printed.

Following is the complete program. Note that we also use loops to print the table header. However, those loops are not nested.

128 Chapter 4 Loops

sec08/powtable.cpp

```cpp
1  #include <iostream>
2  #include <iomanip>
3  #include <cmath>
4
5  using namespace std;
6
7  int main()
8  {
9     const int NMAX = 4;
10    const double XMAX = 10;
11
12    // Print table header
13
14    for (int n = 1; n <= NMAX; n++)
15    {
16       cout << setw(10) << n;
17    }
18    cout << endl;
19    for (int n = 1; n <= NMAX; n++)
20    {
21       cout << setw(10) << "x ";
22    }
23    cout << endl << endl;
24
25    // Print table body
26
27    for (double x = 1; x <= XMAX; x++)
28    {
29       // Print table row
30
31       for (int n = 1; n <= NMAX; n++)
32       {
33          cout << setw(10) << pow(x, n);
34       }
35       cout << endl;
36    }
37
38    return 0;
39 }
```

Program Run

```
         1         2         3         4
         x         x         x         x

         1         1         1         1
         2         4         8        16
         3         9        27        81
         4        16        64       256
         5        25       125       625
         6        36       216      1296
         7        49       343      2401
         8        64       512      4096
         9        81       729      6561
        10       100      1000     10000
```

Table 3 Nested Loop Examples

Nested Loops	Output	Explanation
```cpp\nfor (i = 1; i <= 3; i++)\n{\n for (j = 1; j <= 4; j++) { cout << "*"; }\n cout << endl;\n}\n```	```\n****\n****\n****\n```	Prints 3 rows of 4 asterisks each.
```cpp\nfor (i = 1; i <= 4; i++)\n{\n for (j = 1; j <= 3; j++) { cout << "*"; }\n cout << endl;\n}\n```	```\n***\n***\n***\n***\n```	Prints 4 rows of 3 asterisks each.
```cpp\nfor (i = 1; i <= 4; i++)\n{\n for (j = 1; j <= i; j++) { cout << "*"; }\n cout << endl;\n}\n```	```\n*\n**\n***\n****\n```	Prints 4 rows of lengths 1, 2, 3, and 4.
```cpp\nfor (i = 1; i <= 3; i++)\n{\n for (j = 1; j <= 5; j++)\n {\n if (j % 2 == 0) { cout << "*"; }\n else { cout << "-"; }\n }\n cout << endl;\n}\n```	```\n-*-*-\n-*-*-\n-*-*-\n```	Prints asterisks in even columns, dashes in odd columns.
```cpp\nfor (i = 1; i <= 3; i++)\n{\n for (j = 1; j <= 5; j++)\n {\n if ((i + j) % 2 == 0) { cout << "*"; }\n else { cout << " "; }\n }\n cout << endl;\n}\n```	```\n* * *\n * *\n* * *\n```	Prints a checkerboard pattern.

WORKED EXAMPLE 4.2

Manipulating the Pixels in an Image

Learn how to use nested loops for manipulating the pixels in an image. The outer loop traverses the rows of the image, and the inner loop accesses each pixel of a row. See your E-Text or visit wiley.com/go/bclo3.

Cay Horstmann.

4.9 Problem Solving: Solve a Simpler Problem First

When developing a solution to a complex problem, first solve a simpler task.

As you learn more about programming, the complexity of the tasks that you are asked to solve will increase. When you face a complex task, you should apply an important skill: simplifying the problem, and solving the simpler problem first.

This is a good strategy for several reasons. Usually, you learn something useful from solving the simpler task. Moreover, the complex problem can seem unsurmountable, and you may find it difficult to know where to get started. When you are successful with a simpler problem first, you will be much more motivated to try the harder one.

It takes practice and a certain amount of courage to break down a problem into a sequence of simpler ones. The best way to learn this strategy is to practice it. When you work on your next assignment, ask yourself what is the absolutely simplest part of the task that is helpful for the end result, and start from there. With some experience, you will be able to design a plan that builds up a complete solution as a manageable sequence of intermediate steps.

Let us look at an example. You are asked to arrange pictures, lining them up along the top edges, separating them with small gaps, and starting a new row whenever you run out of room in the current row.

National Gallery of Art (see Credits page for details.)

We use the `Picture` type of Worked Example 4.2. The `add` member function can be used to add one picture to another:

```
pic.add(pic2, x, y);
```

The second picture is added so that its top-left corner is at the given x and y position. The original picture grows to hold all pixels of the added picture. We will use this member function repeatedly in order to build up the result.

Instead of tackling the entire assignment at once, here is a plan that solves a series of simpler problems.

Make a plan consisting of a series of tasks, each a simple extension of the previous one, and ending with the original problem.

1. Draw one picture.

2. Draw two pictures next to each other.

3. Draw two pictures with a gap between them.

4. Draw all pictures in a long row.

5. Draw a row of pictures until you run out of room, then put one more picture in the next row.

Let's get started with this plan.

1. The purpose of the first step is to become familiar with the Picture type. As it turns out, the pictures are in files a.png ... t.png. Let's load the first one:

```
Picture pic("a.png");
pic.save("gallery.png");
```

That's enough to produce the picture.

2. Now let's put the next picture after the first. We need to position it at the rightmost x-coordinate of the preceding picture.

```
Picture pic("a.png");
Picture pic2("b.png");
pic.add(pic2, pic.width(), 0);
```

3. The next step is to separate the two by a small gap when the second is added:

pic.width()

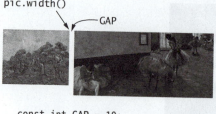

GAP

```
const int GAP = 10;

Picture pic("a.png");
Picture pic2("b.png");
pic.add(pic2, pic.width() + GAP, 0);
```

4. Now let's put all pictures in a row. Read the pictures in a loop, and then put each picture to the right of the one that preceded it. In the loop, you need to track the *x*-coordinate at which the next image should be inserted.

x   pic2

```
const int GAP = 10;
const string names = "abcdefghijklmnopqrst";
const int PICTURES = names.length();

Picture pic("a.png");
int x = pic.width() + GAP;
for (int i = 1; i < PICTURES; i++)
{
   Picture pic2(names.substr(i, 1) + ".png");
   pic.add(pic2, x, 0);
   x = x + pic2.width() + GAP;
}
```

5. Of course, we don't want to have all pictures in a row. The right margin of a picture should not extend past MAX_WIDTH.

```
if (x + pic.width() < MAX_WIDTH)
{
   Place pic on current row.
}
else
{
   Place pic on next row.
}
```

If the image doesn't fit any more, then we need to put it on the next row, below all the pictures in the current row. We'll set a variable max_y to the maximum *y*-coordinate of all placed pictures, updating it whenever a new picture is placed:

```
if (pic2.height() > max_y)
{
   max_y = pic2.height();
}
```

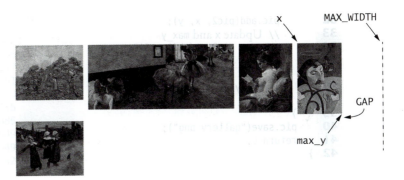

The following statement places a picture on the next row:

```cpp
pic.add(pic2, 0, max_y + GAP);
```

Now we have written complete programs for all preliminary stages. We know how to line up the pictures, how to separate them with gaps, how to find out when to start a new row, and where to start it.

EXAMPLE CODE See sec09 of your companion code for the preliminary stages of the gallery program.

With this knowledge, producing the final version is straightforward. Here is the program listing.

sec09/gallery6.cpp

```cpp
1  #include "picture.h"
2  #include <string>
3
4  using namespace std;
5
6  int main()
7  {
8     const int MAX_WIDTH = 720;
9     const int GAP = 10;
10    const string names = "abcdefghijklmnopqrst";
11    const int PICTURES = names.length();
12
13    // Read the first picture
14    Picture pic("a.png");
15
16    // x and y are the top-left corner of the next picture
17    int x = pic.width() + GAP;
18    int y = 0;
19
20    // max_y is the largest y encountered so far
21    int max_y = pic.height();
22    for (int i = 1; i < PICTURES; i++)
23    {
24       // Read the next picture
25       Picture pic2(names.substr(i, 1) + ".png");
26       if (x + pic2.width() >= MAX_WIDTH) // The picture doesn't fit on the row
27       {
28          // Place the picture on the next row
29          x = 0;
30          y = max_y + GAP;
31       }
```

```
27      @param number an integer between 10 and 19
28      @return the name of the given number ("ten" ... "nineteen")
29   */
30   string teen_name(int number)
31   {
32      if (number == 10) return "ten";
33      if (number == 11) return "eleven";
34      if (number == 12) return "twelve";
35      if (number == 13) return "thirteen";
36      if (number == 14) return "fourteen";
37      if (number == 15) return "fifteen";
38      if (number == 16) return "sixteen";
39      if (number == 17) return "seventeen";
40      if (number == 18) return "eighteen";
41      if (number == 19) return "nineteen";
42      return "";
43   }
44
45   /**
46      Gives the name of the tens part of a number between 20 and 99.
47      @param number an integer between 20 and 99
48      @return the name of the tens part of the number ("twenty" ... "ninety")
49   */
50   string tens_name(int number)
51   {
52      if (number >= 90) return "ninety";
53      if (number >= 80) return "eighty";
54      if (number >= 70) return "seventy";
55      if (number >= 60) return "sixty";
56      if (number >= 50) return "fifty";
57      if (number >= 40) return "forty";
58      if (number >= 30) return "thirty";
59      if (number >= 20) return "twenty";
60      return "";
61   }
62
63   /**
64      Turns a number into its English name.
65      @param number a positive integer < 1,000
66      @return the name of the number (e.g. "two hundred seventy four")
67   */
68   string int_name(int number)
69   {
70      int part = number; // The part that still needs to be converted
71      string name; // The return value
72
73      if (part >= 100)
74      {
75         name = digit_name(part / 100) + " hundred";
76         part = part % 100;
77      }
78
79      if (part >= 20)
80      {
81         name = name + " " + tens_name(part);
82         part = part % 10;
83      }
84      else if (part >= 10)
85      {
```

```
86          name = name + " " + teen_name(part);
87          part = 0;
88      }
89
90      if (part > 0)
91      {
92          name = name + " " + digit_name(part);
93      }
94
95      return name;
96 }
97
98 int main()
99 {
100     cout << "Please enter a positive integer: ";
101     int input;
102     cin >> input;
103     cout << int_name(input) << endl;
104     return 0;
105 }
```

Program Run

```
Please enter a positive integer: 729
seven hundred twenty nine
```

Programming Tip 5.3
Keep Functions Short

There is a certain cost for writing a function. You need to design, code, and test the function. The function needs to be documented. You need to spend some effort to make the function reusable rather than tied to a specific context. To avoid this cost, it is always tempting just to stuff more and more code in one place rather than going through the trouble of breaking up the code into separate functions. It is quite common to see inexperienced programmers produce functions that are several hundred lines long.

As a rule of thumb, a function that is so long that its code will not fit on a single screen in your development environment should probably be broken up.

Programming Tip 5.4
Tracing Functions

When you design a complex set of functions, it is a good idea to carry out a manual **walk-through** before entrusting your program to the computer.

Take an index card, or some other piece of paper, and write down the function call that you want to study. Write the name of the function and the names and values of the parameter variables, like this:

> int_name(number = 416)

Then write the names and initial values of the function variables. Write them in a table, since you will update them as you walk through the code.

int_name(number = 416)	
part	name
416	""

We enter the test `part >= 100`. `part / 100` is 4 and `part % 100` is 16. `digit_name(4)` is easily seen to be `"four"`. (Had `digit_name` been complicated, you would have started another sheet of paper to figure out that function call. It is quite common to accumulate several sheets in this way.)

Now `name` has changed to `name + " " + digit_name(part / 100) + " hundred"`, that is `"four hun-dred"`, and `part` has changed to `part % 100`, or 16.

int_name(number = 416)	
part	name
~~416~~	~~""~~
16	"four hundred"

Now you enter the branch `part >= 10`. `teen_name(16)` is sixteen, so the variables now have the values

int_name(number = 416)	
part	name
~~416~~	~~""~~
~~16~~	~~"four hundred"~~
0	"four hundred sixteen"

Now it becomes clear why you need to set `part` to 0 in line 87. Otherwise, you would enter the next branch and the result would be `"four hundred sixteen six"`. Tracing the code is an effective way to understand the subtle aspects of a function.

Programming Tip 5.5
Stubs

When writing a larger program, it is not always feasible to implement and test all functions at once. You often need to test a function that calls another, but the other function hasn't yet been implemented. Then you can temporarily replace the missing function with a **stub**. A stub is a function that returns a simple value that is sufficient for testing another function. Here are examples of stub functions:

```
/**
    Turns a digit into its English name.
    @param digit an integer between 1 and 9
    @return the name of digit ("one" ... "nine")
```

```
    */
    string digit_name(int digit)
    {
        return "mumble";
    }

    /**
        Gives the name of the tens part of a number between 20 and 99.
        @param number  an integer between 20 and 99
        @return  the tens name of the number ("twenty" ... "ninety")
    */
    string tens_name(int number)
    {
        return "mumblety";
    }
```

If you combine these stubs with the int_name function and test it with an argument of 274, you will get a result of "mumble hundred mumblety mumble", which indicates that the basic logic of the int_name function is working correctly.

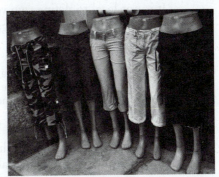
© lillisphotography/iStockphoto.

Stubs are incomplete functions that can be used for testing.

WORKED EXAMPLE 5.3

Calculating a Course Grade

Learn how to use stepwise refinement to solve the problem of converting a set of letter grades into an average grade for a course. See your E-Text or visit wiley.com/go/bclo3.

© paul kline/iStockphoto.

5.8 Variable Scope and Global Variables

> The scope of a variable is the part of the program in which it is visible.

It is possible to define the same variable name more than once in a program. When the variable name is used, you need to know to which definition it belongs. In this section, we discuss the rules for dealing with multiple definitions of the same name.

A variable that is defined within a function is visible from the point at which it is defined until the end of the block in which it was defined. This area is called the **scope** of the variable.

Consider the `volume` variables in the following example:

```cpp
double cube_volume(double side_length)
{
   double volume = side_length * side_length * side_length;
   return volume;
}

int main()
{
   double volume = cube_volume(2);
   cout << volume << endl;

   return 0;
}
```

Each `volume` variable is defined in a separate function, and their scopes do not overlap.

It is not legal to define two variables with the same name in the same scope. For example, the following is *not* legal:

```cpp
int main()
{
   double volume = cube_volume(2);
   double volume = cube_volume(10);
      // ERROR: cannot define another volume variable in this scope
   . . .
}
```

However, you can define another variable with the same name in a **nested block**. Here, we define two variables called `amount`.

```cpp
double withdraw(double balance, double amount)
{
   if (. . .)
   {
      double amount = 10; // Another variable named amount
      . . .
   }
   . . .
}
```

© jchamp/iStockphoto (Railway and Main); © StevenCarrieJohnson/iStockphoto (Main and N. Putnam); © jsmith/iStockphoto (Main and South St.).

In the same way that there can be a street named "Main Street" in different cities, a C++ program can have multiple variables with the same name.

A variable in a nested block shadows a variable with the same name in an outer block.

A local variable is defined inside a function. A global variable is defined outside a function.

The scope of the parameter variable amount is the entire function, *except* inside the nested block. Inside the nested block, amount refers to the variable that was defined in that block. We say that the inner variable *shadows* the variable that is defined in the outer block. You should avoid this potentially confusing situation in the functions that you write, simply by renaming one of the variables.

Variables that are defined inside functions are called **local variables**. C++ also supports **global variables**: variables that are defined outside functions. A global variable is visible to all functions that are defined after it. For example, the `<iostream>` header defines global variables cin and cout.

Here is an example of a global variable:

```cpp
int balance = 10000; // A global variable

void withdraw(double amount)
{
   if (balance >= amount)
   {
      balance = balance - amount;
   }
}

int main()
{
   withdraw(1000);
   cout << balance << endl;
   return 0;
}
```

The scope of the variable balance extends over both the withdraw and the main functions.

Avoid global variables in your programs.

Generally, global variables are not a good idea. When multiple functions update global variables, the result can be difficult to predict. Particularly in larger programs that are developed by multiple programmers, it is very important that the effect of each function be clear and easy to understand. You should avoid global variables in your programs.

Programming Tip 5.6
Avoid Global Variables

There are a few cases where global variables are required (such as cin and cout), but they are quite rare. Programs with global variables are difficult to maintain and extend because you can no longer view each function as a "black box" that simply receives arguments and returns a result. When functions modify global variables, it becomes more difficult to understand the effect of function calls. As programs get larger, this difficulty mounts quickly. Instead of using global variables, use function parameters to transfer information from one part of a program to another.

5.9 Reference Parameters

If you want to write a function that changes the value of an argument, you must use a **reference parameter** in order to allow the change. We first explain why a different parameter type is necessary, then we show you the syntax for reference parameters.

Step 2 Combine solutions with simpler inputs into a solution of the original problem.

> When designing a recursive solution, do not worry about multiple nested calls. Simply focus on reducing a problem to a slightly simpler one.

In your mind, consider the solutions for the simpler inputs that you have discovered in Step 1. Don't worry *how* those solutions are obtained. Simply have faith that the solutions are readily available. Just say to yourself: These are simpler inputs, so someone else will solve the problem for me.

In the case of the digit sum task, ask yourself how you can obtain digit_sum(1729) if you know digit_sum(172). You simply add the last digit (9), and you are done. How do you get the last digit? As the remainder n % 10. The value digit_sum(n) can therefore be obtained as

```
digit_sum(n / 10) + n % 10
```

Don't worry how digit_sum(n / 10) is computed. The input is smaller, and therefore it just works.

Step 3 Find solutions to the simplest inputs.

A recursive computation keeps simplifying its inputs. To make sure that the recursion comes to a stop, you must deal with the simplest inputs separately. Come up with special solutions for them. That is usually very easy.

Look at the simplest inputs for the digit_sum test:

- A number with a single digit
- 0

A number with a single digit is its own digit sum, so you can stop the recursion when n < 10, and return n in that case. Or, if you prefer, you can be even lazier. If n has a single digit, then digit_sum(n / 10) + n % 10 equals digit_sum(0) + n. You can simply terminate the recursion when n is zero.

Step 4 Implement the solution by combining the simple cases and the reduction step.

Now you are ready to implement the solution. Make separate cases for the simple inputs that you considered in Step 3. If the input isn't one of the simplest cases, then implement the logic you discovered in Step 2.

Here is the complete digit_sum function:

```cpp
int digit_sum(int n)
{
   // Special case for terminating the recursion
   if (n == 0) { return 0; }
   // General case
   return digit_sum(n / 10) + n % 10;
}
```

Computing & Society 5.1 **The Explosive Growth of Personal Computers**

In 1971, Marcian E. "Ted" Hoff, an engineer at Intel Corporation, was working on a chip for a manufacturer of electronic calculators. He realized that it would be a better idea to develop a *general-purpose* chip that could be *programmed* to interface with the keys and display of a calculator, rather than to do yet another custom design. Thus, the *microprocessor* was born. At the time, its primary application was

as a controller for calculators, washing machines, and the like. It took years for the computer industry to notice that a genuine central processing unit was now available as a single chip.

Hobbyists were the first to catch on. In 1974 the first computer *kit*, the Altair 8800, was available from MITS Electronics for about $350. The kit consisted of the microprocessor, a circuit board, a very small amount of memory, toggle switches, and a row of

display lights. Purchasers had to solder and assemble it, then program it in machine language through the toggle switches. It was not a big hit.

The first big hit was the Apple II. It was a real computer with a keyboard, a monitor, and a floppy disk drive. When it was first released, users had a $3,000 machine that could play Space Invaders, run a primitive bookkeeping program, or let users program it in BASIC. The original Apple II did not even support lowercase letters, making it worthless for word processing. The breakthrough came in 1979 with a new spreadsheet program, VisiCalc. In a spreadsheet, you enter financial data and their relationships into a grid of rows and columns (see the figure). Then you modify some of the data and watch in real time how the others change. For example, you can see how changing the mix of widgets in a manufacturing plant might affect estimated costs and profits. Corporate managers snapped up VisiCalc and the computer that was needed to run it. For them, the computer was a spreadsheet machine.

More importantly, it was a personal device. The managers were free to do the calculations that they wanted to do, not just the ones that the "high priests" in the data center provided.

Personal computers have been with us ever since, and countless users have tinkered with their hardware and software, sometimes establishing highly successful companies or creating free software for millions of users. This "freedom to tinker" is an important part of personal computing. On a personal device, you should be able to install the software that you want to install to make you more productive or creative, even if that's not the same software that most people use. You should be able to add peripheral equipment of your choice. For the first thirty years of personal computing, this freedom was largely taken for granted.

We are now entering an era where smart phones, tablets, and smart TV sets are replacing functions that were traditionally fulfilled by personal computers. While it is amazing to carry more computing power in your cell phone than in the best personal computers of the 1990s, it is disturbing that we lose a degree of personal control. With some phone or tablet brands, you can install only those applications that the manufacturer publishes on the "app store". For example, Apple rejected MIT's iPad app for the educational language Scratch because it contained a virtual machine. You'd think it would be in Apple's interest to encourage the next generation to be enthusiastic about programming, but they have a general policy of denying programmability on "their" devices, in order to thwart competitive environments such as Flash or Java.

When you select a device for making phone calls or watching movies, it is worth asking who is in control. Are you purchasing a personal device that you can use in any way you choose, or are you being tethered to a flow of data that is controlled by somebody else?

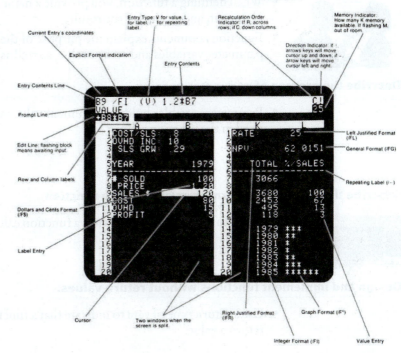

Courtesy of International Business Machines Corporation, © International Business Machines Corporation.

The Visicalc Spreadsheet Running on an Apple II

CHAPTER SUMMARY

Understand the concepts of functions, arguments, and return values.

- A function is a named sequence of instructions.
- Arguments are supplied when a function is called. The return value is the result that the function computes.

Be able to implement functions.

- When defining a function, you provide a name for the function, a variable for each argument, and a type for the result.
- Function comments explain the purpose of the function, the meaning of the parameter variables and return value, as well as any special requirements.

Describe the process of parameter passing.

- Parameter variables hold the argument values supplied in the function call.

Describe the process of returning a value from a function.

- The return statement terminates a function call and yields the function result.

Design and implement functions without return values.

- Use a return type of `void` to indicate that a function does not return a value.

Develop functions that can be reused for multiple problems.

- Eliminate replicated code or pseudocode by defining a function.
- Design your functions to be reusable. Supply parameter variables for the values that can vary when the function is reused.

Apply the design principle of stepwise refinement.

- Use the process of stepwise refinement to decompose complex tasks into simpler ones.
- When you discover that you need a function, write a description of the parameter variables and return values.
- A function may require simpler functions to carry out its work.

Determine the scope of variables in a program.

- The scope of a variable is the part of the program in which it is visible.
- A variable in a nested block shadows a variable with the same name in an outer block.
- A local variable is defined inside a function. A global variable is defined outside a function.
- Avoid global variables in your programs.

Describe how reference parameters work.

- Modifying a value parameter has no effect on the caller.
- A reference parameter refers to a variable that is supplied in a function call.
- Modifying a reference parameter updates the variable that was supplied in the call.

Understand recursive function calls and implement simple recursive functions.

- A recursive computation solves a problem by using the solution of the same problem with simpler inputs.
- For a recursion to terminate, there must be special cases for the simplest inputs.
- The key to finding a recursive solution is reducing the input to a simpler input for the same problem.
- When designing a recursive solution, do not worry about multiple nested calls. Simply focus on reducing a problem to a slightly simpler one.

CHAPTER **6**

ARRAYS AND VECTORS

CHAPTER GOALS

To become familiar with using arrays and vectors to collect values

To learn about common algorithms for processing arrays and vectors

To write functions that process arrays and vectors

To be able to use two-dimensional arrays

© traveler1116/iStockphoto.

CHAPTER CONTENTS

6.1 ARRAYS 180

SYN Defining an Array 181
CE1 Bounds Errors 184
PT1 Use Arrays for Sequences of Related Values 184
C&S Computer Viruses 185

6.2 COMMON ARRAY ALGORITHMS 185

ST1 Sorting with the C++ Library 192
ST2 A Sorting Algorithm 192
ST3 Binary Search 193

6.3 ARRAYS AND FUNCTIONS 194

ST4 Constant Array Parameters 198

6.4 PROBLEM SOLVING: ADAPTING ALGORITHMS 198

HT1 Working with Arrays 200
WE1 Rolling the Dice 203

6.5 PROBLEM SOLVING: DISCOVERING ALGORITHMS BY MANIPULATING PHYSICAL OBJECTS 203

6.6 TWO-DIMENSIONAL ARRAYS 206

SYN Two-Dimensional Array Definition 207
CE2 Omitting the Column Size of a Two-Dimensional Array Parameter 212
WE2 A World Population Table 213

6.7 VECTORS 213

SYN Defining a Vector 213
PT2 Prefer Vectors over Arrays 219
ST5 The Range-Based for Loop 219

In many programs, you need to collect large numbers of values. In standard C++, you use arrays and vectors for this purpose. Arrays are a fundamental structure of the C++ language. The standard C++ library provides the vector construct as a more convenient alternative when working with collections whose size is not fixed. In this chapter, you will learn about arrays, vectors, and common algorithms for processing them.

6.1 Arrays

We start this chapter by introducing the **array** data type. Arrays are the fundamental mechanism in C++ for collecting multiple values. In the following sections, you will learn how to define arrays and how to access array elements.

6.1.1 Defining Arrays

Suppose you write a program that reads a sequence of values and prints out the sequence, marking the largest value, like this:

```
32
54
67.5
29
34.5
80
115 <= largest value
44.5
100
65
```

You do not know which value to mark as the largest one until you have seen them all. After all, the last value might be the largest one. Therefore, the program must first store all values before it can print them.

Could you simply store each value in a separate variable? If you know that there are ten inputs, then you can store the values in ten variables value1, value2, value3, ..., value10. However, such a sequence of variables is not very practical to use. You would

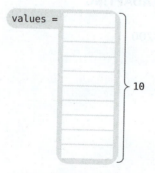

Figure 1   An Array of Size 10

have to write quite a bit of code ten times, once for each of the variables. To solve this problem, use an array: a structure for storing a sequence of values.

Here we define an array that can hold ten values:

```
double values[10];
```

This is the definition of a variable values whose type is "array of double". That is, values stores a sequence of floating-point numbers. The [10] indicates the *size* of the array. (See Figure 1.) The array size must be a constant that is known at compile time.

When you define an array, you can specify the initial values. For example,

```
double values[] = { 32, 54, 67.5, 29, 34.5, 80, 115, 44.5, 100, 65 };
```

When you supply initial values, you don't need to specify the array size. The compiler determines the size by counting the values.

Table 1 Defining Arrays

`int numbers[10];`	An array of ten integers.
`const int SIZE = 10;` `int numbers[SIZE];`	It is a good idea to use a named constant for the size.
`int size = 10;` `int numbers[size];`	**Caution:** In standard C++, the size must be a constant. This array definition will not work with all compilers.
`int squares[5] = { 0, 1, 4, 9, 16 };`	An array of five integers, with initial values.
`int squares[] = { 0, 1, 4, 9, 16 };`	You can omit the array size if you supply initial values. The size is set to the number of initial values.
`int squares[5] = { 0, 1, 4 };`	If you supply fewer initial values than the size, the remaining values are set to 0. This array contains 0, 1, 4, 0, 0.
`string names[3];`	An array of three strings.

Syntax 6.1   Defining an Array

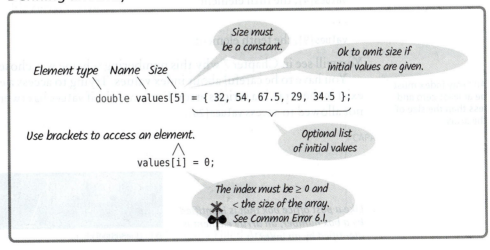

Program Run

```
Please enter values, Q to quit:
12 25 20 Q
24, 50, 40
```

Special Topic 6.4

Constant Array Parameters

When a function doesn't modify an array parameter, it is considered good style to add the const reserved word, like this:

```
double sum(const double values[], int size)
```

The const reserved word helps the reader of the code, making it clear that the function keeps the array elements unchanged. If the implementation of the function tries to modify the array, the compiler issues a warning.

6.4 Problem Solving: Adapting Algorithms

> By combining fundamental algorithms, you can solve complex programming tasks.

In Section 6.2, you were introduced to a number of fundamental array algorithms. These algorithms form the building blocks for many programs that process arrays. In general, it is a good problem-solving strategy to have a repertoire of fundamental algorithms that you can combine and adapt.

Consider this example problem: You are given the quiz scores of a student. You are to compute the final quiz score, which is the sum of all scores after dropping the lowest one. For example, if the scores are

```
8  7  8.5  9.5  7  4  10
```

then the final score is 50.

We do not have a ready-made algorithm for this situation. Instead, consider which algorithms may be related. These include:

- Calculating the sum (Section 6.2.3)
- Finding the minimum value (Section 6.2.4)
- Removing an element (Section 6.2.8)

Now we can formulate a plan of attack that combines these algorithms.

Find the minimum.
Remove the minimum from the array.
Calculate the sum.

Let's try it out with our example. The minimum of

```
     [0] [1] [2] [3] [4] [5] [6]
      8   7  8.5 9.5  7   4   10
```

is 4. How do we remove it?

Now we have a problem. The removal algorithm in Section 6.2.8 locates the element to be removed by using the *position* of the element, not the value.

But we have another algorithm for that:

- Linear search (Section 6.2.7)

We need to fix our plan of attack:

Find the minimum value.
Find the position of the minimum.
Remove the element at the position from the array.
Calculate the sum.

Will it work? Let's continue with our example.

We found a minimum value of 4. Linear search tells us that the value 4 occurs at position 5.

```
     [0] [1] [2] [3] [4] [5] [6]
      8   7  8.5 9.5  7   4   10
```

We remove it:

```
     [0] [1] [2] [3] [4] [5]
      8   7  8.5 9.5  7   10
```

Finally, we compute the sum: $8 + 7 + 8.5 + 9.5 + 7 + 10 = 50$.

This walkthrough demonstrates that our strategy works.

Can we do better? It seems a bit inefficient to find the minimum and then make another pass through the array to obtain its position.

We can adapt the algorithm for finding the minimum to yield the position of the minimum. Here is the original algorithm:

> You should be familiar with the implementation of fundamental algorithms so that you can adapt them.

```
double smallest = values[0];
for (int i = 1; i < size of values; i++)
{
   if (values[i] < smallest)
   {
      smallest = values[i];
   }
}
```

When we find the smallest value, we also want to update the position:

```
if (values[i] < smallest)
{
   smallest = values[i];
   smallest_position = i;
}
```

In fact, then there is no reason to keep track of the smallest value any longer. It is simply values[smallest_position]. With this insight, we can adapt the algorithm as follows:

```
int smallest_position = 0;
for (int i = 1; i < size of values; i++)
{
   if (values[i] < values[smallest_position])
   {
      smallest_position = i;
   }
}
```

With this adaptation, our problem is solved with the following strategy:

Find the position of the minimum.
Remove the element at the position from the array.
Calculate the sum.

EXAMPLE CODE See sec04 of your companion code for a program that implements this strategy. How To 6.1 shows an alternate approach that does not modify the array.

Use two-dimensional arrays for data that is arranged in rows and columns.

- Use a two-dimensional array to store tabular data.
- Individual elements in a two-dimensional array are accessed by using two index values, array[i][j].
- A two-dimensional array parameter must have a fixed number of columns.

Use vectors for managing collections whose size can change.

- A vector stores a sequence of values whose size can change.
- Use the size member function to obtain the current size of a vector.
- Use the push_back member function to add more elements to a vector. Use pop_back to reduce the size.
- Vectors can be function arguments and return values.
- Use a reference parameter to modify the contents of a vector.
- A function can return a vector.

CHAPTER 7

POINTERS AND STRUCTURES

© Suzanne Tucker/Shutterstock.

CHAPTER GOALS

To be able to declare, initialize, and use pointers

To understand the relationship between arrays and pointers

To be able to convert between string objects and character pointers

To become familiar with dynamic memory allocation and deallocation

To use structures to aggregate data items

CHAPTER CONTENTS

7.1 DEFINING AND USING POINTERS 224
SYN Pointer Syntax 226
CE1 Confusing Pointers with the Data to Which They Point 228
PT1 Use a Separate Definition for Each Pointer Variable 229
ST1 Pointers and References 229

7.2 ARRAYS AND POINTERS 230
ST2 Using a Pointer to Step Through an Array 233
CE2 Returning a Pointer to a Local Variable 234
PT2 Program Clearly, Not Cleverly 234
ST3 Constant Pointers 235

7.3 C AND C++ STRINGS 235
ST4 Working with C Strings 238

7.4 DYNAMIC MEMORY ALLOCATION 240
SYN Dynamic Memory Allocation 240

CE3 Dangling Pointers 242
CE4 Memory Leaks 243

7.5 ARRAYS AND VECTORS OF POINTERS 243

7.6 PROBLEM SOLVING: DRAW A PICTURE 246
HT1 Working with Pointers 248
WE1 Producing a Mass Mailing 249
C&S Embedded Systems 250

7.7 STRUCTURES 250
SYN Defining a Structure 251

7.8 POINTERS AND STRUCTURES 254
ST5 Smart Pointers 256

Work with arrays and vectors of pointers.

Draw diagrams for visualizing pointers and the data to which they point.

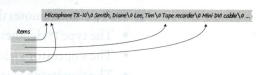

- Draw the data that is being processed, then draw the pointer variables. When drawing the pointer arrows, illustrate a typical situation.

Use structures to aggregate data items.

- A structure combines member values into a single value.
- You use the dot notation to access members of a structure.
- When you assign one structure value to another, all members are assigned.

Work with pointers to structures.

- Use the -> operator to access a structure member through a pointer.

CHAPTER **8**

STREAMS

CHAPTER GOALS

To be able to read and write files

To convert between strings and numbers using string streams

To process command line arguments

To understand the concepts of sequential and random access

James King-Holmes/Bletchley Park Trust/Photo Researchers, Inc.

CHAPTER CONTENTS

8.1   READING AND WRITING TEXT FILES   260

SYN   Working with File Streams   262

8.2   READING TEXT INPUT   265

CE1   Mixing >> and getline Input   268

ST1   Stream Failure Checking   269

8.3   WRITING TEXT OUTPUT   270

ST2   Unicode, UTF-8, and C++ Strings   272

8.4   PARSING AND FORMATTING STRINGS   273

8.5   COMMAND LINE ARGUMENTS   274

C&S   Encryption Algorithms   277

HT1   Processing Text Files   278

WE1   Looking for for Duplicates   281

8.6   RANDOM ACCESS AND BINARY FILES   281

C&S   Databases and Privacy   286

In this chapter, you will learn how to read and write files using the C++ stream library—a very useful skill for processing real world data. As an application, you will learn how to encrypt data. (The Enigma machine shown in the photo is an encryption device used by Germany in World War II. Pioneering British computer scientists broke the code and were able to intercept encoded messages, which was a significant help in winning the war.) Later in the chapter, you will learn to process binary files, such as those that store image data.

8.1 Reading and Writing Text Files

The C++ input/output library is based on the concept of **streams**. An **input stream** is a source of data, and an **output stream** is a destination for data. The most common sources and destinations for data are the files on your hard disk.

© nullplus/iStockphoto.

Data arrive in an input stream just like items on a conveyor belt, one at a time.

To read or write files, you use variables of type fstream, ifstream, or ofstream.

To access a file, you use a file stream. There are three types of file streams: ifstream (for input), ofstream (for output), and fstream (for both input and output). Include the <fstream> header when you use any of these file streams.

In the following sections, you will learn how to process data from files. File processing is a very useful skill in many disciplines because it is exceedingly common to analyze large data sets stored in files.

8.1.1 Opening a Stream

When opening a file stream, you supply the name of the file stored on disk.

To read anything from a file stream, you need to *open* it. When you open a stream, you give the name of the file stored on disk. Suppose you want to read data from a file named input.dat, located in the same directory as the program. Then you use the following function call to open the file:

```
in_file.open("input.dat");
```

This statement associates the variable in_file with the file named input.dat.

Note that all streams are objects, and you use the dot notation for calling functions that manipulate them.

To open a file for writing, you use an ofstream variable. To open the same file for both reading and writing, you use an fstream variable.

File names can contain directory path information, such as

```
~/homework/input.dat (UNIX)
c:\homework\input.dat (Windows)
```

When you specify the file name as a string literal, and the name contains backslash characters (as in a Windows filename), you must supply each backslash *twice*:

```
in_file.open("c:\\homework\\input.dat");
```

Recall that a single backslash inside a string literal is an **escape character** that is combined with another character to form a special meaning, such as \n for a newline character. The \\ combination denotes a single backslash.

In older versions of C++, you must be careful when opening a file with a name that is stored in a string variable. Use the c_str function to convert the C++ string to a C string:

```
cout << "Please enter the file name:";
string filename;
cin >> filename;
ifstream in_file;
in_file.open(filename.c_str()); // Before C++ 11
```

If it is not possible to open a stream, then the stream variable is set to a failed state. You can test for that condition:

```
in_file.open("input.dat");
if (in_file.fail())
{
    cout << "Cannot read from input.dat" << endl;
}
else
{
    Read input.
}
```

When the program ends, all streams that you have opened will be automatically closed. You can also manually close a stream with the close member function:

```
in_file.close();
```

Manual closing is only necessary if you want to use the stream variable again to process another file.

8.1.2 Reading from a File

Read from a file stream with the same operations that you use with cin.

Reading data from a file stream is completely straightforward: You simply use the same functions that you have always used for reading from cin:

```
string name;
double value;
in_file >> name >> value;
```

The fail function tells you whether input has failed. You have already used this function with cin, to check for errors in console input. File streams behave in the same way. When you try to read a number from a file, and the next data item is not a properly formatted number, then the stream fails. After reading data, you should test for success before processing:

```
if (!in_file.fail())
{
    Process input.
}
```

When you read input from a file, number format errors are not the only reason for failure. Suppose you have consumed all of the data contained in a file and try to read more items. A file stream enters the failed state, whereas `cin` would just wait for more user input. Moreover, if you open a file and the name is invalid, or if there is no file of that name, then the file stream is also in a failed state. It is a good idea to test for failure immediately after calling open.

Syntax 8.1 Working with File Streams

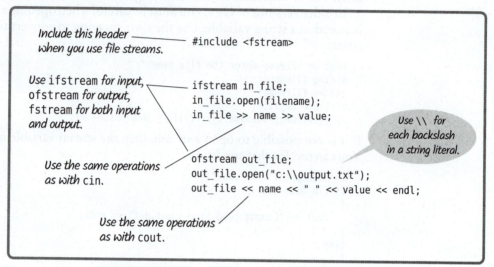

Include this header when you use file streams. ──── `#include <fstream>`

Use `ifstream` for input, `ofstream` for output, `fstream` for both input and output.

```
ifstream in_file;
in_file.open(filename);
in_file >> name >> value;
```

Use `\\` for each backslash in a string literal.

Use the same operations as with `cin`.

```
ofstream out_file;
out_file.open("c:\\output.txt");
out_file << name << " " << value << endl;
```

Use the same operations as with `cout`.

8.1.3 Writing to a File

Write to a file stream with the same operations that you use with cout.

In order to write to a file, you define an `ofstream` or `fstream` variable and open it. Then you send information to the output file, using the same operations that you used with `cout`:

```
ofstream out_file;
out_file.open("output.txt");
out_file << name << " " << value << endl;
```

8.1.4 A File Processing Example

Here is a typical example of processing data in a file. The Social Security Administration publishes lists of the most popular baby names on their web site, http://www.ssa. gov/OACT/babynames/. If you query the 1,000 most popular names for a given decade, the browser displays the result on the screen (see Figure 1).

To save the data as text, simply select it and paste the result into a file. This book's companion code contains a file called `babynames.txt` with the data for the 1990s.

Each line in the file contains seven entries:

- The rank (from 1 to 1,000)

- The name, frequency, and percentage of the male name of that rank

- The name, frequency, and percentage of the female name of that rank

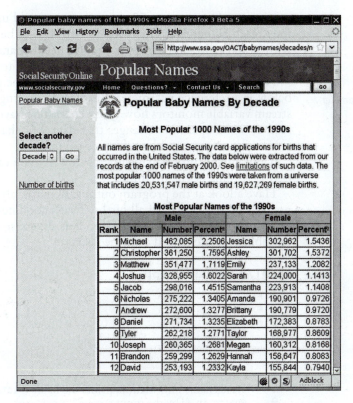

Figure 1 Querying Baby Names

For example, the line

```
10  Joseph  260365  1.2681  Megan  160312  0.8168
```

shows that the 10th most common boy's name was Joseph, with 260,365 births, or 1.2681 percent of all births during that period. The 10th most common girl's name was Megan. Why are there many more Josephs than Megans? Parents seem to use a wider set of girl's names, making each one of them less frequent.

Let us test that conjecture, by determining the names given to the top 50 percent of boys and girls in the list.

To process each line, we first read the rank:

```
int rank;
in_file >> rank;
```

We then read a set of three values for the boy's name:

```
string name;
int count;
double percent;
in_file >> name >> count >> percent;
```

© Nancy Ross/iStockphoto.

Sellers of personalized items can find trends in popular names by processing data files from the Social Security Administration.

Then we repeat that step for girls. Because the actions are identical, we supply a helper function process_name for that purpose. To stop processing after reaching 50 percent, we can add up the frequencies and stop when they reach 50 percent. However, it turns out to be a bit simpler to initialize a total with 50 and subtract the frequencies. We need separate totals for boys and girls. When a total falls below 0, we stop printing. When both totals fall below 0, we stop reading.

Always use a reference parameter for a stream.

Note that the in_file parameter variable of the process_name function in the code below is a reference parameter. Reading or writing modifies a stream variable. The stream variable monitors how many characters have been read or written so far. Any read or write operation changes that data. For that reason, you must always make stream parameter variables reference parameters.

The complete program is shown below. As you can see, reading from a file is just as easy as reading keyboard input.

Have a look at the program output. Remarkably, only 69 boy names and 153 girl names account for half of all births. That's good news for those who are in the business of producing personalized doodads. Exercise P8.3 asks you to study how this distribution has changed over the years.

sec01/babynames.cpp

```cpp
1  #include <iostream>
2  #include <fstream>
3  #include <string>
4
5  using namespace std;
6
7  /**
8     Reads name information, prints the name if total >= 0, and adjusts the total.
9     @param in_file the input stream
10    @param total the total percentage that should still be processed
11 */
12 void process_name(ifstream& in_file, double& total)
13 {
14    string name;
15    int count;
16    double percent;
17    in_file >> name >> count >> percent;
18
19    if (in_file.fail()) { return; } // Check for failure after each input
20    if (total > 0) { cout << name << " "; }
21    total = total - percent;
22 }
23
24 int main()
25 {
26    ifstream in_file;
27    in_file.open("babynames.txt");
28    if (in_file.fail()) { return 0; } // Check for failure after opening
29
30    double boy_total = 50;
31    double girl_total = 50;
32
33    while (boy_total > 0 || girl_total > 0)
34    {
35       int rank;
36       in_file >> rank;
37       if (in_file.fail()) { return 0; }
38
39       cout << rank << " ";
```

```
40
41        process_name(in_file, boy_total);
42        process_name(in_file, girl_total);
43
44        cout << endl;
45     }
46
47     return 0;
48 }
```

Program Run

```
  1 Michael Jessica
  2 Christopher Ashley
  3 Matthew Emily
  4 Joshua Sarah
  5 Jacob Samantha
  6 Nicholas Amanda
  7 Andrew Brittany
  8 Daniel Elizabeth
  9 Tyler Taylor
 10 Joseph Megan
 . . .
 68 Dustin Gabrielle
 69 Noah Katie
 70 Caitlin
 71 Lindsey
 . . .
150 Hayley
151 Rebekah
152 Jocelyn
153 Cassidy
```

8.2 Reading Text Input

In the following sections, you will learn how to process text with complex contents such as that which often occurs in real-life situations.

8.2.1 Reading Words

You already know how to read the next word from a stream, using the >> operator.

```
string word;
in_file >> word;
```

> When reading a string with the >> operator, the white space between words is consumed.

Here is precisely what happens when that operation is executed. First, any input characters that are white space are removed from the stream, but they are not added to the word. White space includes spaces, tab characters, and the newline characters that separate lines. The first character that is not white space becomes the first character in the string word. More characters are added until either another white space character occurs, or the end of the file has been reached. The white space after the word is not removed from the stream.

8.2.2 Reading Characters

Instead of reading an entire word, you can read one character at a time by calling the get function:

```
char ch;
in_file.get(ch);
```

The get function returns the "not failed" condition. The following loop processes all characters in a file:

```
while (in_file.get(ch))
{
    Process the character ch.
}
```

The get function reads white space characters. This is useful if you need to process characters such as spaces, tabs, or newlines. On the other hand, if you are not interested in white space, use the >> operator instead.

```
in_file >> ch; // ch is set to the next non-white space character
```

You can get individual characters from a stream and unget the last one.

If you read a character and you regretted it, you can *unget* it, so that the next input operation can read it again. However, you can unget only the last character. This is called *one-character lookahead.* You get a chance to look at the next character in the input stream, and you can make a decision whether you want to consume it or put it back.

A typical situation for lookahead is to look for numbers:

```
char ch;
in_file.get(ch);
if (isdigit(ch))
{
    in_file.unget(); // Put the digit back so that it is part of the number
    int n;
    in_file >> n; // Read integer starting with ch
}
```

The isdigit function is one of several useful functions that categorize characters—see Table 1. All return true or false as to whether the argument passes the test. You must include the <cctype> header to use these functions.

Table 1 Character Functions in <cctype>	
Function	Accepted Characters
isdigit	0 ... 9
isalpha	a ... z, A ... Z
islower	a ... z
isupper	A ... Z
isalnum	a ... z, A ... Z, 0 ... 9
isspace	White space (space, tab, newline, and the rarely used carriage return, form feed, and vertical tab)

If you read a character from a stream and you don't like what you get, you can unget it.

© altrendo images/Getty Images.

8.2.3 Reading Lines

When each line of a file is a data record, it is often best to read entire lines with the `getline` function:

```
string line;
getline(in_file, line);
```

The next input line (without the newline character) is placed into the string `line`.

The `getline` function returns the "not failed" condition. You can use the following loop to process each line in a file:

```
while (getline(in_file, line))
{
    Process line.
}
```

Note that `getline` is not a member function, but an ordinary function that is not called with the dot notation.

Here is a typical example of processing lines in a file. A file with population data from the CIA World Factbook site (`https://www.cia.gov/library/publications/the-world-factbook/index.html`) contains lines such as the following:

```
China  1330044605
India  1147995898
United States 303824646
. . .
```

Because each line is a data record, it is natural to use the `getline` function for reading lines into a string variable. To extract the data from that string, you need to find out where the name ends and the number starts.

Locate the first digit:

```
int i = 0;
while (!isdigit(line[i])) { i++; }
```

Then go backward and skip white space:

```
int j = i - 1;
while (isspace(line[j])) { j--; }
```

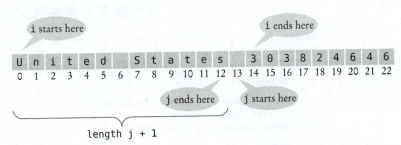

Finally, extract the country name and population:

```
string country_name = line.substr(0, j + 1);
string population = line.substr(i);
```

There is just one problem. The population is stored in a string, not a number. You will see in Section 8.4 how to extract the population number as a number.

Common Error 8.1

Mixing >> and `getline` Input

It is tricky to mix >> and `getline` input. Suppose we place country names and populations on separate lines:

```
China
1330044605
India
1147995898
United States
303824646
```

Now we can use `getline` to read each country name without worrying about spaces:

```
getline(in, country_name);
in >> population;
```

The `getline` function reads an entire line of input, including the newline character at the end of the line. It places all characters except for that newline character into the string `country_name`. The >> operator reads all white space (that is, spaces, tabs, and newlines) until it reaches a number. Then it reads only the characters in that number. It does not consume the character following the number, typically a newline. This is a problem when a call to `getline` immediately follows a call to >>. Then the call to `getline` reads only the newline, considering it as the end of an empty line.

Perhaps an example will make this clearer. Consider the first input lines of the product descriptions. Calling `getline` consumes the darker-colored characters.

```
in = C h i n a \n 1 3 3 0 0 4 4 6 0 5 \n I n d i a \n
```

After the call to `getline`, the first line has been read completely, including the newline at the end. Next, the call to `in >> population` reads the digits.

```
in = 1 3 3 0 0 4 4 6 0 5 \n I n d i a \n
```

After the call to `in >> population`, the digits of the number have been read, but the newline is still unread, because the >> operator never reads any more characters than absolutely necessary. Now we have a problem. The next call to `getline` reads a blank line.

```
in = \n I n d i a \n
```

This is a problem whenever an input with the >> operator is followed by a call to `getline`. The intention, of course, is to skip the rest of the current line and have `getline` read the next line. This purpose is achieved by the following statements, which must be inserted after the last call to the >> operator:

```
string remainder; // Read remainder of line
getline(in, remainder);
// Now you are ready to call getline again
```

Special Topic 8.1

Stream Failure Checking

Given a stream variable, for example,

```
istream in_file;
```

you know that you can use the fail member function to check whether the stream has failed:

```
if (in_file.fail())
{
    Report error.
}
else
{
    Process input.
}
```

Alternatively, you can use the stream variable itself as a condition. The C++ compiler converts the stream to a bool value that is true if the stream has *not* failed, and false if it has failed. Therefore, you can achieve the same effect with the following statement:

```
if (in_file)
{
    Process input.
}
else
{
    Report error.
}
```

This alternative is particularly attractive with input operations that return a stream. In Section 4.5.2, you saw that you can read a sequence of values with the loop

```
cout << "Enter values, Q to quit: ";
int value;
while (cin >> value)
{
    Process value.
}
```

When the user enters a Q, or any other input that is not an integer, the stream state fails.

You can chain the >> operators. Consider this example:

```
while (in_file >> name >> value)
{
    Process the name and value.
}
```

When evaluating the expression

```
in_file >> name >> value;
```

the subexpression in_file >> name executes first, and it returns in_file. Next, the expression in_file >> value executes and again returns in_file. The in_file object is then converted to a bool value and tested in the condition.

As you saw in Section 8.2.1 and Section 8.2.3, you can also use expressions

```
in_file.get(ch)
```

and

```
get_line(in_file, line)
```

as conditions. This works for the same reason. The get and get_line functions return the input stream, and it is converted to a bool value.

8.3 Writing Text Output

You use the << operator to send strings and numbers to a stream. To write a single character to a stream, use

```
out_file.put(ch);
```

To control how the output is formatted, you use stream *manipulators*. A manipulator is a value that affects the behavior of the stream. It is sent to a stream using the << operator. The setw manipulator, which you have already used, is a typical example. The statement

```
out_file << setw(10);
```

does not cause any immediate output, but when the next item is written, it is padded with sufficient spaces so that the output spans ten characters. (If a value does not fit into the given width, it is not truncated.)

Occasionally, you need to pad numbers with leading zeroes, for example to print hours and minutes as 09:01. This is achieved with the setfill manipulator:

```
out_file << setfill('0') << setw(2) << hours
    << ":" << setw(2) << minutes << setfill(' ');
```

Now, a zero is used to pad the field. Afterward, the space is restored as the fill character.

By default, the fill characters appear before the item:

```
out_file << setw(10) << 123 << endl << setw(10) << 4567;
```

produces

```
       123
      4567
```

The numbers line up to the right. That alignment works well for numbers, but not for strings. Usually, you want strings to line up at the left. You use the left and right manipulators to set the alignment. The following example uses left alignment for a string and then switches back to right alignment for a number:

```
out_file << left << setw(10) << word << right << setw(10) << number;
```

The *default floating-point format* displays as many digits as are specified by the *precision* (6 by default), switching to scientific notation for large and small numbers. For example,

```
out_file << 12.3456789 << " " << 123456789.0 << " " << 0.0000123456789;
```

yields

```
12.3457 1.23457e+08 1.23457e-05
```

A manipulator is like a control button on a sound mixer. It doesn't produce an output, but it affects how the output looks.

© iStockphoto.

The *fixed* format prints all values with the same number of digits after the decimal point. In the fixed format, the same numbers are displayed as

```
12.345679 123456789.000000 0.000012
```

Use the fixed manipulator to select that format, and the setprecision manipulator to change the precision.

For example,

```
out_file << fixed << setprecision(2) << 1.2 << " " << 1.235
```

yields

```
1.20 1.24
```

Table 2 summarizes the stream manipulators. Note that all manipulators set the state of the stream object for all subsequent operations, with the exception of setw. After each output operation, the field width is reset to 0. To use any of these manipulators, include the `<iomanip>` header.

> Use the fixed and setprecision manipulators to format floating-point numbers with a fixed number of digits after the decimal point.

Table 2 Stream Manipulators

Manipulator	Purpose	Example	Output

setw	Sets the field width of the next item only.	`out_file << setw(6) << 123 << endl`
		`        << 123 << endl`
		`        << setw(6) << 12345678;`
			`   123`
			`123`
			`12345678`

setfill	Sets the fill character for padding a field. (The default character is a space.)	`out_file << setfill('0') << setw(6)` `        << 123;`	`000123`
left	Selects left alignment.	`out_file << left << setw(6) << 123;`	`123`
right	Selects right alignment (default).	`out_file << right << setw(6) << 123;`	`   123`
fixed	Selects fixed format for floating-point numbers.	`double x = 123.4567;` `out_file << x << endl << fixed << x;`	`123.457` `123.456700`

setprecision	Sets the number of significant digits for the default floating-point format, the number of digits after the decimal point for fixed format.	`double x = 123.4567;`
		`out_file << fixed << x << endl`
		`        << setprecision(2) << x;`
			`123.456700`
			`123.46`

scientific	Selects scientific floating-point format, with one digit before the decimal point and an exponent.	`out_file << scientific` `        << setprecision(3) << 123.4567;`	`1.235e+02`

defaultfloat	(Since C++ 11) Switches back to the default floating-point format.	`double x = 123.4567;`
		`out_file << fixed << x << endl`
		`        << defaultfloat << x;`
			`123.456700`
			`123.457`

Special Topic 8.2

Unicode, UTF-8, and C++ Strings

As described in Computing & Society 2.2, the **Unicode** standard encodes alphabets from many languages. Each Unicode character has a unique 21-bit code that is written using the hexadecimal number system. For example, é (Latin small letter e with acute accent) has the code U+OOE9 and ⛟ (high speed train) has the code U+1F684. However, it would be inefficient to use these codes when characters are saved in files or transmitted over the Internet. Instead, a character encoding is used that represents each Unicode character as a sequence of one or more bytes.

If you process English text, you don't need to worry about character encodings because English characters are encoded with a single byte. The situation is more complex if you want to process text that contains characters such as é or ⛟. Nowadays, most data on the Internet uses the UTF-8 encoding. As it happens, the UTF-8 encoding of the string é takes up two bytes, and the UTF-8 encoding of ⛟ takes four bytes (see Appendix C). Therefore, the text

```
San José ⛟
```

with two spaces, six English characters and these two characters, consists of 14 bytes when encoded with UTF-8.

When you read this text into a C++ string value, you get a string object of length 14, even though it only contains ten Unicode characters. It is not fruitful to look at the individual `char` values in isolation. Instead, work with substrings that are made up of one or more Unicode characters.

For example, suppose you want to find the position of the é. Form a string containing a single Unicode character.

If your C++ compiler uses the UTF-8 encoding, you can make such a string as

```
string e_acute = u8"é";
string high_speed_train = u8"⛟";
```

The `u8` prefix indicates that you want to use the UTF-8 encoding. However, to make sure that your source file is portable to any system, it is a good idea to provide the Unicode value for the letter instead. You can use the `\U` prefix followed by eight hexadecimal digits:

```
string e_acute = u8"\U000000e9";
string high_speed_train = u8"\U0001f684";
```

Now that you know how to specify a string containing an arbitrary Unicode character, you can use the `find` member function to check whether the Unicode character occurs in a given string. We haven't covered this member function before because it is a bit fussy to use. Here is what you need to do:

```
string message = . . .;
size_t pos = message.find(e_acute);
if (pos != string::npos)
{
    // Message has e_acute starting at position pos
}
```

The `size_t` type indicates a non-negative position, and `string::npos` is a special value that denotes no position.

The `locale` library, which we don't cover in this book, gives you additional mechanisms to process UTF-8 strings. Exercise P8.11 provides a simple way of accessing individual characters.

EXAMPLE CODE　See special_topic_2 of your companion code for a sample program using UTF-8 encoding.

8.4 Parsing and Formatting Strings

In the preceding sections, you saw how file streams read characters from a file and write characters to a file. The istringstream class reads characters from a string, and the ostringstream class writes characters to a string. That doesn't sound so exciting—we already know how to access and change the characters of a string. However, the string stream classes have the same **public interface** as the other stream classes. In particular, you can use the familiar >> and << operators to read and write numbers that are contained in strings. For that reason, the istringstream and ostringstream classes are called *adapters*—they adapt strings to the stream interface. Include the <sstream> header when you use string streams.

© iStockphoto.

Like an adapter that converts your power plugs to international outlets, the string stream adapters allow you to access strings as streams.

Here is a typical example. Suppose the string date contains a date such as "January 24, 1973", and we want to separate it into month, day, and year. First, construct an istringstream object. Then use the str function to set the stream to the string that you want to read:

> Use an istringstream to convert the numbers inside a string to integers or floating-point numbers.

```
istringstream strm;
strm.str("January 24, 1973");
```

Next, simply use the >> operator to read the month name, the day, the comma separator, and the year:

```
string month;
int day;
string comma;
int year;
strm >> month >> day >> comma >> year;
```

Now month is "January", day is 24, and year is 1973. Note that this input statement yields day and year as *integers*. Had we taken the string apart with substr, we would have obtained only strings, not numbers.

If you only need to convert a single string to its int or double value, you can instead use the functions stoi and stod:

```
string year = "1973";
int y = stoi(year); // Sets y to the integer 1973
```

These functions are available since C++ 11. If you have an older version of C++, use a helper function for this purpose:

```
int string_to_int(string s)
{
   istringstream strm;
   strm.str(s);
   int n = 0;
   strm >> n;
   return n;
}
```

Use an ostringstream to convert numeric values to strings.

By writing to a string stream, you can convert integers or floating-point numbers to strings. First construct an ostringstream object:

```
ostringstream strm;
```

Next, use the << operator to add a number to the stream. The number is converted into a sequence of characters:

```
strm << fixed << setprecision(5) << 10.0 / 3;
```

Now the stream contains the string "3.33333". To obtain that string from the stream, call the str member function:

```
string output = strm.str();
```

You can build up more complex strings in the same way. Here we build a data string of the month, day, and year:

```
string month = "January";
int day = 4;
int year = 1973;
ostringstream strm;
strm << month << " " << setw(2) << setfill('0') << day << ", " << year;
string output = strm.str();
```

Now output is the string "January 04, 1973". Note that we converted the *integers* day and year into a string.

If you don't need formatting, you can use the to_string function to convert numbers to strings. For example, to_string(1973) is the string "1973".

You can produce a formatted date, without a leading zero for days less than ten, like this:

```
string output = month + " " + to_string(day) + ", " + to_string(year);
```

This function is available since C++ 11. Here is an implementation that you can use with older versions:

```
string int_to_string(int n)
{
   ostringstream strm;
   strm << n;
   return strm.str();
}
```

8.5 Command Line Arguments

Depending on the operating system and C++ development environment used, there are different methods of starting a program—for example, by selecting "Run" in the compilation environment, by clicking on an icon, or by typing the name of the program at a prompt in a command shell window. The latter method is called "invoking the program from the **command line**". When you use this method, you must type the name of the program, of course, but you can also type in additional information that the program can use. These additional strings are called **command line arguments**. For example, if you start a program with the command line

```
prog -v input.dat
```

then the program receives two command line arguments: the strings "-v" and "input.dat". It is entirely up to the program what to do with these strings. It is customary to interpret strings starting with a hyphen (-) as options and other strings as file names.

To receive command line arguments, you need to define the main function in a different way. You define two parameter variables: an integer and an array of string literals of type char*.

```
int main(int argc, char* argv[])
{
    . . .
}
```

Here argc is the count of arguments, and argv contains the values of the arguments. In our example, argc is 3, and argv contains the three strings

```
argv[0]:    "prog"
argv[1]:    "-v"
argv[2]:    "input.dat"
```

Note that argv[0] is always the name of the program and that argc is always at least 1.

Let's write a program that *encrypts* a file—that is, scrambles it so that it is unreadable except to those who know the decryption method. Ignoring 2,000 years of progress in the field of encryption, we will use a method familiar to Julius Caesar, replacing an A with a D, a B with an E, and so on. That is, each character c is replaced with $c + 3$ (see Figure 2).

© xyno/iStockphoto.

The emperor Julius Caesar used a simple scheme to encrypt messages.

The program takes the following command line arguments:

- An optional -d flag to indicate decryption instead of encryption
- The input file name
- The output file name

For example,

```
caesar input.txt encrypt.txt
```

encrypts the file input.txt and places the result into encrypt.txt.

```
caesar -d encrypt.txt output.txt
```

decrypts the file encrypt.txt and places the result into output.txt.

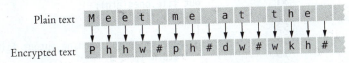

Figure 2 Caesar Cipher

sec05/caesar.cpp

```
1   #include <iostream>
2   #include <fstream>
3   #include <string>
4   #include <sstream>
5
6   using namespace std;
7
8   /**
9       Encrypts a stream using the Caesar cipher.
```

```
10      @param in the stream to read from
11      @param out the stream to write to
12      @param k the encryption key
13  */
14  void encrypt_file(ifstream& in, ofstream& out, int k)
15  {
16      char ch;
17      while (in.get(ch))
18      {
19          out.put(ch + k);
20      }
21  }
22
23  int main(int argc, char* argv[])
24  {
25      int key = 3;
26      int file_count = 0; // The number of files specified
27      ifstream in_file;
28      ofstream out_file;
29
30      for (int i = 1; i < argc; i++) // Process all command-line arguments
31      {
32          string arg = argv[i]; // The currently processed argument
33          if (arg == "-d") // The decryption option
34          {
35              key = -3;
36          }
37          else // It is a file name
38          {
39              file_count++;
40              if (file_count == 1) // The first file name
41              {
42                  in_file.open(arg);
43                  if (in_file.fail()) // Exit the program if opening failed
44                  {
45                      cout << "Error opening input file " << arg << endl;
46                      return 1;
47                  }
48              }
49              else if (file_count == 2) // The second file name
50              {
51                  out_file.open(arg);
52                  if (out_file.fail())
53                  {
54                      cout << "Error opening output file " << arg << endl;
55                      return 1;
56                  }
57              }
58          }
59      }
60
61      if (file_count != 2) // Exit if the user didn't specify two files
62      {
63          cout << "Usage: " << argv[0] << " [-d] infile outfile" << endl;
64          return 1;
65      }
66
67      encrypt_file(in_file, out_file, key);
68      return 0;
69  }
```

Computing & Society 8.1   Encryption Algorithms

The exercises at the end of this chapter give a few algorithms to encrypt text. Don't actually use any of those methods to send secret messages to your lover. Any skilled cryptographer can *break* these schemes in a very short time—that is, reconstruct the original text without knowing the secret keyword.

In 1978 Ron Rivest, Adi Shamir, and Leonard Adleman introduced an encryption method that is much more powerful. The method is called *RSA encryption*, after the last names of its inventors. The exact scheme is too complicated to present here, but it is not actually difficult to follow. You can find the details in `http://people.csail.mit.edu/rivest/Rsapaper.pdf`.

RSA is a remarkable encryption method. There are two keys: a public key and a private key. (See the figure.) You can print the public key on your business card (or in your e-mail signature block) and give it to anyone. Then anyone can send you messages that only you can decrypt. Even though everyone else knows the public key, and even if they intercept all the messages coming to you, they cannot break the scheme and actually read the messages. In 1994, hundreds of researchers, collaborating over the Internet, cracked an RSA message encrypted with a 129-digit key. Messages encrypted with a key of 230 digits or more are expected to be secure.

The inventors of the algorithm obtained a *patent* for it. A patent is a deal that society makes with an inventor. For a period of 20 years, the inventor has an exclusive right for its commercialization, may collect royalties from others wishing to manufacture the invention, and may even stop competitors from using it altogether. In return, the inventor must publish the invention, so that others may learn from it, and must relinquish all claim to it after the monopoly period ends. The presumption is that in the absence

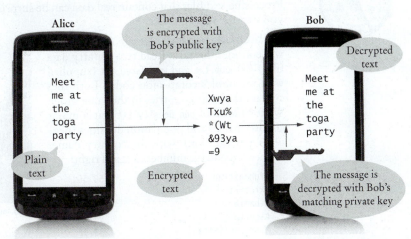

(mobile phone) © Anna Khomulo/iStockphoto.

Public-Key Encryption

of patent law, inventors would be reluctant to go through the trouble of inventing, or they would try to cloak their techniques to prevent others from copying their devices.

There has been some controversy about the RSA patent. Had there not been patent protection, would the inventors have published the method anyway, thereby giving the benefit to society without the cost of the 20-year monopoly? In this case, the answer is probably yes. The inventors were academic researchers, who live on salaries rather than sales receipts and are usually rewarded for their discoveries by a boost in their reputation and careers. Would their followers have been as active in discovering (and patenting) improvements? There is no way of knowing, of course. Is an algorithm even patentable, or is it a mathematical fact that belongs to nobody? The patent office did take the latter attitude for a long time. The RSA inventors and many others described their inventions in terms of imaginary electronic devices, rather than algorithms, to circumvent that restriction.

Nowadays, the patent office will award software patents.

There is another interesting aspect to the RSA story. A programmer, Phil Zimmermann, developed a program called PGP (for *Pretty Good Privacy*) that is based on RSA. Anyone can use the program to encrypt messages, and decryption is not feasible even with the most powerful computers. You can get a copy of a free PGP implementation from the GNU project (`http://www.gnupg.org`). The existence of strong encryption methods bothers the United States government to no end. Criminals and foreign agents can send communications that the police and intelligence agencies cannot decipher. The government considered charging Zimmermann with breaching a law that forbids the unauthorized export of munitions, arguing that he should have known that his program would appear on the Internet. There have been serious proposals to make it illegal for private citizens to use these encryption methods, or to keep the keys secret from law enforcement.

HOW TO 8.1
Processing Text Files

Processing text files that contain real data can be surprisingly challenging. This How To gives you step-by-step guidance.

Problem Statement As an example, we will consider this task: Read two country data files, worldpop.txt and worldarea.txt (supplied with the book's companion code). Both files contain the same countries in the same order. Write a file world_pop_density.txt that contains country names and population densities (people per square km), with the country names aligned left and the numbers aligned right:

© Oksana Perkins/iStockphoto.

Singapore is one of the most densely populated countries in the world.

```
Afghanistan          50.56
Akrotiri            127.64
Albania             125.91
Algeria              14.18
American Samoa      288.92
. . .
```

Step 1 Understand the processing task.

As always, you need to have a clear understanding of the task before designing a solution. Can you carry out the task by hand (perhaps with smaller input files)? If not, get more information about the problem.

The following pseudocode describes our processing task:

> *While there are more lines to be read*
>   *Read a line from each file.*
>   *Extract the country name.*
>   *population = number following the country name in the first line*
>   *area = number following the country name in the second line*
>   *If area != 0*
>   *density = population / area*
>   *Print country name and density.*

Step 2 Determine which files you need to read and write.

This should be clear from the problem. In our example, there are two input files, the population data and the area data, and one output file.

Step 3 Choose a method for obtaining the file names.

There are three options:

- Hard-coding the file names (such as "worldpop.txt")

- Asking the user:
  ```
  cout << "Enter filename: ";
  cin >> filename;
  in_file.open(filename);
  ```

- Using command-line arguments for the file names

In our example, we use hard-coded file names for simplicity.

Step 4 Choose between line, word, and character-based input.

As a rule of thumb, read lines if the input data is grouped by lines. That is the case with tabular data, as in our example, or when you need to report line numbers.

When gathering data that can be distributed over several lines, then it makes more sense to read words. Keep in mind that you lose all white space when you read words.

Reading characters is mostly useful for tasks that require access to individual characters. Examples include analyzing character frequencies, changing tabs to spaces, or encryption.

Step 5 With line-oriented input, extract the required data.

It is simple to read a line of input with the getline function. Then you need to get the data out of that line. You can extract substrings, as described in Section 8.2. Alternatively, you can turn the line into an istringstream and extract its components with the >> operator. The latter approach is easier when the number of items on each line is constant. In our example, that is not the case—country names can consist of more than one string. Therefore, we choose to extract substrings from each input line.

If you need any of the substrings as numbers, you must convert them (see Section 8.4).

Step 6 Place repeatedly occurring tasks into functions.

Processing input files usually has repetitive tasks, such as skipping over white space or extracting numbers from strings. It really pays off to develop a set of functions to handle these tedious operations.

In our example, we have a common task that calls for a helper function: extracting the country name and the value that follows. This task can be implemented in a helper function

```
void read_line(string line, string& country, double& value)
```

We also need a helper function string_to_double to convert the population and area values to floating-point numbers. This function is similar to string_to_int that was developed in Section 8.4.

Step 7 If required, use manipulators to format the output.

If you are asked to format your output, use manipulators, as described in Section 8.3. Usually, you want to switch to fixed format for the output and set the precision. Then use setw before every value, and use left for aligning strings and right for aligning numbers:

```
out << setw(40) << left << country << setw(15) << right << density << endl;
```

Here is the complete program:

how_to_1/popdensity.cpp

```
1  #include <cctype>
2  #include <fstream>
3  #include <iostream>
4  #include <iomanip>
5  #include <sstream>
6  #include <string>
7
8  using namespace std;
9
10 /**
11     Converts a string to a floating-point number, e.g. "3.14" -> 3.14.
12     @param s a string representing a floating-point number
13     @return the equivalent floating-point number
14 */
15 double string_to_double(string s)
16 {
17     istringstream stream;
18     stream.str(s);
```

```
19      double x = 0;
20      stream >> x;
21      return x;
22  }
23
24  /**
25      Extracts the country and associated value from an input line.
26      @param line a line containing a country name, followed by a number
27      @param country the string for holding the country name
28      @param value the variable for holding the associated value
29      @return true if a line has been read, false at the end of the stream
30  */
31  void read_line(string line, string& country, double& value)
32  {
33      int i = 0; // Locate the start of the first digit
34      while (!isdigit(line[i])) { i++; }
35      int j = i - 1; // Locate the end of the preceding word
36      while (isspace(line[j])) { j--; }
37
38      country = line.substr(0, j + 1); // Extract the country name
39      value = string_to_double(line.substr(i)); // Extract the number value
40  }
41
42  int main()
43  {
44      ifstream in1;
45      ifstream in2;
46      in1.open("worldpop.txt"); // Open input files
47      in2.open("worldarea.txt");
48
49      ofstream out;
50      out.open("world_pop_density.txt"); // Open output file
51      out << fixed << setprecision(2);
52
53      string line1;
54      string line2;
55
56      // Read lines from each file
57      while (getline(in1, line1) && getline(in2, line2))
58      {
59          string country;
60          double population;
61          double area;
62
63          // Split the lines into country and associated value
64          read_line(line1, country, population);
65          read_line(line2, country, area);
66
67          // Compute and print the population density
68          double density = 0;
69          if (area != 0) // Protect against division by zero
70          {
71              density = population * 1.0 / area;
72          }
73          out << setw(40) << left << country
74              << setw(15) << right << density << endl;
75      }
76
77      return 0;
78  }
```

WORKED EXAMPLE 8.1

Looking for for Duplicates

Learn how to process a file to locate lines that contain repeated words. See your E-Text or visit wiley.com/go/bclo3.

8.6 Random Access and Binary Files

In the following sections, you will learn how to read and write data at arbitrary positions in a file, and how to edit image files.

At a sit-down dinner, food is served sequentially. At a buffet, you have "random access" to all food items.

© iStockphoto.

8.6.1 Random Access

You can access any position in a random access file by moving the *file pointer* prior to a read or write operation.

So far, you've read from a file an item at a time and written to a file an item at a time, without skipping forward or backward. That access pattern is called **sequential access**. In many applications, we would like to access specific items in a file without first having to read all preceding items. This access pattern is called **random access** (see Figure 3). There is nothing "random" about random access—the term means that you can read and modify any item stored at any location in the file.

Only file streams support random access; the `cin` and `cout` streams, which are attached to the keyboard and the terminal, do not. Each file stream has two special positions: the *get* position and the *put* position (see Figure 4). These positions determine where the next character is read or written.

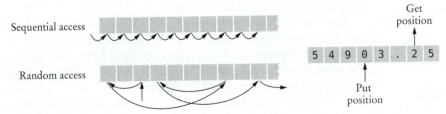

Figure 3 Sequential and Random Access

Figure 4 Get and Put Positions

The following function calls move the get and put positions to a given value, counted from the beginning of the stream.

```
strm.seekg(position);
strm.seekp(position);
```

To determine the current values of the get and put positions (counted from the beginning of the file), use

```
position = strm.tellg();
position = strm.tellp();
```

Whenever you put data to the stream, the get position becomes undefined. Call seekg when you switch back to reading. Call seekp when you switch from reading to writing.

8.6.2 Binary Files

Many files, in particular those containing images and sounds, do not store information as text but as binary numbers. The numbers are represented as sequences of **bytes**, just as they are in the memory of the computer. (Each byte is a value between 0 and 255.) In binary format, a floating-point number always occupies 8 bytes. We will study random access with a binary file format for images.

We have to cover a few technical issues about binary files. To open a binary file for reading and writing, use the following command:

```
fstream strm;
strm.open(filename, ios::in | ios::out | ios::binary);
```

You read a byte with the call

```
int input = strm.get();
```

This call returns a value between 0 and 255. To read an integer, read four bytes b_0, b_1, b_2, b_3 and combine them to $b_0 + b_1 \cdot 256 + b_2 \cdot 256^2 + b_3 \cdot 256^3$. We will supply a helper function for this task.

The >> operator cannot be used to read numbers from a binary file.

8.6.3 Processing Image Files

In this section, you will learn how to write a program for editing image files in the BMP format. Unlike the more common GIF, PNG, and JPEG formats, the BMP format is quite simple because it does not use data compression. As a consequence, BMP files are huge and you will rarely find them in the wild. However, image editors can convert any image into BMP format.

There are different versions of the BMP format; we will only cover the simplest and most common one, sometimes called the 24-bit true color format. In this format, each pixel is represented as a sequence of three bytes, one each for the blue, green, and red value. For example, the color cyan (a mixture of blue and green) is 255 255 0, red is 0 0 255, and medium gray is 128 128 128.

A BMP file starts with a header that contains various pieces of information. We only need the following items:

Position	Item
2	The size of this file in bytes
10	Offset to the start of the image data
18	The width of the image in pixels
22	The height of the image in pixels

The image is stored as a sequence of pixel rows, starting with the pixels of the bottom-most row of the image. Each pixel row contains a sequence of blue/green/red triplets. The end of the row is padded with additional bytes so that the number of bytes in the row is divisible by 4. (See Figure 5.) For example, if a row consisted of merely three pixels, one cyan, one red, and one medium gray one, the row would be encoded as

255 255 0 0 0 255 128 128 128 $x\ y\ z$

where $x\ y\ z$ are padding bytes to bring the row length up to 12, a multiple of 4. It is these little twists that make working with real-life file formats such a joyful experience.

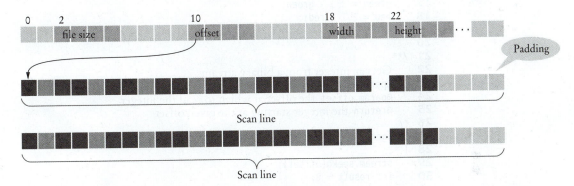

Figure 5 The BMP File Format for 24-bit True Color Images

The sample program at the end of this section reads every pixel of a BMP file and replaces it with its negative, turning white to black, cyan to red, and so on. The result is a negative image of the kind that old-fashioned film cameras used to produce (see Figure 6).

Figure 6
An Image and Its Negative

© Cay Horstmann.

To try out this program, take one of your favorite images, use an image editor to convert to BMP format (or use `queen-mary.bmp` from the code files for this book), then run the program and view the transformed file in an image editor. Exercises P8.16 and P8.17 ask you to produce more interesting effects.

sec06/imagemod.cpp

```cpp
1   #include <iostream>
2   #include <fstream>
3   #include <string>
4   #include <cstdlib>
5
6   using namespace std;
7
8   /**
9       Processes a pixel by forming the negative.
10      @param blue  the blue value of the pixel
11      @param green  the green value of the pixel
12      @param red  the red value of the pixel
13   */
14  void process(int& blue, int& green, int& red)
15  {
16      blue = 255 - blue;
17      green = 255 - green;
18      red = 255 - red;
19  }
20
21  /**
22      Gets an integer from a binary stream.
23      @param stream  the stream
24      @param offset  the offset at which to read the integer
25      @return the integer starting at the given offset
26   */
27  int get_int(fstream& stream, int offset)
28  {
29      stream.seekg(offset);
30      int result = 0;
31      int base = 1;
32      for (int i = 0; i < 4; i++)
33      {
34          result = result + stream.get() * base;
35          base = base * 256;
36      }
37      return result;
38  }
39
40  int main()
41  {
42      cout << "Please enter the file name: ";
43      string filename;
44      cin >> filename;
45
46      fstream stream;
47      // Open as a binary file
48      stream.open(filename, ios::in | ios::out | ios::binary);
49
```

```
50    int file_size = get_int(stream, 2); // Get the image dimensions
51    int start = get_int(stream, 10);
52    int width = get_int(stream, 18);
53    int height = get_int(stream, 22);
54
55    // Scan lines must occupy multiples of four bytes
56    int scanline_size = width * 3;
57    int padding = 0;
58    if (scanline_size % 4 != 0)
59    {
60        padding = 4 - scanline_size % 4;
61    }
62
63    if (file_size != start + (scanline_size + padding) * height)
64    {
65        cout << "Not a 24-bit true color image file." << endl;
66        return 1;
67    }
68
69    int pos = start;
70
71    for (int i = 0; i < height; i++) // For each scan line
72    {
73        for (int j = 0; j < width; j++) // For each pixel
74        {
75            stream.seekg(pos); // Go to the next pixel
76            int blue = stream.get(); // Read the pixel
77            int green = stream.get();
78            int red = stream.get();
79
80            process(blue, green, red); // Process the pixel
81
82            stream.seekp(pos); // Go back to the start of the pixel
83
84            stream.put(blue); // Write the pixel
85            stream.put(green);
86            stream.put(red);
87            pos = pos + 3;
88        }
89
90        stream.seekg(padding, ios::cur); // Skip the padding
91        pos = pos + padding;
92    }
93
94    return 0;
95 }
```

Computing & Society 8.2 **Databases and Privacy**

Most companies use computers to keep huge data files of customer records and other business information. Databases not only lower the cost of doing business; they improve the quality of service that companies can offer. Nowadays it is almost unimaginable how time-consuming it used to be to withdraw money from a bank branch or to make travel reservations.

Today most databases are organized according to the *relational model*. Suppose a company stores your orders and payments. They will probably not repeat your name and address on every order; that would take unnecessary space. Instead, they will keep one file of all their customer names and identify each customer by a unique customer number. Only that customer number, not the entire customer information, is kept with an order record.

To print an invoice, the database program must issue a *query* against both the customer and order files and pull the necessary information (name, address, articles ordered) from both. Frequently, queries involve more than two files. For example, the company may have a file of addresses of car owners and a file of people with good payment history and may want to find all of its customers who placed an order in the last month, drive an expensive car, and pay their bills, so they can send them another catalog.

This kind of query is, of course, much faster if all customer files use the *same* key, which is why so many organizations in the United States try to collect the Social Security numbers of their customers.

Customers			Orders		
Cust. #:	Name		Order #:	Cust. #:	Item
11439	Doe, John		59673	11439	DOS for Historians
			59897	11439	Big C++
			61013	11439	C++ for Everyone

Relational Database Files

The Social Security Act of 1935 provided that each contributor be assigned a Social Security number to track contributions into the Social Security Fund. These numbers have a distinctive format, such as 078-05-1120. (This particular number was printed on sample cards that were inserted in wallets. It actually was the Social Security number of the secretary of a vice president at the wallet manufacturer. When thousands of people used it as their own, the number was voided, and the secretary received a new number.) Although they had not originally been intended for use as a universal identification number, Social Security numbers have become just that.

Some people are very concerned about the fact that just about every organization wants to store their Social Security number and other personal information. There is the possibility that companies and the government can merge multiple databases and derive information about us that we may wish they did not have or that simply may be untrue. An insurance company may deny coverage, or charge a higher premium, if it finds that you have too many relatives with a certain disease. You may be denied a job because of an inaccurate credit or medical report, and you may not even know the reason. These are very disturbing developments that have had a very negative impact for a small but growing number of people.

In many industrialized countries (but not currently in the United States), citizens have a right to control what information about themselves should be communicated to others and under what circumstances.

Social Security Card

CHAPTER SUMMARY

Develop programs that read and write files.

- To read or write files, you use variables of type fstream, ifstream, or ofstream.
- When opening a file stream, you supply the name of the file stored on disk.
- Read from a file stream with the same operations that you use with cin.
- Write to a file stream with the same operations that you use with cout.
- Always use a reference parameter for a stream.

Be able to process text in files.

- When reading a string with the >> operator, the white space between words is consumed.
- You can get individual characters from a stream and unget the last one.
- You can read a line of input with the getline function and then process it further.

Write programs that neatly format their output.

- Use the setw manipulator to set the width of the next output.
- Use the fixed and setprecision manipulators to format floating-point numbers with a fixed number of digits after the decimal point.

Convert between strings and numbers.

- Use an istringstream to convert the numbers inside a string to integers or floating-point numbers.
- Use an ostringstream to convert numeric values to strings.

Process the command line arguments of a C++ program.

- Programs that start from the command line can receive the name of the program and the command line arguments in the main function.

Develop programs that read and write binary files.

- You can access any position in a random access file by moving the file pointer prior to a read or write operation.

CHAPTER 9

CLASSES

CHAPTER GOALS

To understand the concept of encapsulation

To master the separation of interface and implementation

To be able to implement your own classes

To understand how constructors and member functions act on objects

To discover appropriate classes for solving programming problems

To distribute a program over multiple source files

CHAPTER CONTENTS

9.1 OBJECT-ORIENTED PROGRAMMING 290

9.2 IMPLEMENTING A SIMPLE CLASS 292

9.3 SPECIFYING THE PUBLIC INTERFACE OF A CLASS 294
SYN Class Definition 295
CE1 Forgetting a Semicolon 296

9.4 DESIGNING THE DATA REPRESENTATION 297

9.5 MEMBER FUNCTIONS 299
SYN Member Function Definition 301
PT1 All Data Members Should Be Private; Most Member Functions Should Be Public 303
PT2 const Correctness 303

9.6 CONSTRUCTORS 304
CE2 Trying to Call a Constructor 306
ST1 Overloading 306
ST2 Initializer Lists 307
ST3 Universal and Uniform Initialization Syntax 308

9.7 PROBLEM SOLVING: TRACING OBJECTS 308
HT1 Implementing a Class 310
WE1 Implementing a Bank Account Class 314
C&S Electronic Voting Machines 314

9.8 PROBLEM SOLVING: DISCOVERING CLASSES 315
PT3 Make Parallel Vectors into Vectors of Objects 317

9.9 SEPARATE COMPILATION 318

9.10 POINTERS TO OBJECTS 322

9.11 PROBLEM SOLVING: PATTERNS FOR OBJECT DATA 324
C&S Open Source and Free Software 329

This chapter introduces you to object-oriented programming, an important technique for writing complex programs. In an object-oriented program, you don't simply manipulate numbers and strings, but you work with objects that are meaningful for your application. Objects with the same behavior (such as the windmills in the photo) are grouped into classes. A programmer provides the desired behavior by specifying and implementing functions for these classes. In this chapter, you will learn how to discover, specify, and implement your own classes, and how to use them in your programs.

9.1 Object-Oriented Programming

You have learned how to structure your programs by decomposing tasks into functions. This is an excellent practice, but experience shows that it does not go far enough. As programs get larger, it becomes increasingly difficult to maintain a large collection of functions.

To overcome this problem, computer scientists invented **object-oriented programming**, a programming style in which tasks are solved by collaborating objects. Each object has its own set of data, together with a set of functions that can act upon the data. (These functions are called **member functions**).

You have already experienced the object-oriented programming style when you used string objects or streams such as cin and cout. For example, you use the length and substr member functions to work with string objects. The >> and << operators that you use with streams are also implemented as member functions—see Special Topic 9.1.

In C++, a programmer doesn't implement a single object. Instead, the programmer provides a **class**. A class describes a set of objects with the same behavior. For example, the string class describes the behavior of all strings. The class specifies how a string stores its characters, which member functions can be used with strings, and how the member functions are implemented.

> A class describes a set of objects with the same behavior.

A class describes a set of objects with the same behavior. For example, a Car class describes all passenger vehicles that have a certain capacity and shape.

© Media Bakery.

You can drive a car by operating the steering wheel and pedals, without knowing how the engine works. Similarly, you use an object through its member functions. The implementation is hidden.

© Damir Cudic/iStockphoto.

When you develop an object-oriented program, you create your own classes that describe what is important in your application. For example, in a student database you might work with Student and Course classes. Of course, then you must supply member functions for these classes.

> Every class has a public interface: a collection of member functions through which the objects of the class can be manipulated.

When you work with an object, you do not know how it is implemented. You need not know how a string organizes a character sequence, or how the cin object reads input from the console. All you need to know is the **public interface**: the specifications for the member functions that you can invoke. The process of providing a public interface, while hiding the implementation details, is called **encapsulation**.

> Encapsulation is the act of providing a public interface and hiding implementation details.

You will want to use encapsulation for your own classes. When you define a class, you will specify the behavior of the public member functions, but you will hide the implementation details. Encapsulation benefits the programmers who use your classes. They can put your classes to work without having to know their implementations, just as you are able to make use of the string and stream classes without knowing their internal details.

> Encapsulation enables changes in the implementation without affecting users of a class.

Encapsulation is also a benefit for the implementor of a class. When working on a program that is being developed over a long period of time, it is common for implementation details to change, usually to make objects more efficient or more capable. Encapsulation is crucial to enabling these changes. When the implementation is hidden, the implementor is free to make improvements. Because the implementation is hidden, these improvements do not affect the programmers who use the objects.

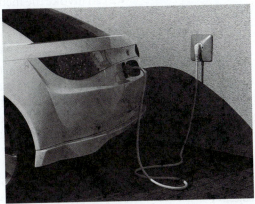

A driver of an electric car doesn't have to learn new controls even though the car engine is very different. Neither does the programmer who uses an object with an improved implementation—as long as the same member functions are used.

© iStockphoto.com/Christian Waadt.

In this chapter, you will learn how to design and implement your own classes in C++, and how to structure your programs in an object-oriented way, using the principle of encapsulation.

9.2 Implementing a Simple Class

In this section, we look at the implementation of a very simple class. You will see how objects store their data, and how member functions access the data of an object. Knowing how a very simple class operates will help you design and implement more complex classes later in this chapter.

Our first example is a class that models a *tally counter*, a mechanical device that is used to count people—for example, to find out how many people attend a concert or board a bus (see Figure 1).

Whenever the operator pushes a button, the counter value advances by one. We model this operation with a count function. A physical counter has a display to show the current value. In our simulation, we use a get_value function instead.

© Jasmin Awad/iStockphoto.

Figure 1 A Tally Counter

Here is an example of using the Counter class. As you know from using classes such as string and ifstream, you use the class name and a variable name to define an object of the class:

```
Counter tally;
```

In Section 9.6, you will learn how to ensure that objects are properly initialized. For now, we will call a member function to ensure that the object has the correct state:

```
tally.reset();
```

Next, we invoke member functions on our object. First, we invoke the count member function twice, simulating two button pushes. Then we invoke the get_value member function to check how many times the button was pushed.

```
tally.count();
tally.count();
int result = tally.get_value(); // Sets result to 2
```

We can invoke the member functions again, and the result will be different.

```
tally.count();
tally.count();
result = tally.get_value(); // Sets result to 4
```

As you can see, the tally object remembers the effect of prior function calls.

By specifying the member functions of the Counter class, we have now specified the **behavior** of Counter objects. In order to produce this behavior, each object needs internal data, called the **state** of the object. In this simple example, the object state is very simple. It is the value that keeps track of how many times the counter has been advanced.

An object stores its state in **data members**. A data member is a storage location that is present in each object of the class.

You specify data members in the class definition:

> The member functions of a class define the behavior of its objects.

> An object's data members represent the state of the object.

```
class Counter
{
public:
   . . .
private:
   int value;
   . . .
};
```

A class definition has a public and private section. As you will see in the following section, we always place data members in the private section.

Each object of a class has its own set of data members. For example, if `concert_counter` and `boarding_counter` are two objects of the `Counter` class, then each object has its own value variable (see Figure 2).

> Each object of a class has its own set of data members.

The member functions are declared in the public section of the class.

```
class Counter
{
public:
   void reset();
   void count();
   int get_value() const;
private:
   int value;
};
```

The `const` reserved word denotes the fact that calling the `get_value` member function, unlike the other member functions, does not change the object. We will discuss this distinction in more detail in the following section.

Next, let us have a quick look at the implementation of the member functions of the `Counter` class. The count member function advances the counter value by 1.

```
void Counter::count()
{
   value = value + 1;
}
```

The function definition can be placed anywhere below the definition of the `Counter` class. The `Counter::` prefix indicates that we are defining the count function of the Counter class.

Now have another look at the implementation of the `Counter::count` member function. Note how the body of the function increments the data member value. Which

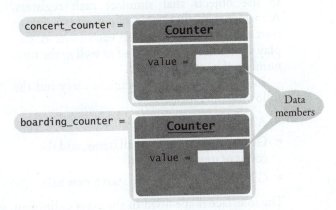

Figure 2   Data Members

data member? The one belonging to the object on which the function is called. For example, consider the call

```
concert_counter.count();
```

This call advances the `value` member of the `concert_counter` object.

The `reset` member function simply sets the value to zero:

```
void Counter::reset()
{
    value = 0;
}
```

A member function can access the data members of the object on which it acts.

Finally, the `get_value` member function returns the current value:

```
int Counter::get_value() const
{
    return value;
}
```

A private data member can only be accessed by the member functions of its own class.

This member function is required so that users of the `Counter` class can find out how often a particular counter has been clicked. A user cannot simply access the `value` data member. That variable has been declared in the private section. The `private` reserved word restricts access to the member functions of the *same class*. For example, the `value` variable can be accessed by the `count` and `get_value` member functions of the `Counter` class but not by a member function of another class. Those other functions need to use the `get_value` member function if they want to find out the counter's value, or the `count` member function if they want to change it.

Private data members are an essential part of encapsulation. They allow a programmer to hide the implementation of a class from a class user.

EXAMPLE CODE See sec02 of your companion code for a program that uses the `Counter` class.

9.3 Specifying the Public Interface of a Class

To define a class, we first need to specify its **public interface**. The public interface of a class consists of all member functions that a user of the class may want to apply to its objects.

Let's consider a simple example. We want to use objects that simulate cash registers. A cashier who rings up a sale presses a key to start the sale, then rings up each item. A display shows the amount owed as well as the total number of items purchased.

In our simulation, we want to carry out the following operations:

- Add the price of an item.
- Get the total amount of all items, and the count of items purchased.
- Clear the cash register to start a new sale.

© James Richey/iStockphoto.

Our first example of a class simulates a cash register.

The interface is specified in the **class definition**, summarized in Syntax 9.1. We will call our class `CashRegister`. (We follow the convention that the name of a programmer-

© GlobalP/iStockphoto.

defined class starts with an uppercase letter, as does each word within the name. This naming convention is called *camel case* because the uppercase letters in the middle of the name look like the humps of a camel.)

Here is the C++ syntax for the CashRegister class definition:

```
class CashRegister
{
public:
    void clear();
    void add_item(double price);

    double get_total() const;
    int get_count() const;

private:
    data members—see Section 9.4
};
```

You can use member function declarations and function comments to specify the public interface of a class.

The member functions are declared in the *public section* of the class. Any part of the program can call the member functions. The data members are defined in the *private section* of the class. Only the member functions of the class can access those data members; they are hidden from the remainder of the program.

It is legal to declare the private members before the public section, but in this book, we place the public section first. After all, most programmers reading a class are class users, not implementors, and they are more interested in the public interface than in the private implementation.

The member function declarations look similar to the declarations of regular functions. These declarations do not provide any implementation. You will see in Section 9.5 how to implement the member functions.

Syntax 9.1   Class Definition

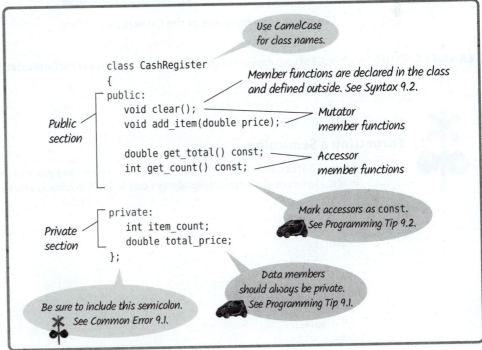

A mutator member function changes the object on which it operates.

There are two kinds of member functions, called **mutators** and **accessors**. A mutator is a function that modifies the data members of the object. The CashRegister class has two mutators: clear and add_item. After you call either of these functions, the total amount and item count are changed.

Accessors just query the object for some information without changing it. The CashRegister class has two accessors: get_total and get_count. Applying either of these functions to a CashRegister object simply returns a value and does not modify the object. In C++, you should use the const reserved word to mark accessor functions (see Programming Tip 9.2), like this:

An accessor member function does not change the object on which it operates. Use const with accessors.

```
double get_total() const;
```

Member functions are invoked using the dot notation that you have already seen with string and stream functions:

```
CashRegister register1; // Defines a CashRegister object
register1.clear(); // Invokes a member function
```

Now we know *what* a CashRegister object can do, but not *how* it does it. Of course, to use CashRegister objects in our programs, we don't need to know. We simply use the public interface. Figure 3 shows the interface of the CashRegister class. The mutator functions are shown with arrows pointing inside the private data to indicate that they modify the data. The accessor functions are shown with arrows pointing the other way to indicate that they just read the data.

Figure 3 The Interface of the CashRegister Class

EXAMPLE CODE   See sec03 of your companion code for the public interface of the CashRegister class.

Common Error 9.1

Forgetting a Semicolon

Braces { } are common in C++ code, and usually you do not place a semicolon after the closing brace. However, class definitions always end in };. A common error is to forget that semicolon:

```
class CashRegister
{
public:
   . . .
private:
   . . .
} // Forgot semicolon

int main()
{
```

```
   // Many compilers report the error in this line
   . . .
}
```

This error can be extremely confusing to many compilers. There is syntax, now obsolete but supported for compatibility with old code, to define class types and variables of that type simultaneously. Because the compiler doesn't know that you don't use that obsolete construction, it tries to analyze the code wrongly and ultimately reports an error. Unfortunately, it may report the error *several lines away* from the line in which you forgot the semicolon.

If the compiler reports bizarre errors in lines that you are sure are correct, check that each of the preceding class definitions is terminated by a semicolon.

9.4 Designing the Data Representation

An object holds data members that are accessed by member functions.

An object stores its data in **data members**. These are variables that are declared inside the class.

When implementing a class, you have to determine which data each object needs to store. The object needs to have all the information necessary to carry out any member function call.

Go through all member functions and consider their data requirements. It is a good idea to start with the accessor functions. For example, a CashRegister object must be able to return the correct value for the get_total function. That means, it must either store all entered prices and compute the total in the function call, or it must store the total.

Now apply the same reasoning to the get_count function. If the cash register stores all entered prices, it can count them in the get_count function. Otherwise, you need to have a variable for the count.

© migin/iStockphoto.

Like a wilderness explorer who needs to carry all items that may be needed, an object needs to store the data required for any function calls.

The add_item function receives a price as an argument, and it must record the price. If the CashRegister object stores an array of entered prices, then the add_item function appends the price. On the other hand, if we decide to store just the item total and count, then the add_item function updates these two variables.

Finally, the clear function must prepare the cash register for the next sale, either by emptying the array of prices or by setting the total and count to zero.

We have now discovered two different ways of representing the data that the object needs. Either of them will work, and we have to make a choice. We will choose the simpler one: variables for the total price and the item count. (Other options are explored in Exercises P9.6 and P9.7.)

The data members are defined in the private section of the class definition:

```
class CashRegister
{
```

```
public:
    // See Section 9.3
private:
    int item_count;
    double total_price;
};
```

Every object has its own set of data members.

Every `CashRegister` object has a separate copy of these data members (see Figure 4).

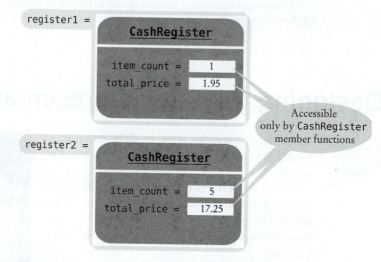

register1 =

CashRegister

item_count = 1
total_price = 1.95

register2 =

CashRegister

item_count = 5
total_price = 17.25

Accessible only by `CashRegister` member functions

Figure 4 Data Members of `CashRegister` Objects

Because the data members are defined to be private, only the member functions of the class can access them. Programmers using the `CashRegister` class cannot access the data members directly:

```
int main()
{
    . . .
    cout << register1.item_count; // Error—use get_count() instead
    . . .
}
```

© Mark Evans/iStockphoto.

These clocks have common behavior, but each of them has a different state. Similarly, objects of a class can have their data members set to different values.

All data access must occur through the public interface. Thus, the data members of an object are effectively hidden from the programmer using the class. While it is theoretically possible in C++ to leave data members unencapsulated (by placing them into the public section), this is very uncommon in practice. We will always make all data members private in this book.

> Private data members can only be accessed by member functions of the same class.

EXAMPLE CODE   See sec04 of your companion code for the CashRegister class with its data members defined.

9.5 Member Functions

The definition of a class declares its member functions. Each member function is defined separately, after the class definition. The following sections show how to define member functions.

9.5.1 Implementing Member Functions

Here is the implementation of the add_item function of the CashRegister class.

```
void CashRegister::add_item(double price)
{
   item_count++;
   total_price = total_price + price;
}
```

> Use the *ClassName::* prefix when defining member functions.

The CashRegister:: prefix makes it clear that we are defining the add_item function of the CashRegister class. In C++ it is perfectly legal to have add_item functions in other classes as well, and it is important to specify exactly which add_item function we are defining. (See Syntax 9.2.) You use the *ClassName*::add_item syntax only when *defining* the function, not when calling it. When you call the add_item member function, the call has the form *object*.add_item(...).

When defining an accessor member function, supply the reserved word const following the closing parenthesis of the parameter list. Here is the get_count member function:

```
int CashRegister::get_count() const
{
   return item_count;
}
```

You will find the other member functions with the example program at the end of this section.

9.5.2 Implicit and Explicit Parameters

Whenever you refer to a data member, such as item_count or total_price, in a member function, it denotes the data member *of the object on which the member function was invoked*. For example, consider the call

```
register1.add_item(1.95);
```

The first statement in the CashRegister::add_item function is

```
item_count++;
```

```
void display_all(const CashRegister registers[])
{
    for (int i = 0; i < NREGISTERS; i++) { registers[i].display(); }
}
```

That programmer is conscientious and declares the registers parameter variable as const. But then the call registers[i].display() will not compile. Because CashRegister::display is not tagged as const, the compiler suspects that the call registers[i].display() may modify registers[i]. But the function promised not to modify the registers array.

If you write a program with other team members who are conscientious about const, it is very important that you do your part as well. You should therefore get into the habit of using const with all accessor member functions.

9.6 Constructors

A constructor is called automatically whenever an object is created.

A **constructor** is a member function that initializes the data members of an object. The constructor is automatically called whenever an object is created. By supplying a constructor, you can ensure that all data members are properly set before any member functions act on an object.

To understand the importance of constructors, consider the following statements:

```
CashRegister register1;
register1.add_item(1.95);
int count = register1.get_count(); // May not be 1
```

Here, the programmer forgot to call clear before adding items. Therefore, the data members of the register1 object were initialized with random values. Constructors guarantee that an object is always fully initialized when it is defined.

The name of a constructor is the same as the class name.

The name of a constructor is identical to the name of its class. You declare constructors in the class definition, for example:

```
class CashRegister
{
public:
    CashRegister(); // A constructor
    . . .
};
```

A constructor is like a set of assembly instructions for an object.

© Ann Marie Kurtz/iStockphoto.

Constructors never return values, but you do not use the void reserved word when declaring them.

Here is the definition of that constructor:

```
CashRegister::CashRegister()
{
    item_count = 0;
    total_price = 0;
}
```

In the constructor definition, the first CashRegister (before the ::) indicates that we are about to define a member function of the CashRegister class. The second CashRegister is the name of that member function.

> A default constructor has no arguments.

The constructor that you just saw has no arguments. Such a constructor is called a **default constructor**. It is used whenever you define an object and do not specify any parameters for the construction. For example, if you define

```
CashRegister register1;
```

then the default constructor is called. It sets register1.item_count and register1.total_price to zero.

> A class can have multiple constructors.

Many classes have more than one constructor. This allows you to define objects in different ways. Consider for example a BankAccount class that has two constructors:

```
class BankAccount
{
public:
    BankAccount(); // Sets balance to 0
    BankAccount(double initial_balance); // Sets balance to initial_balance
    // Member functions omitted
private:
    double balance;
};
```

> The compiler picks the constructor that matches the construction arguments.

Both constructors have the same name as the class, BankAccount. But the default constructor has no parameter variables, whereas the second constructor has a double parameter variable. (This is an example of *overloading*—see Special Topic 9.1.)

When you construct an object, the compiler chooses the constructor that matches the arguments that you supply. For example,

```
BankAccount joes_account;
    // Uses default constructor
BankAccount lisas_account(499.95);
    // Uses BankAccount(double) constructor
```

> Be sure to initialize all number and pointer data members in a constructor.

When implementing a constructor, you need to pay particular attention to all data members that are numbers or pointers. These types are not classes and therefore have no constructors. If you have a data member that is an object of a class (such as a string object), then that class has a constructor, and the object will be initialized. For example, all string objects are automatically initialized to the empty string.

Consider this class:

```
class Item
{
public:
    Item();
    // Additional member functions omitted
private:
    string description;
    double price;
```

```
};
```

In the `Item` constructor, you need to set `price` to 0, but you need not initialize the `description` data member. It is automatically initialized to the empty string.

As of C++ 11, you can specify default values for data members:

```
class Item
{
public:
   // No constructor
   // Member functions
private:
   string description;
   double price = 0;
};
```

If you do not initialize `price` in a constructor, it is set to zero.

If you do not supply any constructor for a class, the compiler automatically generates a default constructor. The automatically generated default constructor initializes the data members that have default constructors or default values, and leaves the other data members uninitialized.

EXAMPLE CODE See sec06 of your companion code for the complete `CashRegister` class with a single constructor, a `BankAccount` class with two constructors, and an `Item` class with three constructors.

Common Error 9.2

Trying to Call a Constructor

The constructor is invoked only when an object is first created. You cannot invoke it again. For example, you cannot call the constructor to clear an object:

```
CashRegister register1;
. . .
register1.CashRegister(); // Error
```

It is true that the default constructor sets a *new* `CashRegister` object to the cleared state, but you cannot invoke a constructor on an *existing* object.

In this case, you can simply invoke the `clear` member function:

```
register1.clear();
```

Alternatively, you can construct a second cash register and assign it to this one:

```
CashRegister cleared_register;
register = cleared_register;
```

Special Topic 9.1

Overloading

When the same function name is used for more than one function, then the name is **overloaded**. In C++ you can overload function names provided the types of the parameter variables are different. For example, you can define two functions, both called `print`:

```
void print(CashRegister r)
void print(Item i)
```

When the print function is called,

```
print(x);
```

the compiler looks at the type of x. If x is a CashRegister object, the first function is called. If x is an Item object, the second function is called. If x is neither, the compiler generates an error.

It is always possible to avoid overloading by giving each function a unique name, such as print_register or print_item. However, we have no choice with constructors. C++ demands that the name of a constructor equal the name of the class. If a class has more than one constructor, then that name must be overloaded.

In addition to name overloading, C++ also supports *operator overloading*. It is possible to give new meanings to the familiar C++ operators such as +, ==, and <<. This is an advanced technique that we will discuss in Chapter 13.

Special Topic 9.2
Initializer Lists

When you construct an object whose data members are themselves objects, those objects are constructed by their class's default constructor. However, if a data member belongs to a class without a default constructor, you need to invoke the data member's constructor explicitly. Here is an example.

This Item class has no default constructor:

```
class Item
{
public:
   Item(string item_description, double item_price);
   // No other constructors
   . . .
};
```

This Order class has a data member of type Item:

```
class Order
{
public:
   Order(string customer_name, string item_description, double item_price);
   . . .
private:
   Item article;
   string customer;
};
```

The Order constructor must call the Item constructor. That is achieved with an *initializer list*. The initializer list is placed before the opening brace of the constructor. The list starts with a colon and contains names of data members with their construction arguments.

```
Order::Order(string customer_name, string item_description, double item_price)
   : article(item_description, item_price)
{
   customer = customer_name;
}
```

Initializers are separated by commas. They can also initialize a data member as a copy of a value of the same type. Here is another way of writing the Order constructor:

```
Order::Order(string customer_name, string item_description, double item_price)
   : article(item_description, item_price), customer(customer_name)
{
}
```

Special Topic 9.3

Universal and Uniform Initialization Syntax

In C++, there are several syntactic variations to initialize a variable, such as

```
double price = 19.25;
int squares[] = { 1, 4, 9, 16 };
BankAccount lisas_account(499.95);
```

C++ 11 introduces a uniform syntax, using braces and no equal sign, like this:

```
double price { 19.25 };
int squares[] { 1, 4, 9, 16 };
BankAccount lisas_account { 499.95 };
```

Use empty braces for default initialization.

```
double balance {}; // Initialized with zero
BankAccount joes_account {}; // Uses default constructor
```

The syntax is universal: it can be used in every context in which variables can be initialized. For example,

```
double* price_pointer = new double { 19.15 };
int result = sum({ 1, 4, 9, 16});
    // where sum has a parameter variable of type vector<int>
```

You can also use the uniform syntax to initialize data members in a constructor. For example, the Order constructor of Special Topic 9.2 can be written as

```
Order::Order(string customer_name, string item_description, double item_price)
   : article{item_description, item_price}, customer{customer_name}
{}
```

There is much to like about this universal and uniform syntax. However, as it is quite different from the traditional syntax, it will likely take some time before it is commonly used.

9.7 Problem Solving: Tracing Objects

You have seen how the technique of hand-tracing is useful for understanding how a program works. When your program contains objects, it is useful to adapt the technique so that you gain a better understanding about object data and encapsulation.

> Write the member functions on the front of a card, and the data member values on the back.

Use an index card or a sticky note for each object. On the front, write the member functions that the object can execute. On the back, make a table for the values of the data members.

Here is a card for a CashRegister object:

				item_count	total_price
CashRegister reg1					
clear					
add_item(price)					
get_total					
get_count					

front   *back*

In a small way, this gives you a feel for encapsulation. An object is manipulated through its public interface (on the front of the card), and the data members are hidden in the back.

When an object is constructed, fill in the initial values of the data members.

item_count	total_price
0	0

Whenever a mutator member function is executed, cross out the old values and write the new ones below. Here is what happens after a call to the add_item member function:

item_count	total_price
~~0~~	~~0~~
1	19.95

If you have more than one object in your program, you will have multiple cards, one for each object:

item_count	total_price
~~0~~	~~0~~
1	19.95

item_count	total_price
~~0~~	~~0~~
1	19.95
2	14.90

These diagrams are also useful when you design a class. Suppose you are asked to enhance the CashRegister class to compute the sales tax. Add a function get_sales_tax to the front of the card. Now turn the card over, look over the data members, and ask yourself whether the object has sufficient information to compute the answer. Remember that each object is an autonomous unit. Any data value that can be used in a computation must be

- A data member.
- A function argument.
- A global constant or variable.

To compute the sales tax, we need to know the tax rate and the total of the taxable items. (Food items are usually not subject to sales tax.) We don't have that information available. Let us introduce additional data members for the tax rate and the taxable total. The tax rate can be set in the constructor (assuming it stays fixed for the lifetime of the object). When adding an item, we need to be told whether the item is taxable. If so, we add its price to the taxable total.

For example, consider the following statements.

```
CashRegister reg2(7.5); // 7.5 percent sales tax
reg2.add_item(3.95, false); // not taxable
reg2.add_item(19.95, true); // taxable
```

When you record the effect on a card, it looks like this:

item_count	total_price	taxable_total	tax_rate
0	0	0	7.5
1	3.95		
2	23.90	19.95	

With this information, it becomes easy to compute the tax. It is *taxable_total x tax_rate / 100*. Tracing the object helped us understand the need for additional data members.

HOW TO 9.1

Implementing a Class

A very common task is to implement a class whose objects can carry out a set of specified actions. This How To walks you through the necessary steps.

Problem Statement   As an example, consider a class Menu. An object of this class can display a menu such as

```
1) Open new account
2) Log into existing account
3) Help
4) Quit
```

Then the menu waits for the user to supply a value. If the user does not supply a valid value, the menu is redisplayed, and the user can try again.

© Mark Evans/iStockphoto.

Step 1   Get an informal list of the responsibilities of your objects.

Be careful that you restrict yourself to features that are actually required in the problem. With real-world items, such as cash registers or bank accounts, there are potentially dozens of features that might be worth implementing. However, your job is not to faithfully model the real world. You need to determine only those responsibilities that you need for solving your specific problem.

In the case of the menu, you need to

Display the menu.
Get user input.

Now look for hidden responsibilities that aren't part of the problem description. How do objects get created? Which mundane activities need to happen, such as clearing the cash register at the beginning of each sale?

In the menu example, consider how a menu is produced. The programmer creates an empty menu object and then adds options "Open new account", "Help", and so on. There is a hidden responsibility:

Add an option.

Step 2   Specify the public interface.

Turn the list in Step 1 into a set of member functions, with specific types for the parameter variables and the return values. Be sure to mark accessors as const. Many programmers find this step simpler if they write out member function calls that are applied to a sample object, like this:

```
Menu main_menu;
main_menu.add_option("Open new account");
// Add more options
int input = main_menu.get_input();
```

Now we have a specific list of member functions.

- `void add_option(string option)`

- `int get_input() const`

What about displaying the menu? There is no sense in displaying the menu without also asking the user for input. However, `get_input` may need to display the menu more than once if the user provides a bad input. Thus, `display` is a good candidate for a private member function.

To complete the public interface, you need to specify the constructors. Ask yourself what information you need in order to construct an object of your class. Sometimes you will want two constructors: one that sets all data members to a default and one that sets them to user-supplied values.

In the case of the menu example, we can get by with a single constructor that creates an empty menu.

Here is the public interface:

```
class Menu
{
public:
    Menu();
    void add_option(string option);
    int get_input() const
private:
    . . .
};
```

Step 3   Document the public interface.

Supply a **documentation comment** for the class, then comment each member function.

```
/**
    A menu that is displayed on a console.
*/
class Menu
{
public:
    /**
        Constructs a menu with no options.
    */
    Menu();
```

```
/**
    Adds an option to the end of this menu.
    @param option the option to add
*/
void add_option(string option);

/**
    Displays the menu, with options numbered starting with 1,
    and prompts the user for input. Repeats until a valid input
    is supplied.
    @return the number that the user supplied
*/
int get_input() const;
private:
    . . .
};
```

Step 4   Determine data members.

Ask yourself what information an object needs to store to do its job. Remember, the member functions can be called in any order! The object needs to have enough internal memory to be able to process every member function using just its data members and the member function arguments. Go through each member function, perhaps starting with a simple one or an interesting one, and ask yourself what you need to carry out the member function's task. Make data members to store the information that the member function needs.

In the menu example, we clearly need to store the menu options so that the menu can be displayed. How should we store them? As a vector of strings? As one long string? Both approaches can be made to work. We will use a vector here. Exercise E9.6 asks you to implement the other approach.

```
class Menu
{
    . . .
private:
    . . .
    vector<string> options;
};
```

When checking for user input, we need to know the number of menu items. Because we store them in a vector, the number of menu items is simply obtained as the size of the vector. If you stored the menu items in one long string, you might want to keep another data member that stores the menu item count.

Step 5   Implement constructors and member functions.

Implement the constructors and member functions in your class, one at a time, starting with the easiest ones. For example, here is the implementation of the add_option member function:

```
void Menu::add_option(string option)
{
    options.push_back(option);
}
```

Here is the get_input member function. This member function is a bit more sophisticated. It loops until a valid input has been obtained, and it calls the private display member function to display the menu.

```
int Menu::get_input() const
{
    int input = 0;
    do
    {
        display();
        cin >> input;
```

```
   }
   while (input < 1 || input > options.size());
   return input;
}
```

Finally, here is the `display` member function:

```
void Menu::display() const
{
   for (int i = 0; i < options.size(); i++)
   {
      cout << i + 1 << ") " << options[i] << endl;
   }
}
```

The `Menu` constructor is a bit odd. We need to construct a menu with no options. A vector is a class, and it has a default constructor. That constructor does exactly what we want, namely to construct an empty vector. Nothing else needs to be done:

```
Menu::Menu()
{
}
```

If you find that you have trouble with the implementation of some of your member functions, you may need to rethink your choice of data members. It is common for a beginner to start out with a set of data members that cannot accurately describe the state of an object. Don't hesitate to go back and rethink your implementation strategy.

Once you have completed the implementation, compile your class and fix any compiler errors.

Step 6   Test your class.

Write a short tester program and execute it. The tester program should carry out the member function calls that you found in Step 2.

```
int main()
{
   Menu main_menu;
   main_menu.add_option("Open new account");
   main_menu.add_option("Log into existing account");
   main_menu.add_option("Help");
   main_menu.add_option("Quit");
   int input = main_menu.get_input();
   cout << "Input: " << input << endl;
   return 0;
}
```

Program Run

```
1) Open new account
2) Log into existing account
3) Help
4) Quit
5
1) Open new account
2) Log into existing account
3) Help
4) Quit
3
Input: 3
```

EXAMPLE CODE   See how_to_1 of your companion code for the complete menu program.

WORKED EXAMPLE 9.1

Implementing a Bank Account Class

Learn how to develop a class that simulates a bank account. See your E-Text or visit wiley.com/go/bclo3.

Computing & Society 9.1 Electronic Voting Machines

In the 2000 presidential elections in the United States, votes were tallied by a variety of machines. Some machines processed cardboard ballots into which voters punched holes to indicate their choices (see photo below). When voters were not careful, remains of paper—the now infamous "chads"—were partially stuck in the punch cards, causing votes to be miscounted. A manual recount was necessary, but it was not carried out everywhere due to time constraints and procedural wrangling. The election was very close, and there remain doubts in the minds of many people whether the election outcome would have been different if the voting machines had accurately counted the intent of the voters.

© Peter Nguyen/iStockphoto.

Punch Card Ballot

Subsequently, voting machine manufacturers have argued that electronic voting machines would avoid the problems caused by punch cards or optically scanned forms. In an electronic voting machine, voters indicate their preferences by pressing buttons or touching icons on a computer screen. Typically, each voter is presented with a summary screen for

review before casting the ballot. The process is very similar to using an automatic bank teller machine.

It seems plausible that these machines make it more likely that a vote is counted in the same way that the voter intends. However, there has been significant controversy surrounding some types of electronic voting machines. If a machine simply records the votes and prints out the totals after the election has been completed, then how do you know that the machine worked correctly? Inside the machine is a computer that executes a program, and, as you may know from your own experience, programs can have bugs.

In fact, some electronic voting machines do have bugs. There have been isolated cases where machines reported tallies that were impossible. When a machine reports far more or far fewer votes than voters, then it is clear that it malfunctioned. Unfortunately, it is then impossible to find out the actual votes. Over time, one would expect these bugs to be fixed in the software. More insidiously, if the results are plausible, nobody may ever investigate.

Many computer scientists have spoken out on this issue and confirmed that it is impossible, with today's technology, to tell that software is error free and has not been tampered with. Many of them recommend that electronic voting machines should employ a *voter verifiable audit trail*. (A good source of information is http://verifiedvoting.org.) Typically, a voter-verifiable machine prints out a ballot. Each voter has a chance to review the printout, and then deposits it in an old-fashioned ballot box. If there is a problem with the electronic

equipment, the printouts can be scanned or counted by hand.

© Lisa F. Young/iStockphoto.

Touch Screen Voting Machine

As this book is written, this concept is strongly resisted both by manufacturers of electronic voting machines and by their customers, the cities and counties that run elections. Manufacturers are reluctant to increase the cost of the machines because they may not be able to pass the cost increase on to their customers, who tend to have tight budgets. Election officials fear problems with malfunctioning printers, and some of them have publicly stated that they actually prefer equipment that eliminates bothersome recounts.

What do you think? You probably use an automatic bank teller machine to get cash from your bank account. Do you review the paper record that the machine issues? Do you check your bank statement? Even if you don't, do you put your faith in other people who double-check their balances, so that the bank won't get away with widespread cheating?

At any rate, is the integrity of banking equipment more important or less important than that of voting machines? Won't every voting process have some room for error and fraud anyway? Is the added cost for equipment, paper, and staff time reasonable to combat a potentially slight risk of malfunction and fraud? Computer scientists cannot answer these questions—an informed society must make these tradeoffs. But, like all professionals, they have an obligation to speak out and give accurate testimony about the capabilities and limitations of computing equipment.

9.8 Problem Solving: Discovering Classes

To discover classes, look for nouns in the problem description.

When you solve a problem using objects and classes, you need to determine the classes required for the implementation. You may be able to reuse existing classes, or you may need to implement new ones. One simple approach for discovering classes and member functions is to look for the nouns and verbs in the problem description. Often, nouns correspond to classes, and verbs correspond to member functions.

Concepts from the problem domain, be it science, business, or a game, often make good classes. Examples are

- Cannonball
- CashRegister
- Monster

Concepts from the problem domain are good candidates for classes.

The name for such a class should be a noun that describes the concept. Other frequently used classes represent system services such as files or menus.

What might not be a good class? If you can't tell from the class name what an object of the class is supposed to do, then you are probably not on the right track. For example, your homework assignment might ask you to write a program that prints paychecks. Suppose you start by trying to design a class PaycheckProgram. What would an object of this class do? An object of this class would have to do everything that the homework needs to do. That doesn't simplify anything. A better class would be Paycheck. Then your program can manipulate one or more Paycheck objects.

© Oleg Prikhodko/iStockphoto.

In a class scheduling system, potential classes from the problem domain include Class, LectureHall, Instructor, and Student.

Another common mistake, particularly by students who are used to writing programs that consist of functions, is to turn an action into a class. For example, if your homework assignment is to compute a paycheck, you may consider writing a class ComputePaycheck. But can you visualize a "ComputePaycheck" object? The fact that "ComputePaycheck" isn't a noun tips you off that you are on the wrong track. On the other hand, a Paycheck class makes intuitive sense. The word "paycheck" is a noun. You can visualize a paycheck object. You can then think about useful member functions of the Paycheck class, such as compute_taxes, that help you solve the assignment.

When you analyze a problem description, you often find that you need multiple classes. It is then helpful to consider how these classes are related. One of the fundamental relationships between classes is the "aggregation" relationship (which is informally known as the "has-a" relationship).

© bojan fatur/iStockphoto.

A car has a motor and tires. In object-oriented design, this "has-a" relationship is called aggregation.

> A class aggregates another if its objects contain objects of the other class.

The **aggregation** relationship states that objects of one class contain objects of another class. Consider a quiz that is made up of questions. Since each quiz has one or more questions, we say that the class Quiz aggregates the class Question. There is a standard notation, called a UML (**Unified Modeling Language**) class diagram, to describe class relationships. In the UML notation, aggregation is denoted by a line with a diamond-shaped symbol (see Figure 6).

Figure 6 Class Diagram

Finding out about aggregation is very helpful for deciding how to implement classes. For example, when you implement the Quiz class, you will want to store the questions of a quiz as a data member. Since a quiz can have any number of questions, you will choose a vector:

```
class Quiz
{
   . . .
private:
   vector<Question> questions;
};
```

In summary, when you analyze a problem description, you will want to carry out these tasks:

- Find the concepts that you need to implement as classes. Often, these will be nouns in the problem description.
- Find the responsibilities of the classes. Often, these will be verbs in the problem description.
- Find relationships between the classes that you have discovered. In this section, we described the aggregation relationship. In the next chapter, you will learn about another important relationship between classes, called inheritance.

Programming Tip 9.3

Make Parallel Vectors into Vectors of Objects

Sometimes, you find yourself using vectors of the same length, each of which stores a part of what conceptually should be an object. In that situation, it is a good idea to reorganize your program and use a single vector whose elements are objects.

For example, suppose an invoice contains a series of item descriptions and prices. One solution is to keep two vectors:

```
vector<string> descriptions;
vector<double> prices;
```

Each of the vectors will have the same length, and the ith *slice*, consisting of `descriptions[i]` and `prices[i]`, contains data that needs to be processed together. These vectors are called **parallel vectors** (see Figure 7).

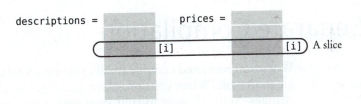

Figure 7 Parallel Vectors

Parallel vectors become a headache in larger programs. The programmer must ensure that the vectors always have the same length and that each slice is filled with values that actually belong together. Moreover, any function that operates on a slice must get all of the vectors as arguments, which is tedious to program.

The remedy is simple. Look at the slice and find the *concept* that it represents. Then make the concept into a class. In this example, each slice contains the description and price of an *item*; turn this into a class.

Avoid parallel vectors by changing them into vectors of objects.

```
class Item
{
public:
   . . .
private:
   string description;
   double price;
};
```

You can now eliminate the parallel vectors and replace them with a single vector:

```
vector<Item> items;
```

Each slot in the resulting vector corresponds to a slice in the set of parallel vectors (see Figure 8).

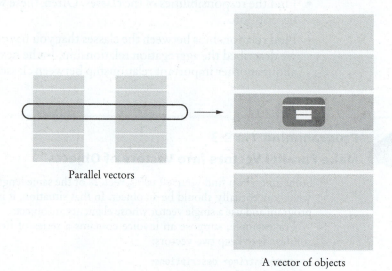

Parallel vectors

A vector of objects

Figure 8 Eliminating Parallel Vectors

9.9 Separate Compilation

The code of complex programs is distributed over multiple files.

When you write and compile small programs, you can place all your code into a single source file. When your programs get larger or you work in a team, that situation changes. You will want to split your code into separate source files. There are two reasons why this split becomes necessary. First, it takes time to compile a file, and it seems silly to wait for the compiler to keep translating code that doesn't change. If your code is distributed over several source files, then only those files that you change need to be recompiled. The second reason becomes apparent when you work with other programmers in a team. It would be very difficult for multiple programmers to edit a single source file simultaneously. Therefore, the program code is broken up so that each programmer is solely responsible for a separate set of files.

If your program is composed of multiple files, some of these files will define data types or functions that are needed in other files. There must be a path of communication between the files. In C++, that communication happens through the inclusion of **header files**.

A header file contains

- Definitions of classes.
- Definitions of constants.
- Declarations of nonmember functions.

The source file contains

- Definitions of member functions.
- Definitions of nonmember functions.

For the `CashRegister` class, you create a pair of files, `cashregister.h` and `cashregister.cpp`, that contain the interface and the implementation, respectively.

The header file contains the class definition:

Header files contain the definitions of classes and declarations of nonmember functions.

sec09/cashregister.h

```
1   #ifndef CASHREGISTER_H
2   #define CASHREGISTER_H
3
4   /**
5      A simulated cash register that tracks the item count and
6      the total amount due.
7   */
8   class CashRegister
9   {
10  public:
11     /**
12        Constructs a cash register with cleared item count and total.
13     */
14     CashRegister();
15
16     /**
17        Clears the item count and the total.
18     */
19     void clear();
20
21     /**
22        Adds an item to this cash register.
23        @param price the price of this item
24     */
25     void add_item(double price);
26
27     /**
28        @return the total amount of the current sale
29     */
30     double get_total() const;
31
32     /**
33        @return the item count of the current sale
34     */
35     int get_count() const;
36
37  private:
38     int item_count;
39     double total_price;
40  };
41
42  #endif
```

You include this header file whenever the definition of the `CashRegister` class is required. Because this file is not a standard header file, you must enclose its name in quotes, not <...>, when you include it, like this:

```
#include "cashregister.h"
```

Note the set of directives that bracket the header file:

```
#ifndef CASHREGISTER_H
#define CASHREGISTER_H
. . .
#endif
```

Suppose a file includes two header files: cashregister.h, and another header file that itself includes cashregister.h. The effect of the directives is to skip the file when it is encountered the second time. If we did not have that check, the compiler would complain when it saw the definition for the CashRegister class twice. (Sadly, it doesn't check whether the definitions are identical.)

The source file for the CashRegister class simply contains the definitions of the member functions (including constructors).

Note that the source file cashregister.cpp includes its own header file, cashregister.h. The compiler needs to know how the CashRegister class is defined in order to compile the member functions.

> Source files
> contain function
> implementations.

sec09/cashregister.cpp

```
 1  #include "cashregister.h"
 2
 3  CashRegister::CashRegister()
 4  {
 5     clear();
 6  }
 7
 8  void CashRegister::clear()
 9  {
10     item_count = 0;
11     total_price = 0;
12  }
13
14  void CashRegister::add_item(double price)
15  {
16     item_count++;
17     total_price = total_price + price;
18  }
19
20  double CashRegister::get_total() const
21  {
22     return total_price;
23  }
24
25  int CashRegister::get_count() const
26  {
27     return item_count;
28  }
```

Note that the function comments are in the header file, because comments are a part of the interface, not the implementation.

The cashregister.cpp file does *not* contain a main function. There are many potential programs that might make use of the CashRegister class. Each of these programs will need to supply its own main function, as well as other functions and classes.

Here is a simple test program that puts the CashRegister class to use. Its source file includes the cashregister.h header file.

sec09/registerdemo2.cpp

```cpp
1  #include <iostream>
2  #include <iomanip>
3  #include "cashregister.h"
4
5  using namespace std;
6
7  /**
8     Displays the item count and total price of a cash register.
9     @param reg  the cash register to display
10 */
11 void display(CashRegister reg)
12 {
13    cout << reg.get_count() << " $" << fixed << setprecision(2)
14       << reg.get_total() << endl;
15 }
16
17 int main()
18 {
19    CashRegister register1;
20    register1.clear();
21    register1.add_item(1.95);
22    display(register1);
23    register1.add_item(0.95);
24    display(register1);
25    register1.add_item(2.50);
26    display(register1);
27    return 0;
28 }
```

To build the complete program, you need to compile both the registerdemo2.cpp and
cashregister.cpp source files (see Figure 9). The details depend on your compiler. For
example, with the GNU compiler, you issue the command

```
g++ -o registerdemo registerdemo2.cpp cashregister.cpp
```

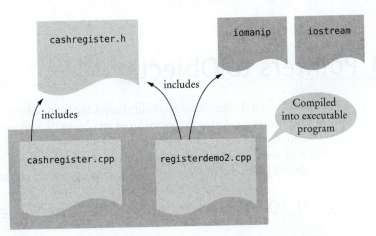

Figure 9 Compiling a Program from Multiple Source Files

You have just seen the simplest and most common case for designing header and source files. There are a few additional technical details that you should know.

- A header file should include all headers that are necessary for defining the class. For example, if a class uses the `string` class, include the `<string>` header as well. Anytime you include a header from the standard library, also include the directive

```
using namespace std;
```

item.h

```
1  #include <string>
2  using namespace std;
3
4  class Item
5  {
6     . . .
7  private:
8     string description
9  };
```

- Place shared constants into a header file. For example,

volumes.h

```
6  const double CAN_VOLUME = 0.355;
```

- To share a nonmember function, place the function declaration into a header file and the definition of the function into the corresponding source file.

cube.h

```
8  double cube_volume(double side_length);
```

cube.cpp

```
1  #include "cube.h"
2
3  double cube_volume(double side_length)
4  {
5     double volume = side_length * side_length * side_length;
6     return volume;
7  }
```

9.10 Pointers to Objects

It is often desirable to provide shared access to objects. This is achieved by **pointers**. A pointer provides the location of an object. When you know where an object is, you can update it without having to receive and return it. In the following sections, you will see how to use pointers for object sharing. In Chapter 10, you will see another use of pointers: for referring to objects of related classes.

9.10.1 Dynamically Allocating Objects

Suppose that we want to model two store employees who share a cash register, or two friends who share a bank account. First, we allocate the shared object on the **free**

store, a storage area that provides memory on demand. Use the new operator together with a constructor invocation:

```
CashRegister* register_pointer = new CashRegister;
BankAccount* lisas_account_pointer = new BankAccount(1000);
```

The type BankAccount* denotes a pointer to a BankAccount object.
Now we can copy the pointer, without copying the object:

```
BankAccount* joes_account_pointer = lisas_account_pointer;
```

Figure 10 shows the result: two pointers that point to the same object.
When you no longer need an object that is allocated on the free store, be sure to delete it:

```
delete register_pointer;
delete lisas_account_pointer;
```

Now the objects are no longer allocated. Be sure not to use any of the pointers afterwards.

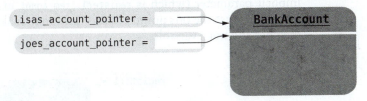

Figure 10 Two Pointers to the Same Object

9.10.2 The -> Operator

Suppose we have a pointer to a CashRegister object:

```
CashRegister* register_pointer = new CashRegister;
```

To refer to the cash register, you can use the * operator: *register_pointer is the Cash-Register object to which register_pointer points. To invoke a member function on that object, you might call

```
(*register_pointer).add_item(1.95);
```

The parentheses are necessary because in C++ the dot operator takes precedence over the * operator. The expression without the parentheses would be a compile-time error:

```
*register_pointer.add_item(1.95); // Error—bad syntax
```

Because the dot operator has higher precedence than *, the dot would be applied to register_pointer, and * would be applied to the result of the member function call. Both of these would be syntax errors.

Because calling a member function through a pointer is very common, there is an operator to abbreviate the "follow pointer and call member function" operation. That operator is written -> and usually pronounced as "arrow". Here is how you use the "arrow" operator:

```
register_pointer->add_item(1.95);
```

This call means: When invoking the add_item member function, set the implicit parameter to *register_pointer and the explicit parameter to 1.95.

9.10.3 The this Pointer

In a member function, the this pointer points to the implicit parameter.

Each member function has a special parameter variable, called this, which is a pointer to the implicit parameter. For example, consider the CashRegister::add_item function. If you call

```
register1.add_item(1.95)
```

then the this pointer has type CashRegister* and points to the register1 object.

You can use the this pointer inside the definition of a member function. For example, you can implement the add_item function as

```
void CashRegister::add_item(double price)
{
    this->item_count++;
    this->total_price = this->total_price + price;
}
```

Here, the expression this->item_count refers to the item_count data member of the implicit parameter (which is register1.item_count in our example). Some programmers like to use the this pointer in this fashion to make it clear that item_count is a data member and not a variable.

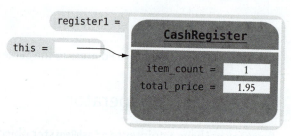

Figure 11 The this Pointer

EXAMPLE CODE See sec10 of your companion code for a program that uses pointers to objects.

9.11 Problem Solving: Patterns for Object Data

When you design a class, you first consider the needs of the programmers who use the class. You provide the member functions that the users of your class will call when they manipulate objects. When you implement the class, you need to come up with the data members for the class. It is not always obvious how to do this. Fortunately, there is a small set of recurring patterns that you can adapt when you design your own classes. We introduce these patterns in the following sections.

9.11.1 Keeping a Total

Many classes need to keep track of a quantity that can go up or down as certain functions are called. Examples:

- A bank account has a balance that is increased by a deposit, decreased by a withdrawal.

- A cash register has a total that is increased when an item is added to the sale, cleared after the end of the sale.
- A car has gas in the tank, which is increased when fuel is added and decreased when the car drives.

In all of these cases, the implementation strategy is similar. Keep a data member that represents the current total. For example, for the cash register:

```
double total_price;
```

A data member for the total is updated in member functions that increase or decrease the total amount.

Locate the member functions that affect the total. There is usually a member function to increase it by a given amount.

```
void add_item(double price)
{
    total_price = total_price + price;
}
```

Depending on the nature of the class, there may be a member function that reduces or clears the total. In the case of the cash register, there is a clear member fucntion:

```
void clear()
{
    total_price = 0;
}
```

There is usually a member function that yields the current total. It is easy to implement:

```
double get_total()
{
    return total_price;
}
```

All classes that manage a total follow the same basic pattern. Find the member functions that affect the total and provide the appropriate code for increasing or decreasing it. Find the member functions that report or use the total, and have those member functions read the current total.

9.11.2 Counting Events

You often need to count how often certain events occur in the life of an object. For example:

A counter that counts events is incremented in member functions that correspond to the events.

- In a cash register, you want to know how many items have been added in a sale.
- A bank account charges a fee for each transaction; you need to count them.

Keep a counter, such as

```
int item_count;
```

Increment the counter in those member functions that correspond to the events that you want to count.

```
void add_item(double price)
{
    total_price = total_price + price;
    item_count++;
}
```

You may need to clear the counter, for example at the end of a sale or a statement period.

```
void clear()
{
    total_price = 0;
    item_count = 0;
}
```

There may or may not be a member function that reports the count to the class user. The count may only be used to compute a fee or an average. Find out which member functions in your class make use of the count, and read the current value in those member functions.

9.11.3 Collecting Values

Some objects collect numbers, strings, or other objects. For example, each multiple-choice question has a number of choices. A cash register may need to store all prices of the current sale.

> An object can collect other objects in an array or vector.

Use a vector or an array to store the values. (A vector is usually simpler because you won't need to track the number of values.) For example,

```
class Question
{
    . . .
private:
    vector<string> choices;
    . . .
};
```

© paul prescott/iStockphoto.

A shopping cart object needs to manage a collection of items.

In the constructor, we want to initialize the data member to an empty collection. The default constructor of the vector class does that automatically. Therefore, the constructor has no explicit actions:

```
Question::Question()
{
}
```

You need to supply some mechanism for adding values. It is common to provide a member function for appending a value to the collection:

```
void Question::add(string choice)
{
    choices.push_back(choice);
}
```

The user of a Question object can call this member function multiple times to add the various choices.

9.11.4 Managing Properties of an Object

A *property* is a value of an object that an object user can set and retrieve. For example, a Student object may have a name and an ID.

An object property can be accessed with a getter member function and changed with a setter member function.

Provide a data member to store the property's value and member functions to get and set it:

```cpp
class Student
{
public:
   string get_name() const;
   void set_name(string new_name);
private:
   string name;
   . . .
};
```

It is common to add error checking to the setter member function. For example, we may want to reject a blank name:

```cpp
void Student::set_name(string new_name)
{
   if (new_name.length() > 0) { name = new_name; }
}
```

Some properties should not change after they have been set in the constructor. For example, a student's ID may be fixed (unlike the student's name, which may change). In that case, don't supply a setter member function.

```cpp
class Student
{
public:
   Student(int an_id);
   string get_id() const;
   // No set_id member function
   . . .
private:
   int id;
   . . .
};
```

EXAMPLE CODE   See sec11_04 of your companion code for a class with getter and setter member functions.

9.11.5 Modeling Objects with Distinct States

If your object can have one of several states that affect the behavior, supply a data member for the current state.

Some objects have behavior that varies depending on what has happened in the past. For example, a Fish object may look for food when it is hungry and ignore food after it has eaten. Such an object would need to remember whether it has recently eaten.

Supply a data member that models the state, together with some constants for the state values:

© John Alexander/iStockphoto.

If a fish is in a hungry state, its behavior changes.

```cpp
class Fish
{
public:
   const int NOT_HUNGRY = 0;
   cont int SOMEWHAT_HUNGRY = 1;
   const int VERY_HUNGRY = 2;
private:
   int hungry;
   . . .
```

Determine which member functions change the state. In this example, a fish that has just eaten food won't be hungry. But as the fish moves, it will get hungrier.

```
void Fish::eat()
{
   hungry = NOT_HUNGRY;
   . . .
}

void Fish::move()
{
   . . .
   if (hungry < VERY_HUNGRY) { hungry++; }
}
```

Finally, determine where the state affects behavior. A fish that is very hungry will want to look for food first.

```
void Fish::move()
{
   if (hungry == VERY_HUNGRY)
   {
      Look for food.
   }
   . . .
}
```

EXAMPLE CODE   See sec11_05 of your companion code for the Fish class.

9.11.6 Describing the Position of an Object

To model a moving object, you need to store and update its position.

Some objects move around during their lifetime, and they remember their current position. For example,

- A train drives along a track and keeps track of the distance from the terminus.
- A simulated bug living on a grid crawls from one grid location to the next, or makes 90 degree turns to the left or right.
- A cannonball is shot into the air, then descends as it is pulled by the gravitational force.

Such objects need to store their position. Depending on the nature of their movement, they may also need to store their orientation or velocity.

If the object moves along a line, you can represent the position as a distance from a fixed point.

```
double distance_from_terminus;
```

A bug in a grid needs to store its row, column, and direction.

If the object moves in a grid, remember its current location and direction in the grid:

```
int row;
int column;
int direction; // 0 = North, 1 = East, 2 = South, 3 = West
```

When you model a physical object such as a cannonball, you need to track both the position and the velocity, possibly in two or three dimensions. Here we model a cannonball that is shot upward into the air:

```
double z_position;
double z_velocity;
```

There will be member functions that update the position. In the simplest case, you may be told by how much the object moves:

```
void move(double distance_moved)
{
    distance_from_terminus = distance_from_terminus + distance_moved;
}
```

If the movement happens in a grid, you need to update the row or column, depending on the current orientation.

```
void move_one_unit()
{
    if (direction == NORTH) { row--; }
    else if (direction == EAST) { column++; }
    . . .
}
```

Exercise P9.21 shows you how to update the position of a physical object with known velocity.

Whenever you have a moving object, keep in mind that your program will simulate the actual movement in some way. Find out the rules of that simulation, such as movement along a line or in a grid with integer coordinates. Those rules determine how to represent the current position. Then locate the member functions that move the object, and update the positions according to the rules of the simulation.

EXAMPLE CODE   See sec11_06 of your companion code for two classes that update position data.

Computing & Society 9.2   Open Source and Free Software

Most companies that produce software regard the source code as a trade secret. After all, if customers or competitors had access to the source code, they could study it and create similar programs without paying the original vendor. For the same reason, customers dislike secret source code. If a company goes out of business or decides to discontinue support for a computer program, its users are left stranded. They are unable to fix bugs or adapt the program to a new operating system. Fortunately, many software packages are distributed as "open source software", giving its users the right to see, modify, and redistribute the source code of a program.

Having access to source code is not sufficient to ensure that software serves the needs of its users. Some companies have created software that spies on users or restricts access to previously purchased books, music, or videos. If that software runs on a server or in an embedded device, the user cannot change its behavior. In the article http://www.gnu.org/philosophy/free-software-even-more-important.en.html, Richard Stallman, a famous computer scientist and winner of a MacArthur "genius" grant, describes the "free software movement" that champions the right of users to control what their software does. This is an ethical position that goes beyond using open source for reasons of convenience or cost savings.

Stallman is the originator of the GNU project (http://gnu.org/gnu/the-gnu-project.html) that has produced an entirely free version of a UNIX-compatible operating system: the GNU operating system. All programs of the GNU project are licensed under the GNU General Public License (GNU GPL). The license allows you to make as many copies as you wish, make any modifications to the source, and redistribute the original and modified programs, charging nothing at all or whatever the market will bear. In return, you must agree that your modifications also fall under the license. You must give out the source code to any changes that you distribute, and anyone else can distribute them under the same conditions. The GNU GPL forms a social contract. Users of the software enjoy the freedom to use and modify the software, and in return they are obligated to share any improvements that they make available.

Some commercial software vendors have attacked the GPL as "viral" and "undermining the commercial software sector". Other companies have a more nuanced strategy, producing free or open source software, but charging for support or proprietary extensions. For example, the Java Development Kit is available under the GPL, but companies that need security updates for old versions or other support must pay Oracle.

Open source software sometimes lacks the polish of commercial software because many of the programmers are volunteers who are interested in solving their own problems, not in making a product that is easy to use by everyone. Open source software has been particularly successful in areas that are of interest to programmers, such as the Linux kernel, Web servers, and programming tools.

The open source software community can be very competitive and creative. It is quite common to see several competing projects that take ideas from each other, all rapidly becoming more capable. Having many programmers involved, all reading the source code, often means that bugs tend to get squashed quickly. Eric Raymond describes open source development in his famous article "The Cathedral and the Bazaar" (http://catb.org/~esr/writings/cathedral-bazaar/cathedral-bazaar/index.html). He writes "Given enough eyeballs, all bugs are shallow".

Courtesy of Richard Stallman published under a CC license.

Richard Stallman, a pioneer of the free source movement.

CHAPTER SUMMARY

Understand the concepts of objects and classes.

- A class describes a set of objects with the same behavior.
- Every class has a public interface: a collection of member functions through which the objects of the class can be manipulated.
- Encapsulation is the act of providing a public interface and hiding implementation details.
- Encapsulation enables changes in the implementation without affecting users of a class.

Understand data members and member functions of a simple class.

- The member functions of a class define the behavior of its objects.
- An object's data members represent the state of the object.
- Each object of a class has its own set of data members.
- A member function can access the data members of the object on which it acts.
- A private data member can only be accessed by the member functions of its own class.

Formulate the public interface of a class in C++.

- You can use member function declarations and function comments to specify the public interface of a class.
- A mutator member function changes the object on which it operates.
- An accessor member function does not change the object on which it operates. Use const with accessors.

Choose data members to represent the state of an object.

- An object holds data members that are accessed by member functions.
- Every object has its own set of data members.
- Private data members can only be accessed by member functions of the same class.

Implement member functions of a class.

- Use the *ClassName*:: prefix when defining member functions.
- The implicit parameter is a reference to the object on which a member function is applied.
- Explicit parameters of a member function are listed in the function definition.
- When calling another member function on the same object, do not use the dot notation.

Design and implement constructors.

- A constructor is called automatically whenever an object is created.
- The name of a constructor is the same as the class name.
- A default constructor has no arguments.
- A class can have multiple constructors.
- The compiler picks the constructor that matches the construction arguments.
- Be sure to initialize all number and pointer data members in a constructor.

Use the technique of object tracing for visualizing object behavior.

- Write the member functions on the front of a card, and the data member values on the back.
- Update the values of the data members when a mutator member function is called.

Discover classes that are needed for solving a programming problem.

- To discover classes, look for nouns in the problem description.
- Concepts from the problem domain are good candidates for classes.
- A class aggregates another if its objects contain objects of the other class.
- Avoid parallel vectors by changing them into vectors of objects.

Separate the interface and implementation of a class in header and source files.

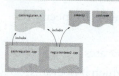

- The code of complex programs is distributed over multiple files.
- Header files contain the definitions of classes and declarations of nonmember functions.
- Source files contain function implementations.

Use pointers to objects and manage dynamically allocated objects.

- Use the new operator to obtain an object that is located on the free store.
- The new operator returns a pointer to the allocated object.
- When an object allocated on the free store is no longer needed, use the delete operator to reclaim its memory.
- Use the -> operator to invoke a member function through a pointer.
- In a member function, the this pointer points to the implicit parameter.

Use patterns to design the data representation of a class.

- An data member for the total is updated in member functions that increase or decrease the total amount.
- A counter that counts events is incremented in member functions that correspond to the events.
- An object can collect other objects in an array or vector.
- An object property can be accessed with a getter member function and changed with a setter member function.
- If your object can have one of several states that affect the behavior, supply a data member for the current state.

- To model a moving object, you need to store and update its position.

CHAPTER 10

INHERITANCE

© Lisa Thornberg/iStockphoto.

CHAPTER GOALS

To understand the concepts of inheritance and polymorphism

To learn how to inherit and override member functions

To be able to implement constructors for derived classes

To be able to design and use virtual functions

CHAPTER CONTENTS

10.1   INHERITANCE HIERARCHIES 334

10.2   IMPLEMENTING DERIVED CLASSES 338

`SYN` Derived-Class Definition 340
`CE1` Private Inheritance 341
`CE2` Replicating Base-Class Members 341
`PT1` Use a Single Class for Variation in Values, Inheritance for Variation in Behavior 342
`ST1` Calling the Base-Class Constructor 342
`SYN` Constructor with Base-Class Initializer 342

10.3   OVERRIDING MEMBER FUNCTIONS 343

`CE3` Forgetting the Base-Class Name 345

10.4   VIRTUAL FUNCTIONS AND POLYMORPHISM 346

`PT2` Don't Use Type Tags 352
`CE4` Slicing an Object 352
`CE5` Failing to Override a Virtual Function 353
`ST2` Virtual Self-Calls 354
`HT1` Developing an Inheritance Hierarchy 354
`WE1` Implementing an Employee Hierarchy for Payroll Processing 359
`C&S` Who Controls the Internet? 360

Objects from related classes usually share common behavior. For example, shovels, rakes, and clippers all perform gardening tasks. In this chapter, you will learn how the notion of inheritance expresses the relationship between specialized and general classes. By using inheritance, you will be able to share code between classes and provide services that can be used by multiple classes.

10.1 Inheritance Hierarchies

> A derived class inherits data and behavior from a base class.

In object-oriented design, **inheritance** is a relationship between a more general class (called the **base class**) and a more specialized class (called the **derived class**). The derived class inherits data and behavior from the base class. For example, consider the relationships between different kinds of vehicles depicted in Figure 1.

Cars share the common traits of all vehicles, such as the ability to transport people from one place to another. We say that the class Car *inherits* from the class Vehicle. In this relationship, the Vehicle class is the base class and the Car class is the derived class.

Informally, the inheritance relationship is called the *is-a* relationship. Contrast this relationship with the *has-a* relationship that we discussed in Section 9.8. Every car *is a* vehicle. Every vehicle *has an* engine.

The inheritance relationship is very powerful because it allows us to reuse algorithms with objects of different classes. Suppose we have an algorithm that

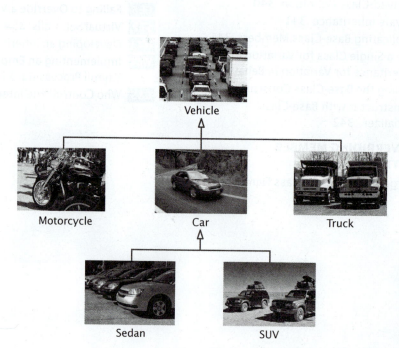

Figure 1 An Inheritance Hierarchy of Vehicle Classes

You can always use a derived-class object in place of a base-class object.

manipulates a Vehicle object. Because a car is a special kind of vehicle, we can supply a Car object to such an algorithm, and it will work correctly. This is an example of the **substitution principle** that states that you can always use a derived-class object when a base-class object is expected.

The inheritance relationship can give rise to hierarchies where classes get ever more specialized, as shown in Figure 1. The C++ stream classes, shown in Figure 2, are another example of such a hierarchy. Figure 2 uses the UML notation for inheritance where the base and derived class are joined with an arrow that points to the base class.

As you can see, an ifstream (an input stream that reads from a file) is a special case of an istream (an input stream that reads data from any source). If you have an ifstream, it can be the argument for a function that expects an istream.

```
void process_input(istream& in) // Can call with an ifstream object
```

Why provide a function that processes istream objects instead of ifstream objects? That function is more useful because it can handle *any* kind of input stream (such as an istringstream, which is convenient for testing). This again is the substitution principle at work.

In this chapter, we will consider a simple hierarchy of classes. Most likely, you have taken computer-graded quizzes. A quiz consists of questions, and there are different kinds of questions:

© paul kline/iStockphoto.

We will develop a simple but flexible quiz-taking program to illustrate inheritance.

- Fill-in-the-blank
- Choice (single or multiple)
- Numeric (where an approximate answer is ok; e.g., 1.33 when the actual answer is 4/3)
- Free response

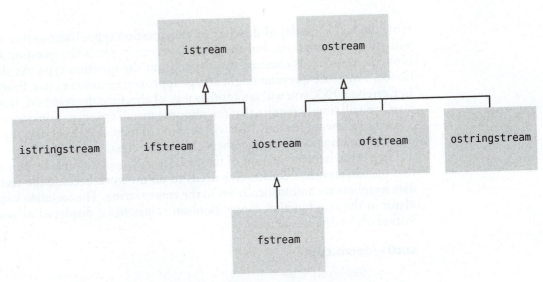

Figure 2 The Inheritance Hierarchy of Stream Classes

Figure 3 shows an inheritance hierarchy for these question types.

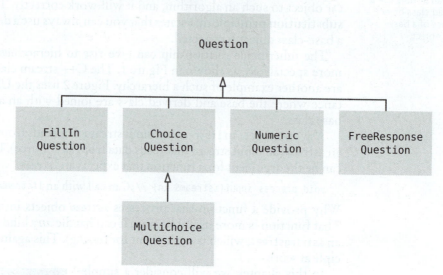

Figure 3 Inheritance Hierarchy of Question Types

At the root of this hierarchy is the Question type. A question can display its text, and it can check whether a given response is a correct answer:

```
class Question
{
public:
   Question();
   void set_text(string question_text);
   void set_answer(string correct_response);
   bool check_answer(string response) const;
   void display() const;
private:
   string text;
   string answer;
};
```

How the text is displayed depends on the question type. Later in this chapter, you will see some variations, but the base class simply sends the question text to cout. How the response is checked also depends on the question type. As already mentioned, a numeric question might accept approximate answers (see Exercise E10.1). In Exercise E10.3, you will see another way of checking the response. But in the base class, we will simply require that the response match the correct answer exactly.

In the following sections, you will see how to form derived classes that inherit the member functions and data members of this base class.

Here is the implementation of the Question class and a simple test program. Note that the Question class constructor needs to do no work because the text and answer data members are automatically set to the empty string. The boolalpha stream manipulator in the main function causes Boolean values to be displayed as true and false instead of the default 1 and 0.

sec01/demo.cpp

```
1  #include <iostream>
2  #include <sstream>
```

```
 3  #include <string>
 4
 5  using namespace std;
 6
 7  class Question
 8  {
 9  public:
10     /**
11         Constructs a question with empty text and answer.
12     */
13     Question();
14
15     /**
16         @param question_text the text of this question
17     */
18     void set_text(string question_text);
19
20     /**
21         @param correct_response the answer for this question
22     */
23     void set_answer(string correct_response);
24
25     /**
26         @param response the response to check
27         @return true if the response was correct, false otherwise
28     */
29     bool check_answer(string response) const;
30
31     /**
32         Displays this question.
33     */
34     void display() const;
35
36  private:
37     string text;
38     string answer;
39  };
40
41  Question::Question()
42  {
43  }
44
45  void Question::set_text(string question_text)
46  {
47     text = question_text;
48  }
49
50  void Question::set_answer(string correct_response)
51  {
52     answer = correct_response;
53  }
54
55  bool Question::check_answer(string response) const
56  {
57     return response == answer;
58  }
59
60  void Question::display() const
61  {
62     cout << text << endl;
```

```
63  }
64
65  int main()
66  {
67     string response;
68     cout << boolalpha; // Show Boolean values as true, false
69
70     Question q1;
71     q1.set_text("Who was the inventor of C++?");
72     q1.set_answer("Bjarne Stroustrup");
73
74     q1.display();
75     cout << "Your answer: ";
76     getline(cin, response);
77     cout << q1.check_answer(response) << endl;
78
79     return 0;
80  }
```

Program Run

```
Who was the inventor of C++?
Your answer: Bjarne Stroustrup
true
```

10.2 Implementing Derived Classes

In C++, you form a derived class from a base class by specifying what makes the derived class different. You define the member functions that are new to the derived class. The derived class inherits all member functions from the base class, but you can change the implementation if the inherited behavior is not appropriate.

The derived class automatically inherits all data members from the base class. You only define the added data members.

Here is the syntax for the definition of a derived class:

```
class ChoiceQuestion : public Question
{
public:
    New and changed member functions
private:
    Additional data members
};
```

The : symbol denotes inheritance. The reserved word `public` is required for a technical reason (see Common Error 10.1).

Like the manufacturer of a stretch limo, who starts with a regular car and modifies it, a programmer makes a derived class by modifying another class.

Media Bakery.

A ChoiceQuestion object differs from a Question object in three ways:

- Its objects store the various choices for the answer.
- There is a member function for adding another choice.
- The display function of the ChoiceQuestion class shows these choices so that the respondent can choose one of them.

When the ChoiceQuestion class inherits from the Question class, it needs only to spell out these three differences:

```cpp
class ChoiceQuestion : public Question
{
public:
    ChoiceQuestion();
    void add_choice(string choice, bool correct);
    void display() const;
private:
    vector<string> choices;
};
```

Figure 4 shows the layout of a ChoiceQuestion object. It inherits the text and answer data members from the Question base object, and it adds an additional data member: the choices vector.

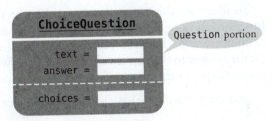

Figure 4 Data Layout of a Derived-Class Object

A derived class can override a base-class function by providing a new implementation.

The derived class inherits all data members and all functions that it does not override.

The add_choice function is specific to the ChoiceQuestion class. You can only apply it to ChoiceQuestion objects, not general Question objects. However, the display function is a redefinition of a function that exists in the base class; it is redefined to take into account the special needs of the derived class. We say that the derived class **overrides** this function. You will see how in Section 10.3.

In the ChoiceQuestion class definition you specify only new member functions and data members. All other member functions and data members of the Question class are automatically inherited by the Question class. For example, each ChoiceQuestion object still has text and answer data members, and set_text, set_answer, and check_answer member functions.

You can call the inherited member functions on a derived-class object:

```cpp
choice_question.set_answer("2");
```

However, the inherited data members are inaccessible. Because these members are private data of the base class, only the base class has access to them. The derived class has no more access rights than any other class.

In particular, the ChoiceQuestion member functions cannot directly access the answer member. These member functions must use the public interface of the Question class to access its private data, just like every other function.

Syntax 10.1 Derived-Class Definition

The : symbol denotes inheritance.

Always place public after the :. See Common Error 10.1.

Derived class

Base class

```
                    class ChoiceQuestion : public Question
Declare functions   {
that are added      public:
to the derived class.  ChoiceQuestion();
                       void add_choice(string choice, bool correct);
Declare functions      void display() const;
that the derived
class overrides.    private:                           Define data members
                       vector<string> choices;          that are added to
                    };                                   the derived class.
```

To illustrate this point, let us implement the add_choice member function. The function has two parameters: the choice to be added (which is appended to the vector of choices), and a Boolean value to indicate whether this choice is correct. If it is true, set the answer to the current choice number. (We use the to_string function to convert the number to a string—see Section 8.4 for details.)

```
void ChoiceQuestion::add_choice(string choice, bool correct)
{
   choices.push_back(choice);
   if (correct)
   {
      // Convert choices.size() to string
      string num_str = to_string(choices.size());
      // Set num_str as the answer
      . . .
   }
}
```

You can't just access the answer member in the base class. Fortunately, the Question class has a set_answer member function. You can call that member function. On which object? The question that you are currently modifying—that is, the implicit parameter of the ChoiceQuestion::add_choice function. As you saw in Chapter 9, if you invoke a member function on the implicit parameter, you don't specify the parameter but just write the member function name:

```
set_answer(num_str);
```

The compiler interprets this call as

implicit parameter.set_answer(num_str);

Common Error 10.1

Private Inheritance

It is a common error to forget the reserved word `public` that must follow the colon after the derived-class name.

```cpp
class ChoiceQuestion : Question // Error
{
    . . .
};
```

The class definition will compile. The `ChoiceQuestion` still inherits from `Question`, but it inherits *privately*. That is, only the member functions of `ChoiceQuestion` get to call member functions of `Question`. Whenever another function invokes a `Question` member function on a `ChoiceQuestion` object, the compiler will flag this as an error:

```cpp
int main()
{
    ChoiceQuestion q;
    . . .
    cout << q.check_answer(response); // Error
}
```

This private inheritance is rarely useful. In fact, it violates the spirit of using inheritance in the first place—namely, to create objects that are usable just like the base-class objects. You should always use public inheritance and remember to supply the `public` reserved word in the definition of the derived class.

Common Error 10.2

Replicating Base-Class Members

A derived class has no access to the data members of the base class.

```cpp
ChoiceQuestion::ChoiceQuestion(string question_text)
{
    text = question_text; // Error—tries to access private base-class member
}
```

When faced with a compiler error, beginners commonly "solve" this issue by adding *another* data member with the same name to the derived class:

```cpp
class ChoiceQuestion : public Question
{
    . . .
private:
    vector<string> choices;
    string text; // Don't!
}
```

Sure, now the constructor compiles, but it doesn't set the correct text! Such a `Choice-Question` object has two data members, both named text. The constructor sets one of them, and the `display` member function displays the other.

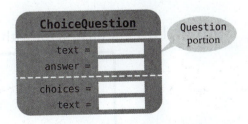

Instead of uselessly replicating a base-class data member, you need to call a member function that updates the base-class member, such as the `set_text` function in our example.

Programming Tip 10.1

Use a Single Class for Variation in Values, Inheritance for Variation in Behavior

The purpose of inheritance is to model objects with different *behavior*. When students first learn about inheritance, they have a tendency to overuse it, by creating multiple classes even though the variation could be expressed with a simple data member.

Consider a program that tracks the fuel efficiency of a fleet of cars by logging the distance traveled and the refueling amounts. Some cars in the fleet are hybrids. Should you create a derived class HybridCar? Not in this application. Hybrids don't behave any differently than other cars when it comes to driving and refueling. They just have a better fuel efficiency. A single Car class with a data member

```
double miles_per_gallon;
```

is entirely sufficient.

However, if you write a program that shows how to repair different kinds of vehicles, then it makes sense to have a separate class HybridCar. When it comes to repairs, hybrid cars behave differently from other cars.

Special Topic 10.1

Calling the Base-Class Constructor

Consider the process of constructing a derived-class object. A derived-class constructor can only initialize the data members of the derived class. But the base-class data members also need to be initialized. Unless you specify otherwise, the base-class data members are initialized with the default constructor of the base class.

Unless specified otherwise, the base-class data members are initialized with the default constructor.

In order to specify another constructor, you use an *initializer list*, as described in Special Topic 9.2. Specify the name of the base class and the construction arguments in the initializer list. For example, suppose the Question base class had a constructor for setting the question text. Here is how a derived-class constructor could call that base-class constructor:

```
ChoiceQuestion::ChoiceQuestion(string question_text)
   : Question(question_text)
{
}
```

The constructor of a derived class can supply arguments to a base-class constructor.

The derived-class constructor calls the base-class constructor before executing the code inside the { }.

In our example program, we used the default constructor of the base class. However, if a base class has no default constructor, you must use the initializer list syntax.

Syntax 10.2 Constructor with Base-Class Initializer

The base-class constructor is called first.

```
ChoiceQuestion::ChoiceQuestion(string question_text)
   : Question(question_text)
{

}
```

This block can contain additional statements.

If you omit the base-class constructor call, the default constructor is invoked.

10.3 Overriding Member Functions

The derived class inherits the member functions from the base class. If you are not satisfied with the behavior of the inherited member function, you can **override** it by specifying a new implementation in the derived class.

Consider the `display` function of the `ChoiceQuestion` class. It needs to override the base-class `display` function in order to show the choices for the answer. Specifically, the derived-class function needs to

A derived class can inherit a function from the base class, or it can override it by providing another implementation.

- *Display the question text.*
- *Display the answer choices.*

The second part is easy because the answer choices are a data member of the derived class.

```
void ChoiceQuestion::display() const
{
    // Display the question text
    . . .
    // Display the answer choices
    for (int i = 0; i < choices.size(); i++)
    {
        cout << i + 1 << ": " << choices[i] << endl;
    }
}
```

But how do you get the question text? You can't access the text member of the base class directly because it is private.

Instead, you can call the `display` function of the base class.

```
void ChoiceQuestion::display() const
{
    // Display the question text
    display(); // Invokes implicit parameter.display()
    // Display the answer choices
    . . .
}
```

However, this won't quite work. Because the implicit parameter of `ChoiceQuestion::display` is of type `ChoiceQuestion`, and there is a function named `display` in the `ChoiceQuestion` class, that function will be called—but that is just the function you are currently writing! The function would call itself over and over.

To display the question text, you must be more specific about which function named `display` you want to call. You want `Question::display`:

```
void ChoiceQuestion::display() const
{
    // Display the question text
    Question::display(); // OK
    // Display the answer choices
    . . .
}
```

Use *BaseClass::function* notation to explicitly call a base-class function.

When you override a function, you usually want to *extend* the functionality of the base-class version. Therefore, you often need to invoke the base-class version before extending it. To invoke it, you need to use the *BaseClass::function* notation. However, you have no obligation to call the base-class function. Occasionally, a derived class overrides a base-class function and specifies an entirely different functionality.

Here is the complete program that displays a plain Question object and a Choice-Question object. (The definition of the Question class, which you have already seen, is placed into question.h, and the implementation is in question.cpp.) This example shows how you can use inheritance to form a more specialized class from a base class.

sec03/demo.cpp

```cpp
1  #include <iostream>
2  #include <sstream>
3  #include <vector>
4  #include "question.h"
5
6  class ChoiceQuestion : public Question
7  {
8  public:
9     /**
10        Constructs a choice question with no choices.
11     */
12     ChoiceQuestion();
13
14     /**
15        Adds an answer choice to this question.
16        @param choice the choice to add
17        @param correct true if this is the correct choice, false otherwise
18     */
19     void add_choice(string choice, bool correct);
20
21     void display() const;
22  private:
23     vector<string> choices;
24  };
25
26  ChoiceQuestion::ChoiceQuestion()
27  {
28  }
29
30  void ChoiceQuestion::add_choice(string choice, bool correct)
31  {
32     choices.push_back(choice);
33     if (correct)
34     {
35        // Convert choices.size() to string
36        string num_str = to_string(choices.size());
37        set_answer(num_str);
38     }
39  }
40
41  void ChoiceQuestion::display() const
42  {
43     // Display the question text
44     Question::display();
45     // Display the answer choices
46     for (int i = 0; i < choices.size(); i++)
47     {
48        cout << i + 1 << ": " << choices[i] << endl;
49     }
50  }
51
```

```
52  int main()
53
54     string response;
55     cout << boolalpha;
56
57     // Ask a basic question
58
59     Question q1;
60     q1.set_text("Who was the inventor of C++?");
61     q1.set_answer("Bjarne Stroustrup");
62
63     q1.display();
64     cout << "Your answer: ";
65     getline(cin, response);
66     cout << q1.check_answer(response) << endl;
67
68     // Ask a choice question
69
70     ChoiceQuestion q2;
71     q2.set_text("In which country was the inventor of C++ born?");
72     q2.add_choice("Australia", false);
73     q2.add_choice("Denmark", true);
74     q2.add_choice("Korea", false);
75     q2.add_choice("United States", false);
76
77     q2.display();
78     cout << "Your answer: ";
79     getline(cin, response);
80     cout << q2.check_answer(response) << endl;
81
82     return 0;
83  }
```

Program Run

```
Who was the inventor of C++?
Your answer: Bjarne Stroustrup
true
In which country was the inventor of C++ born?
1: Australia
2: Denmark
3: Korea
4: United States
Your answer: 2
true
```

Common Error 10.3

Forgetting the Base-Class Name

A common error in extending the functionality of a base-class function is to forget the base-class name. For example, to compute the salary of a manager, get the salary of the underlying Employee object and add a bonus:

```
double Manager::get_salary() const
{
    double base_salary = get_salary();
        // Error—should be Employee::get_salary()
```

```
        return base_salary + bonus;
    }
```

Here get_salary() refers to the get_salary function applied to the implicit parameter of the member function. The implicit parameter is of type Manager, and there is a Manager::get_salary function, so that function is called. Of course, that is a recursive call to the function that we are writing. Instead, you must specify which get_salary function you want to call. In this case, you need to call Employee::get_salary explicitly.

Whenever you call a base-class function from a derived-class function with the same name, be sure to give the full name of the function, including the base-class name.

10.4 Virtual Functions and Polymorphism

In the preceding sections you saw one important use of inheritance: to form a more specialized class from a base class. In the following sections you will see an even more powerful application of inheritance: to work with objects whose type and behavior can vary at run time. This variation of behavior is achieved with **virtual functions**. When you invoke a virtual function on an object, the C++ run-time system determines which actual member function to call, depending on the class to which the object belongs.

In the following sections, you will see why you need to use pointers to access objects whose class can vary at run-time, and how a virtual function selects the member function that is appropriate for a given object.

10.4.1 The Slicing Problem

In this section, we will discuss a problem that commonly arises when you work with a collection of objects that belong to different classes in a class hierarchy.

If you look into the main function of sec03/demo.cpp, you will find that there is some repetitive code to display each question and check the responses. It would be nicer if all questions were collected in an array and one could use a loop to present them to the user:

```
const int QUIZZES = 2;
Question quiz[QUIZZES];
quiz[0].set_text("Who was the inventor of C++?");
quiz[0].set_answer("Bjarne Stroustrup");
ChoiceQuestion cq;
cq.set_text("In which country was the inventor of C++ born?");
cq.add_choice("Australia", false);
. . .
quiz[1] = cq;

for (int i = 0; i < QUIZZES; i++)
{
    quiz[i].display();
    cout << "Your answer: ";
    getline(cin, response);
    cout << quiz[i].check_answer(response) << endl;
}
```

The array `quiz` holds objects of type `Question`. The compiler realizes that a `ChoiceQuestion` is a special case of a `Question`. Thus it permits the assignment from a choice question to a question:

```
quiz[1] = cq;
```

However, a `ChoiceQuestion` object has three data members, whereas a `Question` object has just two. There is no room to store the derived-class data. That data simply gets *sliced away* when you assign a derived-class object to a base-class variable (see Figure 5).

If you run the resulting program, the options are not displayed:

```
Who was the inventor of C++?
Your answer: Bjarne Stroustrup
true
In which country was the inventor of C++ born?
Your answer:
```

When converting a derived-class object to a base class, the derived-class data is sliced away.

This problem is very typical of code that needs to manipulate objects from a mixture of classes in an inheritance hierarchy. Derived-class objects are usually bigger than base-class objects, and objects of different derived classes have different sizes. An array of objects cannot deal with this variation in sizes.

Instead, you need to store the actual objects elsewhere and collect their locations in an array by storing pointers. We will discuss the use of pointers in the next section.

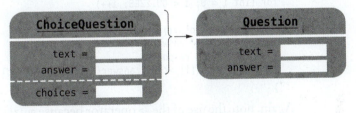

Figure 5 Slicing Away Derived-Class Data

10.4.2 Pointers to Base and Derived Classes

To access objects from different classes in a class hierarchy, use pointers. Pointers to the various objects all have the same size—namely, the size of a memory address—even though the objects themselves may have different sizes.

Here is the code to set up the array of pointers (see Figure 6):

```
Question* quiz[2];
quiz[0] = new Question;
quiz[0]->set_text("Who was the inventor of C++?");
quiz[0]->set_answer("Bjarne Stroustrup");
ChoiceQuestion* cq_pointer = new ChoiceQuestion;
cq_pointer->set_text("In which country was the inventor of C++ born?");
cq_pointer->add_choice("Australia", false);
. . .
quiz[1] = cq_pointer;
```

As the highlighted code shows, you simply define the array to hold pointers, allocate all objects by calling `new`, and use the `->` operator instead of the dot operator.

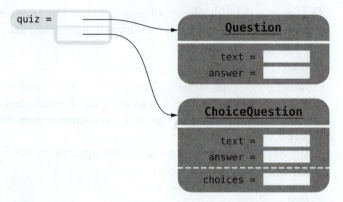

Figure 6 An Array of Pointers Can Store Objects from Different Classes

A derived-class
pointer can be
converted to a base-
class pointer.

Note that the last assignment assigns a derived-class pointer of type ChoiceQuestion*
to a base-class pointer of type Question*. This is perfectly legal. A pointer is the starting address of an object. Because every ChoiceQuestion is a special case of a Question, the
starting address of a ChoiceQuestion object is, in particular, the starting address of a
Question object. The reverse assignment—from a base-class pointer to a derived-class
pointer—is an error.

The code to present all questions is

```
for (int i = 0; i < QUIZZES; i++)
{
    quiz[i]->display();
    cout << "Your answer: ";
    getline(cin, response);
    cout << quiz[i]->check_answer(response) << endl;
}
```

Again, note the use of the -> operator because quiz[i] is a pointer.

10.4.3 Virtual Functions

When you collect objects of different classes in a class hierarchy, and then invoke
a member function, you want the appropriate member function to be applied. For
example, when you call the display member function on a Question* pointer that happens to point to a ChoiceQuestion, you want the choices to be displayed.

For reasons of efficiency, this is not the default in C++. By default, a call

```
quiz[i]->display();
```

always calls Question::display because the type of quiz[i] is Question*.

However, in this case you really want to determine the actual type of the object
to which quiz[i] points, which can be either a Question or a ChoiceQuestion object, and
then call the appropriate function. In C++, you must alert the compiler that the function call needs to be preceded by the appropriate function selection, which can be a
different one for every iteration in the loop. You use the virtual reserved word for
this purpose:

```
class Question
{
```

```
public:
    Question();
    void set_text(string question_text);
    void set_answer(string correct_response);
    virtual bool check_answer(string response) const;
    virtual void display() const;
private:
    . . .
};
```

The `virtual` reserved word must be used in the *base class*. All functions with the same name and parameter variable types in derived classes are then automatically virtual. However, it is considered good taste to supply the `virtual` reserved word for the derived-class functions as well.

```
class ChoiceQuestion : public Question
{
public:
    ChoiceQuestion();
    void add_choice(string choice, bool correct);
    virtual void display() const;
private:
    . . .
};
```

You do not supply the reserved word `virtual` in the function definition:

```
void Question::display() const // No virtual reserved word
{
    cout << text << endl;
}
```

When a virtual function is called, the version belonging to the actual type of the implicit parameter is invoked.

Whenever a virtual function is called, the compiler determines the type of the implicit parameter in the particular call at run time. The appropriate function for that object is then called. For example, when the `display` function is declared virtual, the call

```
quiz[i]->display();
```

always calls the function belonging to the actual type of the object to which `quiz[i]` points—either `Question::display` or `ChoiceQuestion::display`.

10.4.4 Polymorphism

Polymorphism (literally, "having multiple shapes") describes objects that share a set of tasks and execute them in different ways.

The `quiz` array collects a mixture of both kinds of questions. Such a collection is called **polymorphic** (literally, "of multiple shapes"). Objects in a polymorphic collection have some commonality but are not necessarily of the same type. Inheritance is used to express this commonality, and virtual functions enable variations in behavior.

Virtual functions give programs a great deal of flexibility. The question presentation loop describes only the general mechanism: "Display the question, get a response, and check it". Each object knows on its own how to carry out the specific tasks: "Display the question" and "Check a response".

Using virtual functions makes programs *easily extensible*. Suppose we want to have a new kind of question for calculations, where we are willing to accept an approximate answer. All we need to do is to define a new class `NumericQuestion`, with its own `check_answer` function. Then we can populate the `quiz` array with a mixture of plain questions, choice questions, and numeric questions. The code that presents the questions need not be changed at all! The calls to the virtual functions automatically select the correct member functions of the newly defined classes.

© Alpophoto/iStockphoto.

In the same way that vehicles can differ in their method of locomotion, polymorphic objects carry out tasks in different ways.

Here is the final version of the quiz program, using pointers and virtual functions. When you run the program, you will find that the appropriate versions of the virtual functions are called. (The files question.cpp and choicequestion.cpp are included in your book's companion code.)

sec04/question.h

```
 1  #ifndef QUESTION_H
 2  #define QUESTION_H
 3
 4  #include <string>
 5
 6  using namespace std;
 7
 8  class Question
 9  {
10  public:
11     /**
12         Constructs a question with empty question and answer.
13     */
14     Question();
15
16     /**
17         @param question_text the text of this question
18     */
19     void set_text(string question_text);
20
21     /**
22         @param correct_response the answer for this question
23     */
24     void set_answer(string correct_response);
25
26     /**
27         @param response the response to check
28         @return true if the response was correct, false otherwise
29     */
30     virtual bool check_answer(string response) const;
31
32     /**
33         Displays this question.
```

```
34     */
35     virtual void display() const;
36 private:
37     string text;
38     string answer;
39 };
40
41 #endif
```

sec04/choicequestion.h

```
 1 #ifndef CHOICEQUESTION_H
 2 #define CHOICEQUESTION_H
 3
 4 #include <vector>
 5 #include "question.h"
 6
 7 class ChoiceQuestion : public Question
 8 {
 9 public:
10    /**
11        Constructs a choice question with no choices.
12    */
13    ChoiceQuestion();
14
15    /**
16        Adds an answer choice to this question.
17        @param choice the choice to add
18        @param correct  true if this is the correct choice, false otherwise
19    */
20    void add_choice(string choice, bool correct);
21
22    virtual void display() const;
23 private:
24    vector<string> choices;
25 };
26
27 #endif
```

sec04/demo.cpp

```
 1 #include <iostream>
 2 #include "question.h"
 3 #include "choicequestion.h"
 4
 5 int main()
 6 {
 7    string response;
 8    cout << boolalpha;
 9
10    // Make a quiz with two questions
11    const int QUIZZES = 2;
12    Question* quiz[QUIZZES];
13    quiz[0] = new Question;
14    quiz[0]->set_text("Who was the inventor of C++?");
15    quiz[0]->set_answer("Bjarne Stroustrup");
16
17    ChoiceQuestion* cq_pointer = new ChoiceQuestion;
18    cq_pointer->set_text(
19       "In which country was the inventor of C++ born?");
```

```
20      cq_pointer->add_choice("Australia", false);
21      cq_pointer->add_choice("Denmark", true);
22      cq_pointer->add_choice("Korea", false);
23      cq_pointer->add_choice("United States", false);
24      quiz[1] = cq_pointer;
25
26      // Check answers for all questions
27      for (int i = 0; i < QUIZZES; i++)
28      {
29         quiz[i]->display();
30         cout << "Your answer: ";
31         getline(cin, response);
32         cout << quiz[i]->check_answer(response) << endl;
33      }
34
35      return 0;
36   }
```

Programming Tip 10.2
Don't Use Type Tags

Some programmers build inheritance hierarchies in which each object has a tag that indicates its type, commonly a string. They then query that string:

```
if (q->get_type() == "Question")
{
   // Do something
}
else if (q->get_type() == "ChoiceQuestion")
{
   // Do something else
}
```

This is a poor strategy. If a new class is added, then all these queries need to be revised. In contrast, consider the addition of a class NumericQuestion to our quiz program. *Nothing* needs to change in that program because it uses virtual functions, not type tags.

Whenever you find yourself adding a type tag to a hierarchy of classes, reconsider and use virtual functions instead.

Common Error 10.4
Slicing an Object

In C++ it is legal to copy a derived-class object into a base-class variable. However, any derived-class information is lost in the process. For example, when a Manager object is assigned to a variable of type Employee, the result is only the employee portion of the manager data:

```
Manager m;
. . .
Employee e = m; // Holds only the Employee base data of m
```

Any information that is particular to managers is sliced off, because it would not fit into a variable of type Employee. To avoid **slicing**, you can use pointers.

The slicing problem commonly occurs when a function has a polymorphic parameter (that is, a parameter that can belong to a base class or a derived class). In that case, the parameter variable must be a pointer or a reference. Consider this example:

```
void ask(Question q) // Error
{
```

```
        q.display();
        cout << "Your answer: ";
        getline(cin, response);
        cout << q.check_answer(response) << endl;
}
```

If you call this function with a ChoiceQuestion object, then the parameter variable q is initialized with a copy of that object. But q is a Question object; the derived-class information is sliced away. The simplest remedy is to use a reference:

```
void ask(const Question& q)
```

Now only the *address* is passed to the function. A reference is really a pointer in disguise. No slicing occurs, and virtual functions work correctly.

Common Error 10.5

Failing to Override a Virtual Function

In C++, two functions can have the same name, provided they differ in their parameter types. For example, you can define two member functions called display in the Question class:

```
class Question
{
public:
    virtual void display() const;
    virtual void display(ostream& out) const;
    . . .
};
```

These are different functions, each with its own implementation. The C++ compiler considers them to be completely unrelated. We say that the display name is *overloaded*. This is different from overriding, where a derived class function provides an implementation of a base class function with the same name and the same parameter types.

It is a common error to accidentally provide an overloaded function when you actually mean to override a function. Consider this scary example:

```
class ChoiceQuestion : public Question
{
public:
    void display(); // Does not override Question::display() const
    . . .
};
```

The display member function in the Question class has subtly different parameter types: the this pointer that points to the implicit parameter (see Section 9.10.3) has type const Question*, whereas in the ChoiceQuestion class, the this pointer is not const.

In C++ 11, you can use the reserved word override to tag any member function that should override a virtual function:

```
class ChoiceQuestion : public Question
{
public:
    void display() override;
    . . .
};
```

If the member function does not actually override a virtual function, the compiler generates an error. This is good, because you can then have a closer look and add the missing const reserved word.

The compiler also generates an error if you forget to declare the base class member function as virtual. If you use C++ 11, it is a good idea to take advantage of the override reserved word.

Special Topic 10.2
Virtual Self-Calls

Suppose we add the following function to the Question class:

```
void Question::ask() const
{
   display();
   cout << "Your answer: ";
   getline(cin, response);
   cout << check_answer(response) << endl;
}
```

Now consider the call

```
ChoiceQuestion cq;
cq.set_text("In which country was the inventor of C++ born?");
. . .
cq.ask();
```

Which display and check_answer function will the ask function call? If you look inside the code of the Question::ask function, you can see that these functions are executed on the implicit parameter:

```
void Question::ask() const
{
   implicit parameter.display();
   cout << "Your answer: ";
   getline(cin, response);
   cout << implicit parameter.check_answer(response) << endl;
}
```

The implicit parameter in our call is cq, an object of type ChoiceQuestion. Because the display and check_answer functions are virtual, the ChoiceQuestion versions of the functions are called automatically. This happens even though the ask function is defined in the Question class, which has *no knowledge* of the ChoiceQuestion class.

As you can see, virtual functions are a very powerful mechanism. The Question class supplies an ask function that specifies the common nature of asking a question, namely to display it and check the response. How the displaying and checking are carried out is left to the derived classes.

HOW TO 10.1
Developing an Inheritance Hierarchy

When you work with a set of classes, some of which are more general and others more specialized, you want to organize them into an inheritance hierarchy. This enables you to process objects of different classes in a uniform way.

Problem Statement   As an example, we will consider a bank that offers its customers the following account types:

- *A savings account that earns interest. The interest compounds monthly and is computed on the minimum monthly balance.*

- *A checking account that has no interest, gives you three free withdrawals per month, and charges a $1 transaction fee for each additional withdrawal.*

The program will manage a set of accounts of both types, and it should be structured so that other account types can be added without affecting the main processing loop. Supply a menu

```
D)eposit  W)ithdraw  M)onth end  Q)uit
```

For deposits and withdrawals, query the account number and amount. Print the balance of the account after each transaction.

In the "Month end" command, accumulate interest or clear the transaction counter, depending on the type of the bank account. Then print the balance of all accounts.

Step 1   List the classes that are part of the hierarchy.

In our case, the problem description yields two classes: SavingsAccount and CheckingAccount. To express the commonality between them, we will introduce a class BankAccount.

Step 2   Organize the classes into an inheritance hierarchy.

Draw a UML diagram that shows base and derived classes. Here is the diagram for our example:

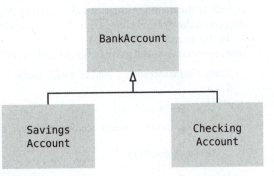

Step 3   Determine the common responsibilities.

In Step 2, you will have identified a class at the base of the hierarchy. That class needs to have sufficient responsibilities to carry out the tasks at hand. To find out what those tasks are, write pseudocode for processing the objects:

For each user command
  If it is a deposit or withdrawal
    Deposit or withdraw the amount from the specified account.
    Print the balance.
  If it is month end processing
    For each account
      Call month end processing.
      Print the balance.

From the pseudocode, we obtain the following list of common responsibilities that every bank account must carry out:

Deposit money.
Withdraw money.
Get the balance.
Carry out month end processing.

Step 4   Decide which functions are overridden in derived classes.

For each derived class and each of the common responsibilities, decide whether the behavior can be inherited or whether it needs to be overridden. Declare any functions that are overridden as virtual in the root of the hierarchy.

Getting the balance is common to all account types. Withdrawing and end of month processing are different for the derived classes, so they need to be declared virtual. Because it is entirely possible that some future account type will levy a fee for deposits, it seems prudent to declare the deposit member function virtual as well.

```
class BankAccount
{
public:
    virtual void deposit(double amount);
    virtual void withdraw(double amount);
    virtual void month_end();
    double get_balance() const;
private:
    . . .
};
```

Step 5 Define the public interface of each derived class.

Typically, derived classes have responsibilities other than those of the base class. List those, as well as the member functions that need to be overridden. You also need to specify how the objects of the derived classes should be constructed.

In this example, we need a way of setting the interest rate for the savings account. In addition, we need to specify constructors and overridden functions.

```
class SavingsAccount : public BankAccount
{
public:
    /**
        Constructs a savings account with a zero balance.
    */
    SavingsAccount();

    /**
        Sets the interest rate for this account.
        @param rate the monthly interest rate in percent
    */
    void set_interest_rate(double rate);

    virtual void withdraw(double amount);
    virtual void month_end();
private:
    . . .
};

class CheckingAccount : public BankAccount
{
public:
    /**
        Constructs a checking account with a zero balance.
    */
    CheckingAccount();

    virtual void withdraw(double amount);
    virtual void month_end();
private:
    . . .
};
```

Step 6   Identify data members.

List the data members for each class. If you find a data member that is common to all classes, be sure to place it in the base of the hierarchy.

All accounts have a balance. We store that value in the BankAccount base class:

```cpp
class BankAccount
{
   . . .
private:
   double balance;
};
```

The SavingsAccount class needs to store the interest rate. It also needs to store the minimum monthly balance, which must be updated by all withdrawals:

```cpp
class SavingsAccount : public BankAccount
{
   . . .
private:
   double interest_rate;
   double min_balance;
};
```

The CheckingAccount class needs to count the withdrawals, so that the charge can be applied after the free withdrawal limit is reached:

```cpp
class CheckingAccount : public BankAccount
{
   . . .
private:
   int withdrawals;
};
```

Step 7   Implement constructors and member functions.

The member functions of the BankAccount class update or return the balance:

```cpp
BankAccount::BankAccount()
{
   balance = 0;
}

void BankAccount::deposit(double amount)
{
   balance = balance + amount;
}

void BankAccount::withdraw(double amount)
{
   balance = balance - amount;
}

double BankAccount::get_balance() const
{
   return balance;
}
```

At the level of the BankAccount base class, we can say nothing about end of month processing. We choose to make that function do nothing:

```cpp
void BankAccount::month_end()
{
}
```

In the `withdraw` member function of the `SavingsAccount` class, the minimum balance is updated. Note the call to the base-class member function:

```
void SavingsAccount::withdraw(double amount)
{
    BankAccount::withdraw(amount);
    double balance = get_balance();
    if (balance < min_balance)
    {
        min_balance = balance;
    }
}
```

In the `month_end` member function of the `SavingsAccount` class, the interest is deposited into the account. We must call the deposit member function because we have no direct access to the balance data member. The minimum balance is reset for the next month:

```
void SavingsAccount::month_end()
{
    double interest = min_balance * interest_rate / 100;
    deposit(interest);
    min_balance = get_balance();
}
```

The `withdraw` function of the `CheckingAccount` class needs to check the withdrawal count. If there have been too many withdrawals, a charge is applied. Again, note how the function invokes the base-class function, using the `BankAccount::` syntax:

```
void CheckingAccount::withdraw(double amount)
{
    const int FREE_WITHDRAWALS = 3;
    const int WITHDRAWAL_FEE = 1;

    BankAccount::withdraw(amount);
    withdrawals++;
    if (withdrawals > FREE_WITHDRAWALS)
    {
        BankAccount::withdraw(WITHDRAWAL_FEE);
    }
}
```

End of month processing for a checking account simply resets the withdrawal count:

```
void CheckingAccount::month_end()
{
    withdrawals = 0;
}
```

Step 8   Allocate objects on the free store and process them.

For polymorphism (that is, variation of behavior) to work in C++, you need to call virtual functions through pointers. The easiest strategy is to allocate all polymorphic objects on the free store, using the new operator.

In our sample program, we allocate 5 checking accounts and 5 savings accounts and store their addresses in an array of bank account pointers. Then we accept user commands and execute deposits, withdrawals, and monthly processing.

```
int main()
{
    cout << fixed << setprecision(2);

    // Create accounts
    const int ACCOUNTS_SIZE = 10;
    BankAccount* accounts[ACCOUNTS_SIZE];
```

```cpp
      for (int i = 0; i < ACCOUNTS_SIZE / 2; i++)
      {
         accounts[i] = new CheckingAccount;
      }
      for (int i = ACCOUNTS_SIZE / 2; i < ACCOUNTS_SIZE; i++)
      {
         SavingsAccount* account = new SavingsAccount;
         account->set_interest_rate(0.75);
         accounts[i] = account;
      }

      // Execute commands
      bool more = true;
      while (more)
      {
         cout << "D)eposit  W)ithdraw  M)onth end  Q)uit: ";
         string input;
         cin >> input;
         if (input == "D" || input == "W")  // Deposit or withdrawal
         {
            cout << "Enter account number and amount: ";
            int num;
            double amount;
            cin >> num >> amount;

            if (input == "D") { accounts[num]->deposit(amount); }
            else { accounts[num]->withdraw(amount); }

            cout << "Balance: " << accounts[num]->get_balance() << endl;
         }
         else if (input == "M")  // Month end processing
         {
            for (int n = 0; n < ACCOUNTS_SIZE(); n++)
            {
               accounts[n]->month_end();
               cout << n << " " << accounts[n]->get_balance() << endl;
            }
         }
         else if (input == "Q")
         {
            more = false;
         }
      }

      return 0;
   }
```

EXAMPLE CODE   See how_to_1 of your companion code for the complete program.

WORKED EXAMPLE 10.1

Implementing an Employee Hierarchy for Payroll Processing

Learn how to implement payroll processing that works for different kinds of employees. See your E-Text or visit wiley. com/go/bclo3.

Jose Luis Pelaez Inc./Getty Images, Inc.

Computing & Society 10.1 Who Controls the Internet?

In 1962, J.C.R. Lick-lider was head of the first computer research program at DARPA, the Defense Advanced Research Projects Agency. He wrote a series of papers describing a "galactic network" through which computer users could access data and programs from other sites. This was well before computer networks were invented. By 1969, four computers—three in California and one in Utah—were connected to the ARPANET, the precursor of the Internet. The network grew quickly, linking computers at many universities and research organizations. It was originally thought that most network users wanted to run programs on remote computers. Using remote execution, a researcher at one institution would be able to access an underutilized computer at a different site. It quickly became apparent that remote execution was not what the network was actually used for. Instead, the "killer application" was electronic mail: the transfer of messages between computer users at different locations.

In 1972, Bob Kahn proposed to extend ARPANET into the *Internet:* a collection of interoperable networks. All networks on the Internet share common *protocols* for data transmission. Kahn and Vinton Cerf developed a protocol, now called TCP/IP (Transmission Control Protocol/Internet Protocol). On January 1, 1983, all hosts on the Internet simultaneously switched to the TCP/IP protocol (which is used to this day).

Over time, researchers, computer scientists, and hobbyists published increasing amounts of information on the Internet. For example, Project Gutenberg makes available the text of important classical books, whose copyright has expired, in computer-readable form (www.gutenberg.org). In 1989, Tim Berners-Lee, a computer scientist at CERN (the European organization for nuclear research) started work on hyperlinked documents, allowing users to browse by following links to related documents. This infrastructure is now known as the World Wide Web.

The first interfaces to retrieve this information were, by today's standards, unbelievably clumsy and hard to use. In March 1993, WWW traffic was 0.1 percent of all Internet traffic. All that changed when Marc Andreesen, then a graduate student working for the National Center for Supercomputing Applications (NCSA), released Mosaic. Mosaic displayed web pages in graphical form, using images, fonts, and colors (see the figure). Andreesen went on to fame and fortune at Netscape, and Microsoft licensed the Mosaic code to create Internet Explorer. By 1996, WWW traffic accounted for more than half of the data transported on the Internet.

The Internet has a very democratic structure. Anyone can publish anything, and anyone can read whatever has been published. This does not always sit well with governments and corporations.

Many governments control the Internet infrastructure in their country. For example, an Internet user in China, searching for the Tiananmen Square massacre or air pollution in their hometown, may find nothing. Vietnam blocks access to Facebook, perhaps fearing that anti-government protesters might use it to organize themselves. The U.S. government has required publicly funded libraries and schools to install filters that block sexually-explicit and hate speech, and its security organizations have spied on the Internet usage of citizens.

When the Internet is delivered by phone or TV cable companies, those companies sometimes interfere with competing Internet offerings. Cell phone companies refused to carry Voice-over-IP services, and cable companies slowed down movie streaming. The Internet has become a powerful force for delivering information—both good and bad. It is our responsibility as citizens to demand of our government that we can control which information to access.

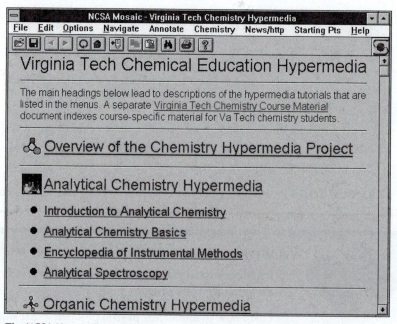

The NCSA Mosaic Browser

CHAPTER SUMMARY

Explain the notions of inheritance, base class, and derived class.

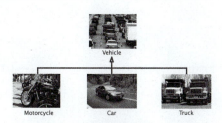

- A derived class inherits data and behavior from a base class.
- You can always use a derived-class object in place of a base-class object.

Implement derived classes in C++.

- A derived class can override a base-class function by providing a new implementation.
- The derived class inherits all data members and all functions that it does not override.
- Unless specified otherwise, the base-class data members are initialized with the default constructor.
- The constructor of a derived class can supply arguments to a base-class constructor.

Describe how a derived class can override functions from a base class.

- A derived class can inherit a function from the base class, or it can override it by providing another implementation.
- Use *BaseClass*::*function* notation to explicitly call a base-class function.

Describe virtual functions and polymorphism.

- When converting a derived-class object to a base class, the derived-class data is sliced away.
- A derived-class pointer can be converted to a base-class pointer.
- When a virtual function is called, the version belonging to the actual type of the implicit parameter is invoked.
- Polymorphism (literally, "having multiple shapes") describes objects that share a set of tasks and execute them in different ways.

RESERVED WORD SUMMARY

Reserved Word	Description	Reference Location
auto	A type that is automatically inferred	Special Topic 2.3 (C++ 11)
bool	The Boolean type	Section 3.7
break	Break out of a loop or switch	Special Topic 3.3, 4.2
case	A label in a switch statement	Special Topic 3.3
char	The character type	Section 7.3
class	Definition of a class	Section 9.2
const	Definition of a constant value, reference, member function, or pointer	Section 2.1.5, Special Topic 5.2, Special Topic 6.4, Programming Tip 9.2
default	The default case of a switch statement	Special Topic 3.3
delete	Return a memory block to the free store	Section 7.4
do	A loop that is executed at least once	Section 4.4
double	The double-precision, floating-point type	Section 2.1.2
else	The alternative clause in an if statement	Section 3.1
false	The false Boolean value	Section 3.7
float	The single-precision, floating-point type	Special Topic 2.1
for	A loop that is intended to initialize, test, and update a variable	Section 4.3
friend	Allows another class or function to access the private features of this class	Section 14.2
if	The conditional branch statement	Section 3.1
int	The integer type	Section 2.1.1
long	A modifier for the int and double types that indicates that the type may have more bytes	Special Topic 2.1
namespace	A name space for disambiguating names	Section 1.5
new	Allocate a memory block from the free store	Section 7.4
nullptr	A pointer that does not point to any value	Section 7.1.3 (C++ 11)

Operator	Description	Reference Location
->*	Dereference and access pointer to member	not covered
*	Multiplication	Section 2.2.1
/	Division or integer division	Section 2.2.1, Section 2.2.3
%	Integer remainder	Section 2.2.3
+	Addition	Section 2.2.1
-	Subtraction	Section 2.2.1
<<	Output	Section 1.5, Section 2.3.2, Appendix F
>>	Input	Section 2.3.1, Appendix F
<	Less than	Section 3.2
<=	Less than or equal	Section 3.2
>	Greater than	Section 3.2
>=	Greater than or equal	Section 3.2
==	Equal	Section 3.2
!=	Not equal	Section 3.2
&	Bitwise *and*	Appendix F
^	Bitwise *xor*	Appendix F
|	Bitwise *or*	Appendix F
&&	Boolean *and*	Section 3.7
||	Boolean *or*	Section 3.7
? :	Conditional operator	Special Topic 3.1
=	Assignment	Section 2.1.4
+= -= *= /= %= &= |= ^= >>= <<=	Combined operator and assignment	Special Topic 2.5
,	Sequencing of expressions	not covered

CHARACTER CODES

These escape sequences can occur in strings (for example, "\n") and characters (for example, '\'') However, the \U escape sequences should only be used inside strings that have an encoding prefix, such as

```
string message = u8"San Jos\U000000e9 \U0001f684";
```

A string is a sequence of bytes. In the UTF-8 encoding, bytes between 0 and 127 correspond to the ASCII character range (see Table 2). Other Unicode characters are encoded into multiple bytes, where the first byte is ≥ 192, and subsequent bytes are between 128 and 191. Table 3 shows the encoding.

Table 1 Escape Sequences	
Escape Sequence	Description
\n	Newline
\r	Carriage return
\t	Tab
\v	Vertical tab
\b	Backspace
\f	Form feed
\a	Alert
\\	Backslash
\"	Double quote
\'	Single quote
\?	Question mark
\U$h_4h_3h_2h_1h_0$	A Unicode character, which will be encoded into a sequence of bytes determined by a character encoding

Table 2 ASCII Code Table

Dec. Code	Hex Code	Character	Dec. Code	Hex Code	Character	Dec. Code	Hex Code	Character	Dec. Code	Hex Code	Character
0	00	\0	32	20	Space	64	40	@	96	60	`
1	01		33	21	!	65	41	A	97	61	a
2	02		34	22	"	66	42	B	98	62	b
3	03		35	23	#	67	43	C	99	63	c
4	04		36	24	$	68	44	D	100	64	d
5	05		37	25	%	69	45	E	101	65	e
6	06		38	26	&	70	46	F	102	66	f
7	07	\a	39	27	'	71	47	G	103	67	g
8	08	\b	40	28	(	72	48	H	104	68	h
9	09	\t	41	29	)	73	49	I	105	69	i
10	0A	\n	42	2A	*	74	4A	J	106	6A	j
11	0B	\v	43	2B	+	75	4B	K	107	6B	k
12	0C	\f	44	2C	,	76	4C	L	108	6C	l
13	0D	\r	45	2D	-	77	4D	M	109	6D	m
14	0E		46	2E	.	78	4E	N	110	6E	n
15	0F		47	2F	/	79	4F	O	111	6F	o
16	10		48	30	0	80	50	P	112	70	p
17	11		49	31	1	81	51	Q	113	71	q
18	12		50	32	2	82	52	R	114	72	r
19	13		51	33	3	83	53	S	115	73	s
20	14		52	34	4	84	54	T	116	74	t
21	15		53	35	5	85	55	U	117	75	u
22	16		54	36	6	86	56	V	118	76	v
23	17		55	37	7	87	57	W	119	77	w
24	18		56	38	8	88	58	X	120	78	x
25	19		57	39	9	89	59	Y	121	79	y
26	1A		58	3A	:	90	5A	Z	122	7A	z
27	1B		59	3B	;	91	5B	[	123	7B	{
28	1C		60	3C	<	92	5C	\	124	7C		
29	1D		61	3D	=	93	5D	]	125	7D	}
30	1E		62	3E	>	94	5E	^	126	7E	~
31	1F		63	3F	?	95	5F	_	127	7F	

Table 3 UTF-8 Encoding

UTF-8				Unicode		
0■■■■■■■				00000 00000000 0■■■■■■■		
110■■■■■ 10■■■■■■				00000 00000■■■ ■■■■■■■■		
1110■■■■ 10■■■■■■ 10■■■■■■				00000 ■■■■■■■■ ■■■■■■■■		
11110■■■ 10■■■■■■ 10■■■■■■ 10■■■■■■				■■■■■ ■■■■■■■■ ■■■■■■■■		

C++ LIBRARY SUMMARY

Standard Code Libraries

\<algorithm\>

- bool **binary_search**(I begin, I end, T x)
  Function: Checks whether the value x is contained in the sorted range [begin, end).
- T **max**(T x, T y)
  Function: The maximum of x and y.
- T **min**(T x, T y)
  Function: The minimum of x and y.
- void **sort**(I begin, I end)
  Function: Sorts the elements in the range [begin, end).

\<cctype\>

- bool **isalnum**(char c)
  Function: Test whether c is a letter or a number.
- bool **isalpha**(char c)
  Function: Tests whether c is a letter.
- bool **isdigit**(char c)
  Function: Tests whether c is a digit.
- bool **islower**(char c)
  Function: Tests whether c is lowercase.
- bool **isspace**(char c)
  Function: Tests whether c is white space.
- bool **isupper**(char c)
  Function: Tests whether c is uppercase.
- char **tolower**(char c)
  Function: Returns the lowercase of c.
- char **toupper**(char c)
  Function: Returns the uppercase of c.

\<cmath\>

- int **abs**(int x)
- double **abs**(double x)
  Function: Absolute value, $|x|$
- double **cos**(double x)
  Function: Cosine, $\cos x$ (x in radians)

- double **log**(double x)
  Function: Natural log, $\log(x), x > 0$
- double **log10**(double x)
  Function: Decimal log, $\log_{10}(x), x > 0$
- double **pow**(double x, double y)
  Function: Power, x^y. If $x > 0$, y can be any value. If x is 0, y must be > 0. If $x < 0$, y must be an integer.
- double **sin**(double x)
  Function: Sine, $\sin x$ (x in radians)
- double **sqrt**(double x)
  Function: Square root, $\sqrt{x}$
- double **tan**(double x)
  Function: Tangent, $\tan x$ (x in radians)

\<cstdlib\>

- int **abs**(int x)
  Function: Absolute value, $|x|$
- void **exit**(int n)
  Function: Exits the program with status code n.
- int **rand**()
  Function: Random integer
- void **srand**(int n)
  Function: Sets the seed of the random number generator to n.

\<ctime\>

- time_t **time**(time_t* p)
  Function: Returns the number of seconds since January 1, 1970, 00:00:00 GMT.
  If p is not nullptr, the return value is also stored in the location to which p points.

\<string\>

- istream& **getline**(istream& in, string& s)
  Function: Gets the next input line from the input stream in and stores it in the string s.
- int **stoi**(const string& s) (C++ 11)
- double **stod**(const string& s) (C++ 11)
  Function: Converts the string to an integer or floating-point number.

Class `string`

- `const char* string::`**`c_str`**`() const`
  Member function: Returns a `char` array with the characters in this string.

- `int string::`**`length`**`() const`
  Member function: Returns the length of the string.

- `string string::`**`substr`**`(int i) const`
  Member function: Returns the substring from index i to the end of the string.

- `string string::`**`substr`**`(int i, int n) const`
  Member function: Returns the substring of length n starting at index i.

`<iomanip>`

- **`boolalpha`**
  Manipulator: Causes Boolean values to be displayed as true and false instead of the default 1 and 0.

- **`defaultfloat`**
  Manipulator: Selects the default floating-point format, which uses scientific format for very large or very small values, and fixed format for all other values.

- **`fixed`**
  Manipulator: Selects fixed floating-point format, with trailing zeroes.

- **`left`**, **`right`**
  Manipulator: Left- or right-justifies values if they are shorter than the field width.

- **`scientific`**
  Manipulator: Selects scientific floating-point format, such as `1.729000e+03`.

- **`setfill`**`(char c)`
  Manipulator: Sets the fill character to the character c.

- **`setprecision`**`(int n)`
  Manipulator: Sets the precision of floating-point values to n digits after the decimal point in fixed and scientific formats.

- **`setw`**`(int n)`
  Manipulator: Sets the width of the next field.

`<iostream>`
Class `istream`

- `bool istream::`**`fail`**`() const`
  Member function: True if input has failed.

- `istream& istream::`**`get`**`(char& c)`
  Member function: Gets the next character and places it into c.

- `istream& istream::`**`seekg`**`(long p)`
  Member function: Moves the get position to position p.

- `long istream::`**`tellg`**`()`
  Member function: Returns the get position.

- `istream& istream::`**`unget`**`()`
  Member function: Puts the last character read back into the stream, to be read again in the next input operation; only one character can be put back at a time.

Class `ostream`

- `ostream& ostream::`**`seekp`**`(long p)`
  Member function: Moves the put position to position p.

- `long ostream::`**`tellp`**`()`
  Member function: Returns the put position.

`<fstream>`
Class `ifstream`

- `void ifstream::`**`open`**`(const string& n)` (C++ 11)
- `void ifstream::`**`open`**`(const char n[])`
  Member function: Opens a file with name n for reading.

Class `ofstream`

- `void ofstream::`**`open`**`(const string& n)` (C++ 11)
- `void ofstream::`**`open`**`(const char n[])`
  Member function: Opens a file with name n for writing.

Class `fstream`

- `void fstream::`**`open`**`(const string& n)` (C++ 11)
- `void fstream::`**`open`**`(const char n[])`
  Member function: Opens a file with name n for reading and writing.

Class `fstreambase`

- `void fstreambase::`**`close`**`()`
  Member function: Closes the file stream.

  Notes: fstreambase is the common base class of ifstream, ofstream, and fstream.
  To open a binary file n both for input and output, use `f.open(n, ios::in | ios::out | ios::binary)`

`<strstream>`
Class `istringstream`

- `istringstream::`**`istringstream`**`(string s)`
  Constructs a string stream that reads from the string s.

Class ostringstream

- string ostringstream::**str**() const
  Member function: Returns the string that was
  collected by the string stream.

  Notes: Call s = string(out.str()) to get a string
  object that contains the characters
  collected by ostringstream out.

<vector>

Class vector<T>

- vector<T>::**vector**()
  Constructs an empty vector.

- vector<T>::**vector**(int n)
  Constructs a vector with n elements.

- T& vector<T>::**operator**[](int n)
  Member function: Accesses the element at index n.

- void vector<T>::**pop_back**()
  Member function: Removes (but does not return)
  the last element.

- void vector<T>::**push_back**(const T& x)
  Member function: Inserts x after the last element.

- int vector<T>::**size**() const
  Member function: Returns the number of elements
  in the container.

C++ LANGUAGE CODING GUIDELINES

Introduction

This coding style guide is a simplified version of one that has been used with good success both in industrial practice and for college courses. It lays down rules that you must follow for your programming assignments.

A style guide is a set of mandatory requirements for layout and formatting. Uniform style makes it easier for you to read code from your instructor and classmates. You will really appreciate the consistency if you do a team project. It is also easier for your instructor and your grader to grasp the essence of your programs quickly.

A style guide makes you a more productive programmer because it *reduces gratuitous choice*. If you don't have to make choices about trivial matters, you can spend your energy on the solution of real problems.

In these guidelines a number of constructs are plainly outlawed. That doesn't mean that programmers using them are evil or incompetent. It does mean that the constructs are of marginal utility and can be expressed just as well or even better with other language constructs.

If you have already programmed in C or C++, you may be initially uncomfortable about giving up some fond habits. However, it is a sign of professionalism to set aside personal preferences in minor matters and to compromise for the benefit of your group.

These guidelines are necessarily somewhat long and dull. They also mention features that you may not yet have seen in class. Here are the most important highlights:

- Tabs are set every three spaces.
- Variable and function names are lowercase.
- Constant names are uppercase. Class names start with an uppercase letter.
- There are spaces after reserved words and between binary operators.
- Braces must line up.
- No magic numbers may be used.
- Every function must have a comment.
- At most 30 lines of code may be used per function.
- No goto, continue, or break is allowed.
- At most two global variables may be used per file.

A note to the instructor: Of course, many programmers and organizations have strong feelings about coding style. If this style guide is incompatible with your own preferences or with local custom, please feel free to modify it. For that purpose, this coding style guide is available in electronic form on the companion web site for this book.

Source Files

Each program is a collection of one or more files or modules. The executable program is obtained by compiling and linking these files. Organize the material in each file as follows:

- Header comments
- `#include` statements
- Constants
- Classes
- Functions

It is common to start each file with a comment block. Here is a typical format:

```
/**
    @file invoice.cpp
    @author Jenny Koo
    @date 2022-01-24
    @version 3.14
*/
```

You may also want to include a copyright notice, such as

```
/* Copyright 2022 Jenny Koo */
```

A valid copyright notice consists of

- the copyright symbol © or the word "Copyright" or the abbreviation "Copr."
- the year of first publication of the work
- the name of the owner of the copyright

(Note: To save space, this header comment has been omitted from the programs in this book as well as the programs on disk so that the actual line numbers match those that are printed in the book.)

Next, list all included header files.

```
#include <iostream>
#include "question.h"
```

Do not embed absolute path names, such as

```
#include "c:\me\my_homework\widgets.h"  // Don't !!!
```

After the header files, list constants that are needed throughout the program file.

```
const int GRID_SIZE = 20;
const double CLOCK_RADIUS = 5;
```

Then supply the definitions of all classes.

```
class Product
{
    . . .
};
```

Order the class definitions so that a class is defined before it is used in another class.

Finally, list all functions, including member functions of classes and nonmember functions. Order the nonmember functions so that a function is defined before it is called. As a consequence, the `main` function will be the last function in your file.

Functions

Supply a comment of the following form for every function.

```
/**
    Explanation.
    @param parameter variable1    explanation
    @param parameter variable2    explanation
    . . .
    @return explanation
*/
```

The introductory explanation is required for all functions except main. It should start with an uppercase letter and end with a period. Some documentation tools extract the first sentence of the explanation into a summary table. Thus, if you provide an explanation that consists of multiple sentences, formulate the explanation such that the first sentence is a concise explanation of the function's purpose.

Omit the @param comment if the function has no parameter variables. Omit the @return comment for void functions. Here is a typical example:

```
/**
    Converts calendar date into Julian day. This algorithm is from Press
    et al., Numerical Recipes in C, 2nd ed., Cambridge University Press, 1992.
    @param year the year of the date to be converted
    @param month the month of the date to be converted
    @param day the day of the date to be converted
    @return the Julian day number that begins at noon of the given
    calendar date
*/
long dat2jul(int year, int month, int day)
{
    . . .
}
```

Parameter variable names must be explicit, especially if they are integers or Boolean.

```
Employee remove(int d, double s); // Huh?
Employee remove(int department, double severance_pay); // OK
```

Of course, for very generic functions, short names may be very appropriate.

Do not write void functions that return exactly one answer through a reference. Instead, make the result into a return value.

```
void find(vector<Employee> c, bool& found); // Don't!
bool find(vector<Employee> c); // OK
```

Of course, if the function computes more than one value, some or all results can be returned through reference parameters.

Functions must have at most 30 lines of code. (Comments, blank lines, and lines containing only braces are not included in this count.) Functions that consist of one long if/else/else statement sequence may be longer, provided each branch is 10 lines or less. This rule forces you to break up complex computations into separate functions.

Local Variables

Do not define all local variables at the beginning of a block. Define each variable just before it is used for the first time.

Every variable must be either explicitly initialized when defined or set in the immediately following statement (for example, through a >> instruction).

```cpp
int pennies = 0;
```

or

```cpp
int pennies;
cin >> pennies;
```

Move variables to the innermost block in which they are needed:

```cpp
while (. . .)
{
   double xnew = (xold + a / xold) / 2;
   . . .
}
```

Do not define two variables in one statement:

```cpp
int dimes = 0, nickels = 0; // Don't
```

When defining a pointer variable, place the * with the type, not the variable:

```cpp
Link* p; // OK
```

not

```cpp
Link *p; // Don't
```

Use auto only with types that are complex and not very informative, such as iterators. For example, prefer

```cpp
unordered_map<string, int> scores = . . .;
auto pos = scores.find("Harry");
```

over

```cpp
unordered_map<string, double>::iterator pos = scores.find("Harry");
```

Constants

In C++, do not use #define to define constants:

```cpp
#define CLOCK_RADIUS 5 // Don't
```

Use const instead:

```cpp
const double CLOCK_RADIUS = 5; // The radius of the clock face
```

You may not use magic numbers in your code. (A magic number is an integer constant embedded in code without a constant definition.) Any number except 0, 1, or 2 is considered magic:

```cpp
if (p.get_x() < 10) // Don't
```

Use a const variable instead:

```cpp
const double WINDOW_XMAX = 10;
if (p.get_x() < WINDOW_XMAX) // OK
```

Even the most reasonable cosmic constant is going to change one day. You think there are 365 days per year? Your customers on Mars are going to be pretty unhappy about your silly prejudice.

Make a constant

```
const int DAYS_PER_YEAR = 365;
```

so that you can easily produce a Martian version without trying to find all the 365's, 364's, 366's, 367's, and so on in your code.

Classes

Lay out the items of a class as follows:

```
class ClassName
{
public:
   constructors
   mutators
   accessors
private:
   data
};
```

All data members of classes must be private.

Control Flow

The for Statement

Use for loops only when a variable runs from somewhere to somewhere else with some constant increment/decrement.

```
for (i = 0; i < a.size(); i++)
{
   cout << a[i] << endl;
}
```

Do not use the for loop for weird constructs such as

```
for (xnew = a / 2; count < ITERATIONS; cout << xnew) // Don't
{
   xold = xnew;
   xnew = xold + a / xold;
   count++;
}
```

Make such a loop into a while loop, so the sequence of instructions is much clearer.

```
xnew = a / 2;
while (count < ITERATIONS) // OK
{
   xold = xnew;
   xnew = xold + a / xold;
   count++;
   cout << xnew;
}
```

Consider using the range-based for loop when traversing a container such as a vector or list:

```
vector<int> values = . . .;
for (int v : values)
{
   cout << v << " ";
}
```

Nonlinear Control Flow

Don't use the switch statement. Use if/else instead.

Do not use the break, continue, or goto statement. Use a bool variable to control the execution flow.

Lexical Issues

Naming Conventions

The following rules specify when to use upper- and lowercase letters in identifier names.

1. All variable and function names and all data members of classes are in lowercase, sometimes with an underscore in the middle. For example, first_player.

2. All constants are in uppercase, with an occasional underscore. For example, CLOCK_RADIUS.

3. All class names start with uppercase and are followed by lowercase letters, with an occasional uppercase letter in the middle. For example, BankTeller.

Names must be reasonably long and descriptive. Use first_player instead of fp. No drppng f vwls. Local variables that are fairly routine can be short (ch, i) as long as they are really just boring holders for an input character, a loop counter, and so on. Also, do not use ctr, c, cntr, cnt, c2 for five counter variables in your function. Surely each of these variables has a specific purpose and can be named to remind the reader of it (for example, ccurrent, cnext, cprevious, cnew, cresult).

Indentation and White Space

Use tab stops every three columns. Save your file so that it contains no tabs at all. That means you will need to change the tab stop setting in your editor! In the editor, make sure to select "3 spaces per tab stop" and "save all tabs as spaces". Every programming editor has these settings. If yours doesn't, don't use tabs at all but type the correct number of spaces to achieve indentation.

Use blank lines freely to separate logically distinct parts of a function.

Use a blank space around every binary operator:

```
x1 = (-b - sqrt(b * b - 4 * a * c)) / (2 * a); // Good
x1=(-b-sqrt(b*b-4*a*c))/(2*a); // Bad
```

Leave a blank space after (and not before) each comma, semicolon, and reserved word, but not after a function name.

```
if (x == 0) . . .
f(a, b[i]);
```

Every line must fit in 80 columns. If you must break a statement, add an indentation level for the continuation:

```
a[n] = ......................................................
       + ................;
```

Braces

Opening and closing braces must line up, either horizontally or vertically.

```
while (i < n) { cout << a[i] << endl; i++; }  // OK
while (i < n)
{
   cout << a[i] << endl;
   i++;
} // OK
```

Some programmers don't line up vertical braces but place the { *behind* the while:

```
while (i < n) {   // Don't
   cout << a[i] << endl;
   i++;
}
```

This style saves a line, but it is difficult to match the braces.

Always use braces with if, while, do, and for statements, even if the body is only a single statement.

```
if (floor > 13)
{             // OK
   floor--;
}
if (floor > 13)
   floor--;   // Don't
```

Unstable Layout

Some programmers take great pride in lining up certain columns in their code:

```
class Employee
{
   . . .
private:
   string  name;
      int  age;
   double  hourly_wage;
};
```

This is undeniably neat, and we recommend it if your editor does it for you, but *don't* do it manually. The layout is not *stable* under change. A data type that is longer than the pre-allotted number of columns requires that you move *all* entries around.

Some programmers like to start every line of a multiline comment with **:

```
/* This is a comment
** that extends over
** three source lines
*/
```

Again, this is neat if your editor has a command to add and remove the asterisks, and if you know that all programmers who will maintain your code also have such an editor. Otherwise, it can be a powerful method of *discouraging* programmers from editing the comment. If you have to choose between pretty comments and comments that reflect the current facts of the program, facts win over beauty.

GLOSSARY

Access specifier   A reserved word that indicates the accessibility of a feature, such as private or public.

Accessor function   A member function that accesses an object but does not change it.

Address   A value that specifies the location of a variable in memory.

Aggregation   The *"has-a"* relationship between classes.

Algorithm   An unambiguous, executable, and terminating specification of a way to solve a problem.

ANSI/ISO C++ Standard   The standard for the C++ language that was developed by the American National Standards Institute and the International Standards Organization.

API (Application Programming Interface)   A code library for building programs.

Argument   A value supplied in a function call, or one of the values combined by an operator.

Array   A collection of values of the same type stored in contiguous memory locations, each of which can be accessed by an integer index.

Arrow operator   The -> operator. p->m is the same as (*p).m.

ASCII code   The American Standard Code for Information Interchange, which associates code values between 0 and 127 to letters, digits, punctuation marks, and control characters.

Assignment   Placing a new value into a variable.

Assignment statement   A statement that places a new value into an existing variable.

Asymmetric bounds   Bounds that include the starting index but not the ending index.

Base class   A class from which another class is derived.

Behavior (of an object)   The actions taken by an object when its functions are invoked.

Binary file   A file in which values are stored in their binary representation and cannot be read as text.

Binary search   A fast algorithm for finding a value in a sorted array. It narrows the search down to half of the array in every step.

Bit   Binary digit; the smallest unit of information, having two possible values: 0 and 1. A data element consisting of n bits has 2^n possible values.

Black Box   A device with a given specification but unknown implementation.

Block   A group of statements bracketed by {}.

Body   All statements of a function or block.

Boolean operator   An operator that can be applied to Boolean values. C++ has three Boolean operators: &&, ||, and !.

Boolean type   A type with two possible values: true and false.

Boundary test case   A test case involving values that are at the outer boundary of the set of legal values. For example, if a function is expected to work for all nonnegative integers, then 0 is a boundary test case.

Bounds error   Trying to access an array element that is outside the legal range.

break statement   A statement that terminates a loop or switch statement.

Breakpoint   A point in a program, specified in a debugger, at which the debugger stops executing the program and lets the user inspect the program state.

Bug   A programming error.

Byte   A number made up of eight bits. Essentially all currently manufactured computers use a byte as the smallest unit of storage in memory.

Call stack   The ordered set of all functions that currently have been called but not yet terminated, starting with the current function and ending with main.

Capacity   The number of values that a data structure such as an array can potentially hold, in contrast to the size (the number of elements it currently holds).

Case sensitive   Distinguishing upper- and lowercase characters.

Cast   Explicitly converting a value from one type to a different type. For example, the cast from a floating-point number x to an integer is expressed in C++ by the static cast notation static_cast<int>(x).

Central processing unit (CPU)   The part of a computer that executes the machine instructions.

Character   A single letter, digit, or symbol.

Class   A programmer-defined data type.

Command line   The line the user types to start a program in DOS or UNIX or a command window in Windows. It consists of the program name followed by any necessary arguments.

Command line arguments   Additional strings of information provided at the command line that the program can use.

Comment   An explanation to help the human reader understand a section of a program; ignored by the compiler.

Compiler   A program that translates code in a high-level language (such as C++) to machine instructions.

Compile-time error   An error that is detected when a program is compiled.

Compound statement   A statement such as if or for that is made up of several parts (for example, condition, body).

Computer program   A sequence of instructions that is executed by a computer.

Concatenate   To place one string after another to form a new string.

Constant   A value that cannot be changed by a program. In C++, constants are marked with the reserved word const.

Construction   Setting a newly allocated object to an initial state.

Constructor   A sequence of statements for initializing a newly allocated object.

CPU (Central Processing Unit)   The part of a computer that executes the machine instructions.

Dangling pointer   A pointer that does not point to a valid location.

Data member   A variable that is present in every object of a class.

Delimiter   A character or sequence of characters used to specify the beginning or end of a text segment.

De Morgan's Law   A law about logical operations that describes how to negate expressions formed with *and* and *or* operations.

Debugger   A program that lets a user run another program one or a few steps at a time, stop execution, and inspect the variables in order to analyze it for bugs.

Declaration   A statement that announces the existence of a variable, function, or class but does not define it.

Default constructor   A constructor that can be invoked with no parameters.

#define directive   A directive that defines constant values and macros for the preprocessor. Values can be queried during the preprocessing phase with the #if and #ifndef directives. Macros are replaced by the preprocessor when they are encountered in the program file.

Definition   A statement or series of statements that fully describes a variable, a function and its implementation, a type, or a class and its properties.

delete operator   The operator that recycles memory to the free store.

Dereferencing   Locating an object when a pointer to the object is given.

Derived class   A class that modifies a base class by adding data members, adding member functions, or redefining member functions.

Directory   A structure on a disk that can hold files or other directories; also called a folder.

Documentation comment   A comment in a source file that can be automatically extracted into the program documentation by a program such as javadoc.

Dot notation   The notation *object.function(parameters)* used to invoke a member function on an object.

Dynamic memory allocation   Allocating memory as a program runs as required by the program's needs.

Editor   A program for writing and modifying text files.

Element   A storage location in an array.

Embedded system   The processor, software, and supporting circuitry that is included in a device other than a computer.

Encapsulation   The hiding of implementation details.

Escape character   A character in text that is not taken literally but has a special meaning when combined with the character or characters that follow it. The \\ character is an escape character in C++ strings.

Escape sequence   A sequence of characters that starts with an escape character, such as \\n or \\".

Exception   A class that signals a condition that prevents the program from continuing normally. When such a condition occurs, an object of the exception class is thrown.

Executable file   The file that contains a program's machine instructions.

Explicit parameter A parameter of a member function other than the object on which the function is invoked.

Expression A syntactical construct that is made up of constants, variables, function calls, and the operators combining them.

Extension The last part of a file name, which specifies the file type. For example, the extension .cpp denotes a C++ file.

Failed stream state The state of a stream after an invalid operation has been attempted, such as reading a number when the next stream position yielded a nondigit, or reading after the end of file was reached.

Fibonacci numbers The sequence of numbers 1, 1, 2, 3, 5, 8, 13, . . . , in which every term is the sum of its two predecessors.

File A sequence of bytes that is stored on disk.

File pointer The position within a random-access file of the next byte to be read or written. It can be moved so as to access any byte in the file.

Flag A type with two possible values: true and false.

Floating-point number A number that can have a fractional part.

Folder A structure on a disk that can hold files or other folders; also called a directory.

Free store A reservoir of storage from which memory can be allocated when a program runs.

Function A sequence of statements that can be invoked multiple times, with different values for its parameter variables.

Function signature The name of a function and the types of its parameters.

Garbage collection Automatic reclamation of memory occupied by objects that are no longer referenced. C++ does not have garbage collection

Global variable A variable whose scope is not restricted to a single function.

grep The "global regular expression print" search program, useful for finding all strings matching a pattern in a set of files.

Hard disk A device that stores information on rotating platters with magnetic coating.

Hardware The physical equipment for a computer or another device.

Header file A file that informs the compiler of features that are available in another module or library.

High-level programming language A programming language that provides an abstract view of a computer and allows programmers to focus on their problem domain.

HTML (Hypertext Markup Language) The language in which web pages are described.

IDE (Integrated Development Environment) A programming environment that includes an editor, compiler, and debugger.

#if directive A directive to the preprocessor to include the code contained between the #if and the matching #endif if a condition is true.

Implicit parameter The object on which a member function is invoked. For example, in the call x.f(y), the object x is the implicit parameter of the function f.

#include directive An instruction to the preprocessor to include a header file.

Index The position of an element in an array.

Inheritance The "*is-a*" relationship between a general base class and a specialized derived class.

Initialization Setting a variable to a well-defined value when it is created.

Input stream An abstraction for a sequence of bytes from which data can be read.

Instance of a class An object whose type is that class.

Integer A number that cannot have a fractional part.

Integer division Taking the quotient of two integers and discarding the remainder. In C++ the / symbol denotes integer division if both arguments are integers. For example, 11/4 is 2, not 2.75.

Integrated Development Environment (IDE) A programming environment that includes an editor, compiler, and debugger.

Internet A worldwide collection of networks, routing equipment, and computers using a common set of protocols that define how participants interact with each other.

Lexicographic ordering Ordering strings in the same order as in a dictionary, by skipping all matching characters and comparing the first non-matching characters of both strings. For example, "orbit" comes before "orchid" in lexicographic ordering. Note that in C++, unlike a dictionary, the ordering is case sensitive: Z comes before a.

Library A set of precompiled classes and functions that can be included in programs.

Linear search   Searching a container (such as an array or list) for an object by inspecting each element in turn.

Linker   The program that combines object and library files into an executable file.

Literal   A constant value in a program that is explicitly written as a number, such as –2 or 6.02214115E23, or as a character sequence, such as "Harry".

Local variable   A variable whose scope is a block.

Logic error   An error in a syntactically correct program that causes it to act differently from its specification. (A form of run-time error.)

Logical operator   An operator that can be applied to Boolean values. C++ has three Boolean operators: &&, ||, and !.

Loop   A sequence of instructions that is executed repeatedly.

Loop and a half   A loop whose termination decision is neither at the beginning nor at the end.

Machine code   Instructions that can be executed directly by the CPU.

Magic number   A number that appears in a program without explanation.

main function   The function that is first called when a program executes.

Member function   A function that is defined by a class and operates on objects of that class.

Memory   The circuitry that stores code and data in a computer.

Memory location   A value that specifies the location of data in computer memory.

Modulus   The % operator that computes the remainder of an integer division.

Mutator function   A member function that changes the state of an object.

Nested block   A block that is contained inside another block.

Nested loop   A loop that is contained in another loop.

new operator   The operator that allocates new memory from the free store.

Newline   The '\n' character, which indicates the end of a line.

null pointer   The value nullptr that indicates that a pointer does not point to any object.

Number literal   A constant value in a program that is explicitly written as a number, such as –2 or 6.02214115E23.

Object   A value of a class type.

Object-oriented programming   Designing a program by discovering objects, their properties, and their relationships.

Off-by-one error   A common programming error in which a value is one larger or smaller than it should be.

Operating system   The software that launches application programs and provides services (such as a file system) for those programs.

Operator   A symbol denoting a mathematical or logical operation, such as + or &&.

Operator associativity   The rule that governs in which order operators of the same precedence are executed. For example, in C++ the - operator is left-associative because a - b - c is interpreted as (a - b) - c, and = is right-associative because a = b = c is interpreted as a = (b = c).

Operator precedence   The rule that governs which operator is evaluated first. For example, in C++ the && operator has a higher precedence than the || operator. Hence a || b && c is interpreted as a || (b && c).

Output stream   An abstraction for a sequence of bytes to which data can be written.

Overloading   Giving more than one meaning to a function name or operator.

Overriding   Redefining a function from a base class in a derived class.

Parallel arrays   Arrays of the same length, in which corresponding elements are logically related.

Parallel vectors   Vectors of the same length, in which corresponding elements are logically related.

Parameter   An item of information that is specified to a function when the function is called.

Parameter passing   Specifying expressions to be arguments for a function when it is called.

Parameter variable   A variable of a function that is initialized with a value when the function is called.

Partially filled array   An array that is not filled to capacity, together with a companion variable that indicates the number of elements actually stored.

Path (to a file or directory)   The sequence of directory names and, for a file, a file name at the end, that describes how to reach the file or directory from a given starting point.

Permutation A rearrangement of a set of values.

Pointer A value that denotes the memory location of an object.

Polymorphism Selecting a function among several functions that have the same name on the basis of the actual type of the implicit parameter.

Postfix operator A unary operator that is written after its argument.

Prefix operator A unary operator that is written before its argument.

Programming The act of designing and implementing computer programs.

Prompt A string that tells the user to provide input.

Prototype The declaration of a function, including its parameter types and return type.

Pseudocode A high-level description of the actions of a program or algorithm, using a mixture of English and informal programming language syntax.

Pseudorandom number A number that appears to be random but is generated by a mathematical formula.

Public interface The features (functions, variables, and nested types) of a class that are accessible to all clients.

RAM (random-access memory) Electronic circuits in a computer that can store code and data of running programs.

Random access The ability to access any value directly without having to read the values preceding it.

Recursion A technique for computing a result by decomposing the inputs into simpler values and applying the same function to them.

Recursive function A function that can call itself with simpler values. It must handle the simplest values without calling itself.

Redirection Linking the input or output of a program to a file instead of the keyboard or display.

Reference A value that denotes the location of an object in memory.

Reference parameter A parameter that is bound to a variable supplied in the call. Changes made to the parameter within the function affect the variable outside the function.

Regular expression A string that defines a set of matching strings according to their content. Each part of a regular expression can be a specific required character; one of a set of permitted characters such as [abc], which can be a range such as [a-z]; any character not in a set of forbidden characters, such as [^0-9]; a repetition of one or more matches, such as [0-9]+, or zero or more, such as [ACGT]; one of a set of alternatives, such as and|et|und; or various other possibilities. For example, [A-Za-z][0-9]+ matches Cloud9 or 007 but not Jack.

Relational operator An operator that compares two values, yielding a Boolean result.

Reserved word A word that has a special meaning in a programming language and therefore cannot be used as a name by the programmer.

Return value The value returned by a function through a return statement.

Roundoff error An error introduced by the fact that the computer can store only a finite number of digits of a floating-point number.

Run-time error An error in a syntactically correct program that causes it to act differently from its specification.

Run-time stack The data structure that stores the local variables of all called functions as a program runs.

Scope The part of a program in which a variable is defined.

Secondary storage Storage that persists without electricity, e.g., a hard disk.

Sentinel A value in input that is not to be used as an actual input value but to signal the end of input.

Sequential access Accessing values one after another without skipping over any of them.

Shadowing Hiding a variable by defining another one with the same name.

Shell window A window for interacting with an operating system through textual commands.

Short-circuit evaluation Evaluating only a part of an expression if the remainder cannot change the result.

Slicing an object Copying an object of a derived class into a variable of the base class, thereby losing the derived-class data.

Software The intangible instructions and data that are necessary for operating a computer or another device.

A

abs function, 39t
access member operator (.), 52–53, 251, 253, 255, 323, A-3
accessors, 296, 296f
  data representation, 297–299
account.cpp, 169, 228
actual parameters, 146–147
adapters, string stream, 273–274
addition, 12, 36
addition operator (+), 12, 52, A-4
address operator (&), 225, A-3
adjacent values, comparing, 122, 122f
Adleman, Leonard, 277
aggregation, 316–317
algorithm(s), 16–22
  for arrays, 185–206. *See also* array(s), algorithms for
  adapting, 198–203
  definition, 17
  designing, 17–22
  discovering by manipulating physical objects, 203–206
  encryption, 277
  executable, 17, 19
  filling, 186
  for investment problem, 17–18
  loops, 119–122
  patents for, 277
  pseudocode and, 18–22, 49
  search, 188, 193–194
  sorting, 192–194
  terminating, 17, 19
  unambiguous, 16–17, 19
  for vectors, 216–217. *See also* vector(s), algorithms for
<algorithm> library, A-8
alphabets. *See also* character(s)
  international, 55–56
American National Standards Institute (ANSI), 7
ampersand (&)
  address operator, 225, A-3
  reference parameter indicator, 165, 195
ampersands (&&), *and* operator, 85, 86, 88, 89–90, A-4
and (&&) operator, 85, 86, 88, 89–90, A-4. *See also* Boolean operators
Andreesen, Marc, 360
angle brackets (< >), vectors, 214

Apple computers. *See also* computer(s)
  development of, 174–175
applications: programs and simulations
  average salary, 112–113, 116–117
  bank accounts
    deposits, 224–230
    multiple, 355–359
    opening, 310–313
    withdrawal, 166–169
  cash register, 294–310, 319–324
  coin sequence, 204–206
  die toss, 135–136
  elevator floors, 60–68, 90–92
  encryption, 275–277
  Galton board, 244–246, 244f, 245f
  "Hello, World!", 7–8, 11–14, 53
  income tax, 76–78, 80
  investing, 17–19, 96–102
  Monte Carlo method, 136–137
  Olympic medal counts, 206–212, 218–219
  photocopier user accounts, 248–249
  printing a check, 156–161
  printing a table, 126–129
  printing triangles, 171–173
  quizzes
    scoring, 198–203
    taking, 335–354
  random number generator, 134–137
  Richter scale, 73–75
  series of pictures, 130–134
  shipping charges, 82–83, 89–90
  Social Security baby names list, 262–265
  street addresses, 250–256
  tally counter, 292–294
  tiling a floor, 21–22, 47–48
  vending machines, 48–51
  volume
    bottles and cans, 26–47
    cubes, 147–150
    pyramids, 151–152
arguments, 142–143
  command line, 274–281
    encryption, 275–277
    main function, 275
    processing text files, 259
  parameter passing, 146–148
  vectors as, 216
argv function, 275

arithmetic, 36–43. *See also* number types
  addition, 36
  analyzing expressions, 38–39, 39t
  with assignment, 42–43
  common errors, 39–43
  converting floating-point numbers to integers, 37–38
  division, 36–37
  functions, 38–39
  hand calculation, 48–51
  increment and decrement, 36
  multiplication, 12, 36, A-4
  operators, 36–37, A-4. *See also* operator(s)
  order of operations, 36
  pointer, 230–231
  powers and roots, 38–39
  subtraction, 36
  symbols, 36
  vs. logical expressions, 88
ARPANET, 360
array(s), 179–213
  algorithms for, 185–194, 198–206
    adapting, 198–203
    binary search, 193–194
    combining, 198–203
    copying, 186
    counting matches, 187
    discovering by manipulating physical objects, 203–206
    element separators, 187
    filling, 186
    functions and, 194–198
    inserting elements, 189
    linear search, 188, 198–199
    maximum and minimum, 187, 198–199
    reading input, 191–192
    removing elements, 188, 198–199
    sorting, 192–193
    sum and average value, 186–187, 198–199
    swapping elements, 190
  array/pointer duality, 231, 240
  bounds errors, 183, 184
  capacity, 183, 196
  character, 236–237, 236t. *See also* string(s)
  dynamic memory allocation, 240–243
  collecting objects in, 326
  common errors, 184, 212–213

companion variables, 183–184
copying, 186, 186f
counting matches, 187
defining, 180–181, 181t
dynamic memory allocation, 240–243
elements, 182–183, 182f
    accessing, 182–183, 207–208
    computing sum of, 186–187, 194–195
    copying, 186, 186f
    inserting, 189, 189f
    locating neighboring, 208, 208f
    position, 188, 193–194
    removing, 188, 188f, 198–199
    separators for, 187
    sorting, 192–194
    swapping, 190, 190f, 193
    in two-dimensional arrays, 207–208, 207f, 208f
filling, 186
index, 182–183, 182f
    array/pointer duality law, 231, 231t
    row and column, 207, 208–209. *See also* two-dimensional arrays (matrices)
index operator, A-3
maximum/minimum values, 187
partially filled, 183–184, 183f
    vs. vectors, 213
passing to function, 194–195, 232–235
pointers as, 230–235, 243–246
    array/pointer duality, 231, 240
    parameter variables, 232–233
    sequences in arrays, 243–246
    two-dimensional, 243–246
polymorphic, 349
processing with functions, 194–198. *See also* function(s), arrays and
range-based for loop, 219
reading input, 191–192
searching
    binary search, 193–194
    linear search, 188, 198–199
for sequences of related values, 184
size of, 181, 183–184
    modifying, 195–196
stepping through, using pointer, 233–234, 233f
structures, 252–253, 252f, 253f

sum and average value, 186–187
syntax, 181
triangular, 243–244, 243f
two-dimensional, 206–213, 243–246. *See also* two-dimensional arrays (matrices)
values in, 180–181, 182
    vs. pointers, 233
    vs. vectors, 213, 219
    when to use, 180–181
array parameters, 195
    constant, 198, 210
    as pointers, 232–235. *See also* pointer(s)
    reference parameters as, 195
    two-dimensional, 210–213
array/pointer duality law, 231, 240
arrow operator (->), 255, 323, A-3
artificial intelligence, 92–93
ASCII codes, 55–56, 235, 235t, A-5
assignment, 30–31
    with arithmetic, 42–43
    combined operators, 42–43, A-4
    syntax, 30
assignment operator (=), 30, 31f, A-4
    vs. equality relational operator (==), 66, 68, 251–252
assignment statement, 30–31, 31f
assignments, class, time management for, 84
asterisk (*)
    indirection (dereferencing) operator, 225, A-3
    multiplication operator, 12, 36, A-4
    pointers, 249, 254–255, 323
asymmetric bounds, 110
atoi function, 237
auto (reserved word), 35, A-1
automobiles, self-driving, 93
average values, computing, 119
average salary simulation, 112–113, 116–117

B

babynames.cpp, 264
baby names program, 262–265
backslash (\)
    displaying on screen, 261
    displaying quotation marks, 14
    in escape sequence, 14, 261
backslash and zero (\0), null terminator, 236–237

backup copies, 10
bank account simulation
    deposits, 224–230
    multiple, 355–359
    opening, 310–313
    printing triangles, 171–173
    withdrawal, 166–169
base class. *See* inheritance, base class
BaseClass::function notation, 343
behavior, of class objects, 292
Berners-Lee, Tim, 360
binary files, 282
binary search, of array, 193–194
binary system, roundoff errors, 41–42
bitwise *not* operator, A-3
black boxes, functions as, 142–143, 143f, 146
BMP format, 282–285, 283f
body, of function, 144
bool data type, 85
boolalpha stream manipulator, 336
Boole, George, 85
Boolean operators, 85–90, 86t, 87t
    && *(and)*, 85, 86, 88, 89–90
    common errors, 88
    De Morgan's Law, 89–90
    definition, 85
    evaluation of, 86–87, 86f, 87t
        short-circuit, 89
    ! *(not)*, 86, A-3
    negating conditions, 89–90
    || *(or)*, 85, 86, 88, 89
    precedence of, 86
Boolean truth tables, 86t
Boolean values, true and false, 86, 87f, 87t, 88
Boolean variables, 85–90, 86t, 87t
    loop control, 114, 116
bottles, volume calculation, 26–47
boundary conditions, test cases for, 83, 84
bounds errors, 183, 184
braces ({ })
    alignment, 63–64
    body of function, 144
    if statements, 61, 61f, 63–64
    language coding guidelines, A-17
    semicolon after, 296
brackets
    angle (< >), vectors, 214

brackets, cont.
  square ([ ])
    accessing arrays, 230, 232–233
    accessing pointer variables, 249
    accessing string characters, 238
    index operator, A-3
branches, 61, 61f, 81–83
  avoiding spaghetti code, 82–83
  default, 76
  else, 61, 61f, 62, 75
  nested, 76–83
  pointing arrow into another
    branch, 82–83, 82f, 83f
  test cases for, 83–85
break (reserved word), A-1
break statement, 76, 116
bug
  origin of term, 102
  Pentium floating-point, 43

C

C++ language coding guidelines,
    A-11–17
  braces, A-17
  classes, A-15
  constants, A-14–A-15
  control flow, A-15–A-16
  functions, A-13
  indentation, A-16–A-17
  lexical issues, A-16–A-17
  local variables, A-14
  naming conventions, A-16
  overview, A-11
  source files, A-12
  for statement, A-15
  unstable layout, A-17
  white space, A-16–A-17
C++ libraries, 9, 260, A-8–A-10
  streams and, 260. See also file
    streams; string streams
C++ programs. See also applications:
    programs and simulations;
    programming
  basic structure, 11, 12f
  case sensitivity, 8, 15–16, 29, 31,
    66
  development, 6
  standardization, 6
  style guide. See C++ language
    coding guidelines
  syntax, 12
  writing first program, 7–10
C strings, 236–239. See also string(s)
  converting to/from C++,
    236–239, 261

functions, 239t
  null terminator, 236–237
  working with, 238–239
caesar.cpp, 275
Caesar cipher, 275–276, 275f
  calculating by hand, 47–51
calling, functions, 142–143, 142f,
    146–148, 195–196
camel case, 295
cans, volume calculation, 26–47
capitalization errors, 15–16
cars, self-driving, 93
case (reserved word), A-1
case sensitivity, 8, 15–16
  comparisons, 66
  variables, 29, 31
cash register simulation, 294–310,
    319–324
cashregister.cpp 302, 320
cashregister.h, 319
casts, 42
<cctype> library, 266, 266t, A-8
central processing unit (CPU), 3, 3f,
    4, 4f
  microprocessors and, 174–175
char (reserved word), A-1
char* pointer, 236, 237
char values, 235–237. See also
    string(s)
character(s)
  alphabetic, 55–56
  ASCII codes, 55–56, 235, 235t,
    A-5, A-6
  definition, 51
  escape, 13–14, 261
  ideographic, 56
  international alphabets, 55–56
  newline, 14
  reading, 266, 279
  sequence of, 51–56. See also
    string(s)
character arrays, 236–237, 236t. See
    also string(s)
  dynamic memory allocation,
    240–243
character codes
  ASCII, 55–56, 235, 235t, A-5, A-6
  escape sequences, 13–14, 261, A-5
  Unicode, 56, 272, A-5, A-7
  UTF-8, 56, 272, A-5, A-7
character functions, 266, 266t

character literals, 235, 236t. See also
    literal(s)
char_array, 237
check printing program, 156–161
chips, 3
choicequestion.h, 351
ChoiceQuestion class. See inheritance,
    derived class
cin (>>). See also input
  reading input, 52, 114
    random access, 281
    from stream file, 261–262
  strings and, 52, 290
ciphers. See encryption
class(es), 289–332
  aggregation, 316–317
  base, 334. See also inheritance,
    base class
  common errors, 296
  definition, 291, 292–293, 297–298
    class, 294–295
    in header file, 319
  derived. See inheritance, derived
    class
  diagramming, 316, 316f
  diagrams, 316
  discovering, 315–318
  encapsulation, 291, 294, 309
  forgetting semicolon, 296
  header files, 318–322
  implementing, 291, 292–294,
    310–313
    data representation, 297–299
  inheritance, 333–361. See also
    inheritance
  language coding guidelines, A-15
  main function, 320
  names/naming, 294–295, 315
    as nouns, 316–317
  objects in, 290–291
    allocation of, 322–323
    behavior of, 292
    collecting in values and arrays,
      326
    collecting in vectors, 317–318,
      317f, 318f
    data members in, 292–294,
      293f, 297–299
    pointers to, 290, 322–324. See
      also pointer(s), to objects
    position of, 328–329
    properties of, 326–327
    state of, 292, 327–328
    string, 290, 305

public interface, 291, 294–299
    relationship between, 315–316
    stream, inheritance, 335–336,
        335f, 336f, 352. *See also*
        inheritance hierarchies
    vectors, 316–318, 317f, 318f
    vs. actions, 316
class (reserved word), A-1
class assignments, time management
    for, 84
class definition, 294–295
ClassName:: prefix, 299
clearing the failure state, 115
close function, 261
<cmath> header, 38, 39, 40–41, 69
<cmath> library, A-8
code
    hand-tracing, 79–80, 103–105
        functions, 161–162
        if statements, 79–80
        loops, 103–105, 125
        objects, 308–310
    machine, 6, 9, 9f
    source, 9, 9f
    spaghetti, 82–83, 112
code libraries, 9, 60, 260, A-8–A-10
    streams and, 260
coding guidelines. *See* C++ language
    coding guidelines
coin sequence simulation, 204–206
colon (:), inheritance indicator, 338
colons (::), scope resolution
    operator, A-3
columns
    formatting, 45–46
    in two-dimensional arrays,
        206–213. *See also* two-
        dimensional arrays (matrices)
combined operators, 42–43, A-4
command line arguments, 274–281
    encryption, 275–277
    main function, 275
    processing text files, 259
comment delimiters (//, /*, */),
    31–32
comments, 31–32
    function, 145–146
companion variables, 183–184
comparisons, 66–72
    common errors, 68–69
    double numbers, 69
    floating-point numbers, 68–69

    inside and outside tests, 66, 68
    numbers, 66–69
    relational operators in, 66–68, 66t,
        67f, 67t
    strings, 66–70
compilers, 6, 8–9, 9f
    warnings, 68, 69
compile-time errors, 14–15
computer(s)
    components, 3–4, 3f, 4f
    development and explosive
        growth of, 174–175
    in everyday life, 5
    peripheral devices, 4, 4f
computer networks, 4
computer programs
    applications. *See* applications:
        programs and simulations
    definition, 2
    starting, 274–275. *See also*
        command line arguments
computer systems, untested/
    dysfunctional, 72
computer viruses, 185
computing average value, 119
computing by hand, 47–51
concatenation, 52, 54, 54f
condition, inverting, 86
conditional operator (?:), 65–66, A-4
console window, 7
const (reserved word), 31, A-1
    arrays, 198, 293
    member functions, 293, 299, 303
constant(s), 31, 33
    language coding guidelines,
        A-14–A-15
    magic number, 34
constant array parameters, 198
    two-dimensional, 210
    vs. constant pointers, 235
constant pointers, 235, 236
constructors, 304–308
    base-class, 342
    calling, 306
    default, 305, 306
    derived-class, 342
    initializer list, 307
    initializing numbers and pointers,
        305–306
    multiple, 305
    overloading, 305, 306–307
copies, backup, 10
copying algorithm

    for arrays, 186
    for vectors, 217
cos function, 39t
count-controlled loops, 106, 124
counter++, 36
counter--, 36
counters, in member functions,
    325–326
counting matches
    for arrays, 187
    for loops, 120
cout (<<), 12, 13, 13f. *See also* output
    random access, 281
    stream files, 262
CPU (central processing unit), 3, 3f,
    4, 4f
    microprocessors and, 174–175
<cstdlib> library, A-8
c_str function, 237, 261
<ctime> library, A-8
cube.cpp, 145, 322
cube.h, 322
cubes, volume calculation, 147–150

D

dangling else, 79
dangling pointers, 242
data, private
    accessing with public interface,
        293–299, 303, 339, 341
    inheritance, 339, 341
data members, of class objects,
    292–294, 293f
databases
    privacy concerns, 286
    relational model, 286
De Morgan's Law, 89–90
decisions, 59–94
    comparing numbers and strings,
        66–72
    if statements, 60–94. *See also* if
        statements
    with multiple alternatives, 73–76,
        73t
    nested, 76–82. *See also* nested
        branches
    test cases, 83–85
declarations, 150
    member functions, 295–296
decrement operator (--), 36, A-3
default (reserved word), A-1, 76
default constructors, 305, 306
default floating-point format, 270

defaultfloat manipulator, 271t
Defense Advanced Research Projects
    Agency (DARPA), 93
definite loops, 106
delete operator, 240, 323, A-3
    reserved word, A-1
delete[] operator, 240
delimiters, 31–32
demo.cpp, 336, 344, 351
dereference and access member (->),
    A-3
dereferencing operator (*), 225, A-3
derived class. *See* inheritance,
    derived class
diagrams. *See also* flowcharts; hand-
    tracing
    classes, 316
    pointer, 246–249
dice.cpp, 135
die toss simulation, 135–136
digital piracy, 138
directories, 10
display
    escape sequences and, 13–14
    of literals, 13–14
    of values, 12, 13f
division, 36–37
    common errors, 39–40
division operator (/), 36, 39–40, A-3
do (reserved word), A-1
do loops, 111–112, 124. *See also*
    loop(s)
dongles, 138
dot notation, 52–53
    member functions, 53, 296, 301,
        323
    streams, 260
    structures, 251, 253, 255
dot operator (.), 52–53, 251, 253, 255,
    323, A-3
double (reserved word), A-1
double number type, 28–29, 28t, 34,
    35, 35t
    comparisons, 69
double quotation marks ("). *See*
    quotation marks ('...'/"...")
doublinv.cpp, 98
Doxygen tool, 146
drawing. *See also* diagrams; hand-
    tracing
    flowcharts, 81–83
    pictures, 246–249

duplication, in if statements, 65
dynamic memory allocation. *See*
    memory allocation, dynamic
dysfunctional computer systems, 72

E
editor, 7
electronic voting machines, 314–315
elements. *See* array(s), elements;
    vector(s), elements
elevator floor simulation, 60–68,
    90–92
elevator1.cpp, 62
elevator2.cpp, 91
else (reserved word), A-1
else branch, 61, 61f, 62, 75
    dangling, 79
embedded systems, 250
empty string literal, 51
encapsulation, 291, 294, 309
encryption, 275–277
    algorithms, 277
    Caesar cipher, 275–276, 275f
    command line arguments,
        275–277
    PGP, 277
    public key, 277
    RSA, 277
endl (end of line marker), 12, 13f, 44
ENIAC, 5, 5f
Enigma machine, 260
epsilon (ε), in comparisons, 69
equal sign (=), assignment operator,
    30, 31f, 66, 68, 251–252, A-4
equal signs (==), equality relational
    operator, 66–70, 66t, 67f, 67t,
    251–252, A-4
equality testing, 66–70
errors, 14–16. *See also specific errors*
    arithmetic, 39–43
    capitalization, 15–16
    checking for, 83
    compile-time, 14–15
    hand-tracing revealing, 105
    logic, 15
    misspellings, 15–16
    roundoff, 35, 41–42
        floating-point numbers, 68–69
    run-time, 15
    syntax, 14–15
    vs. warnings, 69
escape character, 13–14, 261
escape sequences, 13–14, 261, A-5

even numbers, testing for with %, 37
event-controlled loops, 106, 124
exclamation point (!), *not* Boolean
    operator, 86, A-3
exclamation point and equal sign
    (!=), *not equal* operator, 86,
    A-3
executable file, 9, 9f
expert-system program, 92
explicit parameters, member
    functions, 299–301, 300f
extensions, 9
extraction operator (>>), 44, 52,
    265–269, 279, 282, A-4
    binary files, 282
    as member function, 290
    reading characters, 266
    reading string from console, 52
    reading words, 265, 268
    vs. getline function, 268
    vs. getline input, 268

F
fail function
    input validation for if statements,
        91–92
    reading input from file, 261–262,
        269
false (Boolean value), 86, 87f, 87t,
    88, A-1
fence post error, 110
file(s), 9–10. *See also specific types*
    backing up, 10
    binary, 282
    executable, 9, 9f
    header, 38, 39, 40–41, 41f, 45,
        318–322
    multiple, compiling from,
        318–322
    source, 9, 318–322, A-12
    splitting, 318
file extensions, 9
file folders and directories, 10, 10f
file names, 8, 9, 260–261. *See also*
    names/naming
file pointer. *See* pointer(s)
file streams. *See also* string streams
    C++ libraries and, 9, 260,
        A-8–A-10
    closing, 261
    failed state, 261–262, 269
    file name, 260
    get position, 281–282, 281f
    inheritance hierarchy, 335

input, 260
    `fail` function, 91–92, 261–262,
      269
    `fstream` variable, 260
    `ifstream` variable, 260
    reading, 261–262, 265–269,
      278–281. *See also* reading
      input
manipulators, 45–46, 47t,
    270–271, 271t. *See also*
    manipulators
opening, 260–261
output, 260
    formatting, 45–47, 47t,
      270–273, 279
    `fstream` variable, 260
    `ofstream` variable, 260
    writing, 270–273, 278–281. *See*
      also writing output
processing example, 262–265,
    263f
public interface, 273
put position, 281–282, 281f
random access, 281–282
reference parameters, 264
syntax, 262
types, 260
filling algorithm, for arrays, 186
`fixed` manipulator, 45, 47t, 271, 271t
flags, 124. *See also* Boolean variables
`float` (reserved word), 34, 35t, A-1
floating-point numbers, 28–29, 28t,
    34, 34t–35t
    comparing, 68–69
    converting to integers, 37–38, 42
    converting to strings, 273–274
    division, 36, 39–40
    fractional parts, 28, 37–38
    Pentium bug, 43
    random, 137
    rounding, 38
    roundoff errors, 35, 41–42, 68–69
    vs. integers, 28–29, 28t
    vs. truth values, 88
floor tiling simulation, 21–22, 47–48
flowcharts, 81–83
    avoiding spaghetti code, 82–83
    Boolean operators, 87f
    constructing, 81–83
    elements of, 81, 81f
    for `if` statements, 61–62, 61f, 62f,
      74f
    for loops, 97, 97f, 108, 108f,
      111–112

with more than two cases, 73–76,
    73t, 74f, 81, 81f
stepwise refinement, 156, 157f
storyboards and, 117–119
test cases for, 83–85
with two cases, 61–62, 61f, 62f,
    73–76, 73t, 74f, 81, 81f
vs. pseudocode, 83
folders, 10, 10f
`for` (reserved word), A-1
`for` loops, 106–110. *See also* loop(s)
    common errors, 110
    count-controlled, 106
    counting iterations, 110
    examples, 108t
    execution, 107, 107f
    flowchart for, 108–109
    range-based, 219
    symmetric vs. asymmetric
      bounds, 110
    syntax, 106
    uses, 106, 108, 109
    vectors, 219
    `while` loops and, 106–110, 124
`for` statement, 106
    language coding guidelines, A-15
foreign languages, 55–56, 272, A-5,
    A-7
formal parameters, 146–147
formatting output, 45–47, 47t,
    270–273, 279. *See also*
    manipulators; writing output
forward slash (/)
    as comment delimiter, 31–32
    division operator, 36, 39–40, A-3
fractional parts, floating-point
    numbers and, 28, 37–38
free software, 329–330
free store, 240–241, 322–323
    returning allocated memory to,
      240–243
free store allocation operator, A-3
free store recycling operator, A-3
`friend` (reserved word), A-1
`fstream` class, 260
    inheritance hierarchy, 335, 335f
`<fstream>` library, A-9
function(s), 11, 38–39, 39t, 141–178.
    See also specific functions
    arguments, 142–143, 146–147,
      216, 259, 274–281. *See also*
      arguments
    arrays and, 194–198

    capacity, 196
    constant array parameter, 198
    modifying size, 195–196
    `multiply` function, 196, 197
    parameter variables, 195
    passing array to function,
      194–195, 232–235
    `print` function, 196, 197
    `read_inputs` function, 196–197
    return type, 195
as black boxes, 142–143, 143f, 146
body of, 144
braces, 144
calling, 142–143, 142f, 146–148,
    195–196, A-3
character, 266, 266t
comments, 145–146
constant references, 170
declarations, 150, 295
definition, 141, 142, 145, 150
designing, 154–155
documentation, 41, 41f
dot notation, 52–53, 296, 301, 323
hand-tracing, 161–162
helper, 157–158, 279
implementing, 143–146, 151–154
    with absent return value,
      153–154
inputs, 142–143, 151
language coding guidelines, A-13
length, 161
member. *See* member functions
power and root calculation, 38–39
prototypes, 150
recursive, 170–174
reference parameters, 165–170,
    167f, 196. *See also* reference
    parameters
    pointers, 229–230
return statements, 144, 148–149
return values, 142–143, 148–154.
    See also return values
    absent, 153–154
    arrays, 195
    vs. reference parameters,
      169–170
reusable, 154–155
stepwise refinement, 156–163
string, 51, 52–54, 55t
stub, 162–163
syntax, 145
unit test, 152
variables
    defined within function,
      163–165

function(s), cont.
  variables, cont.
    global, 165
    local, 165
    in nested blocks, 164
    parameter, 143, 146–147, 148,
      155. *See also* parameter
      variables
  vectors and, 216
  virtual, 348–349
    failing to override, 353
    self-calls, 354
    vs. type tags, 352
  when to use, 154–155
function call operator (()), 11, 40,
  A-3
functions.cpp, 196

G

gallery6.cpp, 133
galton.cpp, 245
Galton board, 244–246, 244f, 245f
General Public License, 330
get function, 266, 269
get position, 281–282, 281f
getline function, 267, 269
  vs. extraction (>>) operator, 268
get_value member function, 293, 294
global variables, 165
GNU operating system, 329–330
greater than operator (>), 66, 66t, 67f,
  67t, A-4
greater than or equal operator (>=),
  66, 66t, 67f, 67t, A-4

H

hand calculations, 47–51
hand-tracing
  functions, 161–162
  if statements, 79–80
  loops, 103–105, 125
  objects, 308–310
hard disk, 3–4, 3f
hardware, 2, 3–4, 3f, 4f
"has-a" vs. "is-a" relationships, 334
header files, 38, 39, 40–41, 41f, 45,
  318–322
  contents of, 318
"Hello, World!" program, 7–8,
  11–14, 53
hello.cpp, 8–9, 11
hello.exe, 9
helper functions, 157–158, 279

hierarchies. *See* inheritance
  hierarchies
high-level programming languages,
  6. *See also* C++ language
  coding guidelines; C++
  programs
Hoff, Marcian E. (Ted), 174
homework assignments, time
  management for, 84
hyphen (-), in option names, 274
hyphens (--), decrement operator,
  36, A-3

I

ideographic characters, 56
if (reserved word), A-1
if statements, 60–66
  braces, 61, 61f, 63–64
  break statement, 76, 116
  common errors, 63, 70, 79
  comparisons, 66–72. *See also*
    comparisons
  conditions in, 66, 70
    order of, 74–75
    selection of, 70
  default branch, 76
  definition, 60
  duplication in, 65, 71
  else branch, 61, 61f, 62, 75
    dangling, 79
  flowcharts for, 61–62, 61f, 62f, 74f
  implementing, 70–72
  input validation, 90–93
  with more than two cases, 73–76,
    73t, 74f, 81, 81f
  nested branches, 76–83
  relational operators, 66–68, 66t,
    67f, 68t, 71
  semicolons, 61f, 63
  switch statements, 75–76
  syntax, 61
  tabs, 64
  with two cases, 60–66, 61f, 62f,
    81, 81f
  warnings, 70
ifstream class, inheritance hierarchy,
  335, 335f, A-9
ifstream variable, 260
image files, 282–285
imagemod.cpp, 284
implicit parameters
  member functions, 299–301, 300f
  this pointer, 324
#include, 11

income tax simulation, 76–78, 80
increment operator (++), 36, A-3
indefinite loops, 106
indentation
  language coding guidelines, A-16
  tabs for, 64
index operator, vector or array, A-3
index values, array, 182–183, 182f
  array/pointer duality law, 231,
    231f
  row and column, 207–209. *See
    also* two-dimensional arrays
    (matrices)
indirection (dereferencing) operator
  (*), 225, A-3
infinite loops, 100–101
information loss warnings, 42
inheritance, 333–361
  base class, 334, 338
    calling constructor, 342
    conversion from derived class,
      346–347, 347f
    derived-class overriding
      functions of, 339, 343–346,
      353
    forgetting name, 345
    forming derived class from,
      338
    initializing data members, 342
    pointers to, 347–348, 348f
    replicating members, 341
  common errors, 341, 345–346,
    352–353
  constructors, 342
  data member accessibility,
    339–340
  definition, 334
  derived class, 334, 338–342
    constructors, 342
    converting to base class,
      346–347, 347f
    defining, 338, 340
    formed from base class, 338
    implementing, 338–342
    initializing data members, 342
    object, layout of, 339, 339f
    overriding base-class
      functions, 339, 343–346,
      353
    pointers to, 347–348, 348f
    slicing data, 346–347, 347f,
      352–353
    syntax, 338, 340

unget function, 266
Unicode, 56, 272, A-5, A-7
unit test, 152
universal and uniform syntax, 308
unsigned (reserved word), A-2
unsigned number type, 34, 34t
unsigned short, 34, 35t
unstable layout, language coding
    guidelines, A-17
user input. *See* input
using (reserved word), A-2
UTF-8 encoding, 56, 272, A-5, A-7

V

value(s), 166–170, 167f
    in arrays, 180–181, 182. *See also*
        array(s)
    displaying on screen, 12, 13f
value member function, 293–294
value parameters, 166–170, 167f
variables, 25–35. *See also specific*
    variables
    assignment statement, 30–31, 31f
    Boolean, 85–90, 86f, 86t, 87t
        loop control, 114, 116
    case sensitivity, 29, 31
    common errors, 33–34
    companion, 183–184
    constants, 31, 33
        language coding guidelines,
            A-14–A-15
        magic number, 34
    data types and, 27
    defining, 26–28, 28t, 33, 35
        within functions, 163–165
    floating point, 28–29, 28t. *See also*
        floating-point numbers
    functions and, 143, 146–148, 155,
        163–165
    global, 165
    initializing, 27, 30, 33, 44, 51–52
        syntax, 308
    local, 165, A-14
        language coding guidelines,
            A-14
    loops and, 97, 98, 100–102
    names/naming, 26, 29, 33
        multiple definitions of same
            name, 163–165
        reserved words, 29, 31, 35
        underscore (_) in, 29
    in nested blocks, 164–165
    parameter. *See* parameter
        variables

placing input into, 44–45
pointer, 225. *See also* pointer(s)
scope of, 163–165
storing adjacent value in, 122
string, 51–52
    name inside, 261
syntax, 27
value in, 26
    assignment statement, 30, 30f
    initializing, 27, 30
    replacing, 30, 30f
vector(s), 213–219, 316–318, 317f,
    318f
    advantages of, 219
    algorithms for, 216–217
        copying, 217
        finding matches, 217
        inserting element, 217
        removing element, 217
    as arguments, 216
    classes, 316–318, 317f, 318f
    collecting objects in, 326
    copying, 217
    defining, 213–214, 213t, 214t
    dynamic memory allocation, 241
    elements
        inserting, 217
        removing, 217
        sorting, 192–194
    index operator, A-3
    of objects, 317–318
    parallel, 317–318
    pointers as, 243–246
    pop_back function, 215, 217
    push_back function, 215, 217
    range-based for loop, 219
    as reference parameters, 216
    as return values, 216
    returned by functions, 216
    size of
        increasing or reducing, 215
        specifying, 214
    syntax, 213
    two-dimensional, 218–219
    vs. arrays, 213, 219
    when to use, 219
<vector> library, A-10
vehicles, self-driving, 93
vending.cpp, 50
vending machine simulation, 48–51
virtual (reserved word), 348–349,
    A-2

virtual functions, 348–349
    failing to override, 353
    self-calls, 354
    vs. type tags, 352
viruses, 185
VisiCalc spreadsheet, 175, 175f
void (reserved word), 153–154, 305,
    A-2
volume calculations
    bottles and cans, 26–47
    cubes, 147–150
    pyramids, 151–152
volume1.cpp, 32
volume2.cpp, 46
volumes.h, 322
voter verifiable audit trail, 314
voting machines, 314–315

W

warnings, 68, 69
while (reserved word), A-2
while loops, 96–103. *See also* loop(s)
    common errors, 97, 100–102
    event-controlled, 106
    examples, 99–100
    execution of, 98–99
    flowchart for, 97
    for loops and, 106–110, 124
    syntax, 97
    uses, 97, 106–110, 124
    variables and, 98, 100–101
while statements, 96–97
white space
    language coding guidelines, A-16
    reading, 265, 266, 266t
Wilkes, Maurice, 102
words, reading, 265
World Wide Web, 360. *See also*
    Internet
writing output, 125, 260, 262,
    270–273, 278–281. *See also* file
    streams, output
    formatting, 45–47, 47t, 270–273,
        279
    random access file, 281–282
    screen display, 12, 13, 13f
    sequential access, 281, 281f
    syntax, 13

Z

zero, leading, 270
zero (\0), null terminator, 236–237
zero digit, 236, 236t
Zimmermann, Phil, 277

ILLUSTRATION CREDITS

Icons

Common Error icon: © Scott Harms/iStockphoto.
How To icon: © Steve Simzer/iStockphoto.
Paperclip: © Yvan Dubé/iStockphoto.
Programming Tip icon: © Macdaddy/Dreamstime.com.
Computing and Society icon: © Mishella/ Dreamstime.com.
Self Check icon: © Nicholas Homrich/iStockphoto.
Special Topic icon: ©Nathan Winter/iStockphoto.
Worked Example icon: © Tom Horyn/iStockphoto.

Chapter 4

Page 130-133 (left to right, top to bottom):
Gogh, Vincent van *The Olive Orchard:* Chester Dale Collection 1963.10.152/National Gallery of Art.
Degas, Edgar *The Dance Lesson:* Collection of Mr. and Mrs. Paul Mellon 1995.47.6/National Gallery of Art.
Fragonard, Jean-Honoré *Young Girl Reading:* Gift of Mrs. Mellon Bruce in memory of her father, Andrew W. Mellon 1961.16.1/National Gallery of Art.
Gauguin, Paul *Self-Portrait:* Chester Dale Collection 1963.10.150/National Gallery of Art.
Gauguin, Paul *Breton Girls Dancing, Pont-Aven:* Collection of Mr. and Mrs. Paul Mellon 1983.1.19/ National Gallery of Art.
Guigou, Paul *Washerwomen on the Banks of the Durance:* Chester Dale Fund 2007.73.1/National Gallery of Art.

Guillaumin, Jean-Baptiste-Armand *The Bridge of Louis Philippe:* Chester Dale Collection 1963.10.155/National Gallery of Art.
Manet, Edouard *The Railway:* Gift of Horace Havemeyer in memory of his mother, Louisine W. Havemeyer 1956.10.1/National Gallery of Art.
Manet, Edouard *Masked Ball at the Opera:* Gift of Mrs. Horace Havemeyer in memory of her mother-in-law, Louisine W. Havemeyer 1982.75.1/National Gallery of Art.
Manet, Edouard *The Old Musician:* Chester Dale Collection 1963.10.162/National Gallery of Art.
Monet, Claude *The Japanese Footbridge:* Gift of Victoria Nebeker Coberly, in memory of her son John W. Mudd, and Walter H. and Leonore Annenberg 1992.9.1/ National Gallery of Art.
Monet, Claude *Woman with a Parasol—Madame Monet and Her Son:* Collection of Mr. and Mrs. Paul Mellon 1983.1.29/National Gallery of Art.
Monet, Claude *The Bridge at Argenteuil:* Collection of Mr. and Mrs. Paul Mellon 1983.1.24/National Gallery of Art.
Monet, Claude *The Artist's Garden in Argenteuil (A Corner of the Garden with Dahlias):* Gift of Janice H. Levin, in Honor of the 50th Anniversary of the National Gallery of Art 1991.27.1/National Gallery of Art.